Narrative Play Therapy

of related interest

Narrative Approaches in Play with Children
Ann Cattanach
ISBN 978 1 84310 588 6

The Story So Far
Play Therapy Narratives
Edited by Ann Cattanach
ISBN 978 1 84310 063 8

Children's Stories in Play Therapy
Ann Cattanach
ISBN 978 1 85302 362 0

Play as Therapy
Assessment and Therapeutic Interventions
Edited by Karen Stagnitti and Rodney Cooper
Foreword by Ann Cattanach
ISBN 978 1 84310 637 1

Introduction to Developmental Playtherapy
Playing and Health
Sue Jennings
Foreword by Mooli Lahad
ISBN 978 1 85302 635 5

The Creation of Imaginary Worlds
The Role of Art, Magic and Dreams in Child Development
Claire Golomb
ISBN 978 1 84905 852 0

Narrative Play Therapy

Theory and Practice

Edited by Aideen Taylor de Faoite

Jessica Kingsley *Publishers*
London and Philadelphia

Table 3.2 from Lahad 1993 on p.62 is adapted by permission of Mooli Lahad.

First published in 2011
by Jessica Kingsley Publishers
116 Pentonville Road
London N1 9JB, UK
and
400 Market Street, Suite 400
Philadelphia, PA 19106, USA

www.jkp.com

Library of Congress Cataloging in Publication Data
Narrative play therapy : theory and practice / edited by Aideen Taylor de Faoite.
p. cm.
Includes bibliographical references and index.
ISBN 978-1-84905-142-2 (alk. paper)
1. Narrative therapy. 2. Play therapy. 3. Child psychotherapy. I. Taylor de Faoite, Aideen.
RJ505.S75N35 2011
618.92'891653--dc22
2011002401

British Library Cataloguing in Publication Data
A CIP catalogue record for this book is available from the British Library

ISBN 978 1 84905 142 2

Printed and bound in Great Britain

Dedicated to the memory of Ann Cattanach

Do not go where the path may lead, go instead where there is no path and leave a trail.

Ralph Waldo Emerson

Contents

Part II: Narrative Play Therapy Practice

Part I
Theory and Background

Chapter 1

An Introduction to Social Construction and Narrative Theories

Aideen Taylor de Faoite and Ann Marie John

Introduction

This chapter aims to set Narrative Play Therapy in the context of post-modern and social constructionist thought. We will explore the foundations of the philosophy on which social constructionist thinking was built and make reference to the different ways it has influenced thinking in therapy and research. We will trace how the premise has been interpreted by family therapists and psychotherapy in general.

The issue of power is central to social constructionist thinking in the context of therapy research and philosophy. As our journey through the theory will take us to various landscapes; they all have in common the theme of power. Power is a common path that takes us from Foucault's concept of the influence of *social discourse* to the mutual influence of therapist and child making a story together. For the sake of beginning our journey with a good map we will begin with some of the early terminology and the basic philosophical ideas that are embedded in the theory.

Foundations

Narrative Play Therapy has developed in the context of a new paradigm of psychotherapy which is often described as 'post modern'. The term post modern has been used in different contexts: art, theatre, research and psychotherapy but fundamentally in philosophy. The modern aspect refers to the scientific Age of the Enlightenment, sometimes called the Age of Reason. At this time the scientific method was developed and, of course, Darwinism, which led ultimately to the questioning of God as the creator and regulator of nature. Descartes' system, often referred to as 'Cartesian dualism', suggested that there was a metaphysical relationship between mind and body that allowed us to take an observer position in our observation of the natural world. Post-modern and constructionist thinkers questioned this ability to separate the observer from the self (Descartes 1983). Van Foerster's (1981) studies into the natural word demonstrated that perception is not an act where the object presents itself to the senses but where the brain constructs images of objects based on past experience. This had a fundamental impact on thinking about the philosophy of knowledge and how we come to know things. The idea that knowing or experiencing something is an objective process was challenged. This development in theoretical thinking was referred to as constructivism. Social constructionism takes this further in suggesting that the way we know things is not only constructed by our brain but by the social contexts in which we operate. The creation of knowledge then is socially constructed by social processes. The philosophy of knowledge inevitably leads us to thinking about the development of social constructionist research.

Social constructionist research

At the time one of the authors (AMJ) was at college the term 'social sciences' was popular as sociology struggled to replicate the scientific method to attain the 'credibility' of the traditional sciences. It emerged that the process of measuring within these sciences did not fit with trying to understand social phenomena and sociology began to develop its own methods. Memorable studies such as the exciting participant observation study of drug taking that Jock Young carried out in the 1960s began this process of developing new methods of research, suitable to the study of social phenomena (Young 1971). The approach in these studies recognised that the achievement of objectivity was neither possible nor desirable when studying the social world. One could not be purely an observer in any context because one's experience colours one's view of what one is seeing. Later this critique of social research was extended to a critique of the natural sciences. For example Jungk (1958) researched the ethical position and personal accounts of the workers involved with the splitting of the first atom. His work begs the question of how the notion of objectivity allowed scientists to split the atom despite the potential consequences.

'What has all this to do with Narrative Play Therapy?', you may well ask. Allow me one more reference from my past and all will be revealed. Thomas Kuhn questioned the whole idea of science 'as set in stone', suggesting that scientific theory develops in cycles. He gives as his main example the story of Copernicus, who was persecuted for suggesting that the planets move around the sun. Kuhn (1962) suggests that science changes as new evidence emerges to disprove previous theories. This led to Karl Popper's (1959) work paving the way for the null hypothesis: theories cannot be proved, only disproved, and that good science should be the process of trying to disprove one's hypothesis, for if one tries to do so and fails one can find some credence in the original idea. These examples of critique of the notion of western science are included as they are an important element in the development of social constructionist thinking.

Deconstruction of research and knowledge is very important in social constructionist thought. The knowledge created is only one story. This deconstruction tells us a great deal about the processes by which the knowledge is created. Controlled trials, for example, show us that a medicine or treatment works, but they do not tell us how it works, how the people experiencing the treatment feel or what they understand about how it works, or how they feel about the treatment. The research method one uses determines the kind of knowledge one produces. Social constructionist research favours a hermeneutic approach where layers of meaning are uncovered in a reflexive loop like a double helix. The researcher, of course, is part of the layers of meaning and the research process moves between researcher and research participant. A researcher would therefore make no attempt to be objective as this is neither positive nor desirable. This has implications for the choices we make in researching Narrative Play Therapy and indeed for the position we take as therapists.

The impact of a critique of the manner in which knowledge is created, and what is considered to be 'true', leads to further critiques, determining who has the power to create knowledge and to sanction what is regarded as 'true or useful', and who is to be regarded as expert in that knowledge.

Philosophy and therapy as 'confession'

Philosopher Michel Foucault (1975) took the idea that knowledge is socially constructed further by suggesting that some groups in any society have the power to decide what kind of knowledge is valuable and who is qualified to disseminate such knowledge. He termed the ideas created by powerful groups in society as 'social discourses'. Foucault refers to the most powerful ideas as dominant discourses. Conventional medical discourses are much more powerful than those of, say, homeopathy and are an example of a dominant discourse. Others have suggested that the construction of ideas or discourses is intentionally directed in order to subjugate (Gramsci 1971). In Foucault's view social discourses are inevitable because they are the stories of more powerful groups in society. Foucault was particularly interested in the process of professionalisation and how the role of an expert in medicine, for example, discounted the knowledge that a patient might have about getting well, in favour of their own expertise. Foucault also refers to the discourses concerning psychotherapy as pertaining to confession and disputes the idea that the key to psychological recovery lies in revisiting the past to disclose a trauma that needs to be cathartically reworked. This development is key in understanding the processes in Narrative Play Therapy, as the process to recovery in this model is through co-construction of more satisfactory stories.

Kenneth Gergen (1992) and Lynn Hoffman (1992) began to apply these ideas to thinking about family therapy. We now refer to this as a social constructionist approach. A social constructionist approach to therapy acknowledges that problems are socially constructed, in other words, people come to therapy with stories about a problem and referrers may have similar or different stories about the problems. Key to this is that discourses are often created around a problem that involves blaming the clients. The essence of working within a social constructionist frame is that the process of therapy is a process of finding a story that fits the family rather than one that fits with the therapist. Michael White's (White and Epston 1990) work on narrative therapy is key in that he suggests that families often come with 'problem saturated stories' rather than stories of resilience. The process of narrative therapy is therefore to uncover new stories or to co-construct with the therapist non-blaming stories. The issue of power is central to narrative therapy because the client is considered to have expertise rather than be in a 'one down' position (a situation whereby both client and therapist behave in a way that assumes the therapist is the expert and therefore has more power in terms of 'prescribing' a solution).

Social construction stance

Gergen, in his *Invitation to Social Construction* (2009), identified five assumptions that form the backbone of social constructionism. These are as follows:

1. *The way in which we understand the world is not required by 'what there is'.* We use language to construct a range of concepts that explain our experiences. 'There is nothing about "what there is" that demands these particular accounts' (Gergen 2009, p.5). He goes on to suggest that there is 'no truth – words that truly map the world' (p.5). We have lots of different ways of talking about our experiences with different possible outcomes. Traditional truths can become some of the possible ways of talking and as such these don't have to be abandoned but can be seen as options instead.

2. *The ways in which we describe and explain the world are the outcomes of relationship.* We understand and describe our experiences in the context of the relationships we have experienced in the past, the present and into the future. Think of the question 'How are you?' The respondent will reply to this question in different ways depending on the context of the relationship. For example, if it is a nurse or a doctor who is asking the question following surgery, your response to this may include a consideration of the physical pain you are experiencing, your feelings about successfulness of the operation, etc. This same question asked by a therapist, shop assistant or a family member will be responded to in a different way, depending on the relationship and when the question is asked in the context of the relationship.

3. *Constructions gain their significance from their social utility.* We interact with each other in a relatively co-ordinated way and follow a rough set of conventions of what is acceptable or not. It is socially useful for children to interact with their teacher in a certain predictable fashion. How children interact with their teacher will be different depending on the cultural construction of the role of teacher but the roles that both child and teacher take are relatively consistent

across that culture, whether it is the culture of the school or the wider social and political environment in which the child lives.

4. *As we describe and explain, so do we fashion our future.* The language we use is bound up in our relationships and this in turn has a wider impact on our practice. Consider a recession with all the associated cutbacks. These can be described as devastating for a society and be blamed on a group or groups within that society. This can lead to a 'them and us' mentality, social derision and chaos. Alternatively a recession can be described as a time of change, a time to reflect on the environment that one wishes to create and cutbacks can be described as the changing landscape of this environment. The choice of language, the descriptions and the explanations offered impact on the future.

5. *A reflection on our taken-for-granted worlds is vital to our future well-being.* This challenges the social constructionist to reflect on what is taken for granted, to begin to listen to alternatives and to grapple with comparing multiple perspectives. It requires the person to question what is known and to see traditional values and truths as one of the multiple options to be considered.

These five assumptions influence the stance taken by the social constructionist. In the practice of therapy, these influence the role of the therapist, challenging him or her to consider taken for granted knowledge and also challenging the client's perception of the role of the therapist in facilitating change. Clients may come to therapy with an understanding of a professional relationship, into which they have come with a problem or an illness, and the therapist, as expert, is expected to duly solve the problem or cure the illness. Instead the client, in a relationship with the therapist, begins to identify how descriptions and explanations of events, in the context of relationships in his or her lived worlds, have fashioned the problem. Being able to change these explanations and descriptions facilitates change and begins to fashion a new future for the client. These changes are outcomes of the relationship between the therapist and client. The focus of therapy is not to gain a clear picture of 'what really happened' but to understand from the client's perspective, the 'constructed meaning' the client has made of his or her world (Gergen 2009).

The social construction of the problem

The 'problem' is identified as a problem and is differentiated from the person so that the person is not seen as the problem. It is seen as socially constructed and defined (McLeod 1997). What brings the client to therapy at this time are problematic stories about him- or herself. This story has often become stuck, resulting in the client being blind to alternative stories.

White's work is important as it applies social construction thinking to our understanding of problems and the position of client and families in relation to problems in therapy (White and Epston 1990). White created the term 'problem saturated' narratives as he noticed how families came to therapy speaking about how the problem dominated their lives. It was 'as if' the coping, healthy, positive aspects of the family or the identified client had been forgotten or taken over by the problem. White suggested that these 'problem saturated stories' are oppressive to families and disempowering. Crucially he distinguishes the person from the problem, identifying that the problem is the problem. This has enabled him to develop a specific technique which he has called 'externalisation'. Using this technique, the therapist helps children to create a character to externalise the problem and then harnesses the family to 'outsmart' the problem (White and Epston 1990). This development is key to addressing some of the issues raised by Foucault. Externalisation and narrative practices serve to re-write stories for families which are anti-oppressive and non-blaming. For White and Epston (1990) therapy is a process of 're-authoring' and helping the client to re-discover untold stories that are more useful to them.

Cattanach (1997) used narrative ideas and adapted them into a model for play therapy. In Narrative Play Therapy the child creates stories through play and re-stories their experiences in the safety of the metaphor. The play therapist's role is co-author, asking questions to facilitate plot line character or expression. In family therapy the therapist is also looking for new stories that are helpful to the family, and perhaps less often in the metaphor (i.e. therapists work more in the realm of literal stories of what has happened to the clients, while play therapists enable the child to make up an imaginary story in order to include more therapeutic distance). This method was especially pertinent to work with children particularly in the field of abuse. Therapy for these children could be fun and the children could be resourceful and enjoy playing and did not have to talk about their abuse, which often made them feel labelled and victimised.

The social construction of the self

Social constructionists assume that knowledge is socially constructed and that there are many and diverse ways of understanding ourselves and others. They assume that all knowledge, including 'scientific knowledge', is 'perspectival' (Smith 1997). Gergen suggests that in perspectival knowing, people make interpretations and conclusions based on 'a particular community of interpretation' (1991, p.104). Within therapy attention is focused on the social world of the person with an emphasis on intersubjectivity and therapeutic curiosity. The narratively oriented therapist assumes that people's actions are guided by culturally diverse meanings and stories that they continuously construct about themselves (Smith 1997).

From the constructionist perspective the view of 'self' differs from that of other orientations. The 'self' is not perceived as an entity but as a social construction. The 'person' is identified as an active agent engaged in intentional activity, a relational being who is constituted in the context of their mutual relations with one another (Macmurray 1961). The person is situated within a culture and a social setting and in relation to other persons. Stories are the means by which we can express ourselves and our relationship. Spence proposed that 'part of my sense of self depends on my being able to go backwards and forwards in time and weave a story about who I am, how I got that way and where I am going, a story that is continuously nourishing and self-sustaining. Take that away from me and I am significantly less' (1982, cited in McLeod 1997, p.458).

In social construction theory, the self is therefore constricted in the dialogue between the relating people. Within this process a social constructionist approach conceptualises 'the self' as relational, according to psychologist John Schotter (1984). We construct ourselves in our interactions with others. The self is not a fixed entity but is constantly changing. For example, I (AMJ) consider myself to be good at my job (this is through working hard rather than a belief in any innate talent). I recently had a conversation with an Ofsted inspector[1] as part of an

---

1   The role of the Office for Standards in Education (Ofsted) inspector is to inspect and report on standards in education and social care in public and sometimes private organisations. Organisations are graded according to the quality of service they provide, and this information is published in the public domain.

inspection of a fostering agency for which I work. As I spoke about my work I developed more of a story or narrative of myself as doing a good job and as we received an outstanding report. This further reinforced my perception of myself as being competent. I had another conversation with the director of the hospital I work at in which I spoke about my work and about my views about working at the hospital and about what changes needed to be made. These ideas were listened to and taken on board. My sense of myself as a therapist evolves through the interaction with the young people and their families and also through working with other professionals. Although I may have stories from the past that do not support the idea that I am good at my job, these are not fixed in the idea of who I am (I believe I was a terrible teacher). Social constructionist psychologist Romme Harré (1986) challenges the idea that our emotions are internal entities. He suggests that, instead, they are acted out relationally and may be different in different contexts. The implication for therapy is that the self and emotions are created in the present and therefore past experience need not be 'oppressive' or labelling.

The position (role) of the therapist

The role of the therapist is to adopt a 'not knowing' but curious stance. On opening a therapeutic conversation with the client the therapist does not make any presumptions about how the conversation is going to evolve. Instead the therapist remains open to seeing where the conversation will be taken by the client. The therapist refrains from asking questions that are going to close down the conversation or that might be based on clinical or theoretical assumptions. The meaning and the understanding of the story that the client brings are socially constructed by the two people in conversation with one another (Anderson and Goolishian 1992). The therapist begins to understand the difficulties from the client's perspective, not some theoretical perspective. The therapist's actions communicate an abundance of genuine curiosity as the therapist has a dialogue with the client to learn more about what is being said. The therapist questions to gain an understanding from the client's perspective of intentions of his or her actions. In this way questioning clarifies the story being told from the client's perspective, and begins to identify the intentions and motivations of the client. By taking the client's story seriously the therapist joins the client in a mutual exploration of the client's experience and their understanding of their experiences.

The therapist's task is therefore to attempt to understand from the changing perspective of the client. In adopting a 'not knowing' but curious to learn stance open conversational spaces are created for the client thus increasing the likelihood of narrative development that includes new agency and personal freedom. In this open conversational space new meaning and ideas emerge and are co-created in the dialogue between the therapist and the client (Anderson and Goolishian 1992). The therapist's expertise is to develop a free conversational space and facilitate an emerging dialogue in which newness can occur.

The goal of therapy

In a relational approach the therapist is concerned with helping the client to create or co-author new meanings and not cathartically revisit past traumas. Stories take a central role in constructionist narrative therapies. The goal of therapy is 'not to replace a story with another' but to 'enable the client to participate in the continuous process of creating and transforming meaning' (Gergen 1996, p.215). The therapist aims to develop 'local' knowledge of the client, his or her social and cultural history and the stock of stories the client brings with him or her. McLeod proposes that 'it is through stories that we best express our sense of ourselves as active, relational beings' (1997, p.92). The person is the author of the story and therapy is an opportunity to re-author stories. This happens in the safe space that is opened up between the therapist and the person, as the therapist listens to the story and the person tells his or her story to the therapist as a listener. It is in this space that the relationship is developed that allows for the co-construction of new or alternative selves. McLeod (1997) identifies four elements of narrative therapy, namely:

1. The ambiguity of stories – the therapist does not know where the story will lead or what alternative stories will emerge.

2. The co-construction of the therapy narrative – through skilful listening and questioning on the part of the therapist, therapy narratives are co-constructed.

3. The story is a purposeful act – the structure of a story with a beginning, middle and end supports the engagement in the purposeful act of re-authoring stories.

4. The existence of a cultural stock of stories is acknowledged and exploring these is seen as part of the therapy process.

In summary the role of therapy from a narrative social construction perspective is to offer the client a space to tell stories and to have these stories valued and affirmed. In telling these stories the client maintains or repairs life narratives. The role of therapy is to deconstruct those stories that are destructive to the client and to co-construct new and alternative stories through a process of communication (Dallos 2006) and in the context of the relationship.

The goal of therapy is therefore to offer a space and a 'curious' audience and to review the function of the stories that the client lives by. These stories are structured by the client's understanding and beliefs and contain events, actions, experiences and beliefs over time. In altering these stories the client's experience of him- or herself and others can be dramatically altered. This leads to an adjustment or realignment of the client's life narratives. The client feels freed from old stories. This is often accompanied by an emotional sense of release (Dallos 2006). In this space the client can also create stories that are radically new and different. In looking at these stories in the context of the therapeutic relationship 'meaning is generated and patterns of action become reasonable and desirable' (Gergen 2009, p.138). The therapy offers the client a space to explore the network of relationships in which he or she is a participant.

The assessment and evaluation of social constructionist therapy

Assessing a client coming for therapy would involve identifying and deconstructing the narratives that accompany him or her into the therapy space. These may not be the client's narratives but those generated within the systems in the client's lived in world. Examples could include teacher's stories (threat of exclusion), stories about behaviour, or stories that label families as unreachable, difficult to work with and problematic. The therapist may also need to identify and deconstruct blaming and unhelpful stories within the client's network of relationships. Crucial to this is to co-construct a story of the purpose of the therapy with the client. Discussing with the client his or her experience of therapeutic or helping relationships in the past can be useful to identify the approach that is more helpful to the client. The therapist is not prescribing a treatment. He or she is making a respectful agreement as to what might be helpful. However, often the context of one's work means that one has to make a treatment formulation. This means that one must do 'both/and': 'both' make a respectful agreement, 'and' prescribe a treatment. Being transparent in sharing one's formulation and involving the client as much as possible in this process is used as an approach to meet these, often competing, requirements of practice.

Evaluation in a social constructionist frame also requires deconstruction and a 'both/and approach'. Although a hermeneutic approach is the best fit with the social constructionist approach the contexts in which we work require 'hard evidence' – the numbers of people that get better and stay better are important but social constructionists see this only as one aspect of evaluation. Like the process of formulation, the social construction therapist is more likely to include the client in the evaluation of what was useful. Creative techniques such as video interviews or simple scaling (how bad is the problem on a scale of 1 to 10) at the beginning and end of therapy are used. This type of mix of measures tends to be used. It is important to be aware that, while each measure tells a story, there are other stories equally relevant that form a part of the evaluation of therapy from a Social Construction perspective.

A critique of the social constructionist approach

Social constructionism offers a critique of other approaches. In this approach self critique and reflexivity in thinking is advocated. However, social constructionism is itself a social construction and Lyddon proposes that it begs a number of critical questions including:

> What historical, cultural and/or social forces contribute to the construction of social constructionism?
>
> If power relationships exist in social interactions, then what might be the values and power hidden in social constructionism?
>
> What alternative views might be marginalised by social construction thinking?

> (Lyddon 1998, p.218)

Lyddon goes on to propose that social constructionism presents a 'privileged view of the way things really are (i.e. the real truth is that reality is socially constructed)' (1998, p.219). Gergen addresses some of these criticisms of social constructionism by suggesting that it is one perspective in the range of post-modern and traditional perspectives that are available to the person to consider when assessing information or information presented as a 'truth' (Gergen 2009).

Social constructionist approaches to therapy have been criticised on several fronts. First, the process is so much about deconstruction that it is difficult to create a conceptual framework for what we do. Mason (2005) has argued, with regards to a 'not knowing position', that expertise is useful and that some families want an expert. Therefore it is not helpful to throw the baby out with the bath water and indeed in some cases a 'not knowing' position can be unhelpful. Mason presents what he calls 'relational risk taking' in which he advocates a balanced approach to using expertise in a way that does not present it as truth.

Linked to this criticism is the criticism of social construction's concept of the client as the expert, and the resultant reluctance of the therapist to take an expert stance, as this has become associated with privileged knowledge. Lyddon queries if the therapist can instead be an expert in 'drawing the client's attention to the problematic patterns and themes observed in the client's story or life narrative' (1998, p.219) and helping the client to see how these problems and identities might be socially constructed. The social construction of problems and its juxtaposition with the personal agency of the client also need to be considered in a critique of social constructionism. The role of empowerment, both personal and political, needs to be considered. The role of therapy is to support the client's personal agency and personal empowerment to gain control over his or her life and to effect change. Should the therapist also consider the potential therapeutic value of political activity to bring about significant political/social change (Lyddon 1998)?

Narrative therapy has also come in for critique. Minuchin (1998) has criticised White's approach for not involving the family in the process of externalisation and, in so doing, deserting the family and the person within the system, in favour of the externalisation of the story. This has been countered by many family therapists, writing about how narrative approaches recruit family stories of resilience rather than exclude the family (Hayward 2003). Others have been critical of the privileging of the individual and the construction of the individual's story over the relationship (Gergen 2009).

In conclusion, social construction theory and narrative therapy are new and developing approaches. In forming a distinct identity, some of the stories or narratives that are generated offer a contrasting picture of post-modern perspective to modern or traditional perspectives (Neimeyer 1998, as cited in Lyddon 1998). These can be seen as challenging to such traditions. More recent writings on these post-modern approaches have offered a middle ground where the social construction perspective is one of many perspectives that are available for consideration, with traditional perspectives being another (Gergen 2009).

Conclusion

This chapter identified some of the main concepts and practices in social construction theory and narrative therapy. The concept of the self and the problem, the role of story and narrative in therapy, and the stance of the therapist in facilitating the telling of the client's story from his or her perspective, were discussed. The change process of co-constructing more satisfactory stories and life narratives was presented. The next chapter presents Narrative Play Therapy as a branch of play therapy that was developed and practised by Ann Cattanach. These ideas and practices are now understood in light of the more recent and developing theories of social constructionism and narrative therapy.

References

Anderson, H. and Goolishian, H. (1992) 'The Client is the Expert: A Not-knowing Approach to Therapy.' In S. McNamee and K.J. Gergen (eds) *Therapy as Social Construction*. London: SAGE Publications.

Cattanach, A. (1997) *Children's Stories in Play Therapy*. London: Jessica Kingsley Publishers.

Dallos, R. (2006) *Attachment Narrative Therapy: Integrating Narrative, Systemic and Attachment Therapies*. Buckingham: Open University Press.

Descartes, R. (1983) *Principles of Philosophy*, trans. V.R. Miller and R.P. Miller. Dordrecht: D. Reidel.

Foucault, M. (1975) *The Archaeology of Knowledge*. London: Tavistock.

Gergen, K.J. (1991) *The Saturated Self: Dilemmas of Identity in a Contemporary Life*. New York: Basic Books.

Gergen, K.J. (1992) 'Beyond Narrative in the Negotiation of Therapeutic Meaning.' In S. McNamee and K.J. Gergen (eds) *Therapy as a Social Construction*. London: SAGE Publications.

Gergen, K.J. (1996) 'Beyond Life Narratives in the Therapeutic Encounter.' In J.E. Birren, G.M. Keyton, J.-K. Ruth, J.J. F. Schroots and T. Svensson (eds) *Aging and Biography: Explorations in Adult Development*. New York: Springer.

Gergen, K.J. (2009) *An Invitation to Social Construction*, 2nd edn. London: SAGE Publications.

Gramsci, A. (1971) *Selections from the Prison Notebooks*. In Q. Hoare and G. Norwell Smith (eds) New York: International Publishers.

Harré, R. (1986) 'An Outline of the Social Constructionist Viewpoint.' In R. Harré (ed.) *The Social Construction of Emotions*. Oxford: Blackwell.

Hayward, M. (2003) 'Critiques of narrative therapy: A personal response.' *Australian and New Zealand Journals of Family Therapy 24*, 4, 183–189.

Hoffman, L. (1992) 'A Reflexive Stance for Family Therapy.' In S. McNamee and K.J. Gergen (eds) *Therapy as a Social Construction.* London: SAGE Publications.

Jungk, R. (1958) *Brighter than a Thousand Suns: A Personal History of the Atomic Scientists.* New York: Houghton Mifflin Harcourt.

Kuhn, T.S. (1962) *The Structure of Scientific Revolutions.* Chicago, IL: University of Chicago Press.

Lyddon, W.J. (1998) 'Social construction in counselling psychology: A comment and critique.' *Counselling Psychology Quarterly 11*, 2, 215–223.

Macmurray, J. (1961) *Persons in Relation.* London: Faber.

Mason, B. (2005) 'Relational risk-taking and the training of supervisors.' *Journal of Family Therapy 27*, 3, 298–301.

McLeod, J. (1997) *Narrative and Psychotherapy.* London: SAGE Publications.

Minuchin, S. (1998) 'Where is the family in family therapy.' *Journal of Marital and Family Therapy 24*, 397–403.

Neimeyer, R.A. (1998) 'Social constructionism in the counselling context.' *Counselling Psychology Quarterly 11*, 2, 135–149.

Popper, K. (1959) *The Logic of Scientific Method.* London: Routledge.

Schotter, J. (1984) *Social Accountability and Selfhood.* London: Blackwell.

Smith, C. (1997) 'Comparing Traditional Therapies with Narrative Approaches.' In C. Smith and D. Nylund (eds) *Narrative Therapies with Children and Adolescents.* New York: Guilford Press.

Van Foerster, H. (1981) *Observing Systems.* Seaside, CA: Intersystems Publications.

White, M. and Epston, D. (1990) *Narrative Means to Therapeutic Ends.* New York: Norton.

Young, J. (1971) *The Drug Takers: The Social Meaning of Drug Use.* London: McGibbon and Kee.

Chapter 2

The Theory of Narrative Play Therapy

Aideen Taylor de Faoite

Introduction

Narrative Play Therapy has evolved over the last two decades, so here a historical perspective is presented. This identifies the main contributors and tracks the development of their ideas, as presented in their published works. The research on brain development, its contribution to our understanding of neurodevelopment, enriched environments, the centrality of relationship and the impact of stress will be considered. The chapter will end with a current conceptualisation of Narrative Play Therapy, the role of play and narrative in the development of the self and in supporting change, and the role of the therapist within Narrative Play Therapy.

Historical perspective

Narrative Play Therapy has its roots in play therapy and creative arts therapies. Its origins can be identified in the writings of Ann Cattanach and her collaborations with colleagues, including Sue Jennings and Brenda Meldrum, in the development of a professional training in play therapy in the UK in the early 1990s. All three were dramatherapists, and the role of drama and dramatic play is evident throughout the development of Narrative Play Therapy.

In her book on play therapy, Cattanach proposed a 'new model of play therapy' and gave four core assumptions that underpinned this model. These were:

1. The centrality of play as the child's way of understanding the world.

2. Play is a developmental process. In therapy the child moves back and forth along the developmental continuum of play as a way of discovering individuality and separation.

3. Play is a symbolic process through which the child can experiment with imaginary choices, appropriately distanced from the consequences of these choices in the 'real' world.

4. The play in play therapy happens in a therapeutic space. This space defines what is 'me' and 'not me'. This space is seen as one where creative life begins, a space where we experience the psychological significance of art.

                                                         (Cattanach 1992, p.41)

In these early writings the role of the play therapist was identified as:

- helping the child to use play and play materials to express him- or herself effectively

- to play with the child at the child's direction

- to be an audience and an empathic listener

- to record, for the child, any stories or explanations the child might offer of his or her play

- to give meaning and importance to the child's stories so the child may feel valued.

                                                         (Cattanach 1992, p.69)

- to facilitate and contain the process, thus supporting the child through their journey

- to provide boundaries and rules for safety.

                                                         (Cattanach 1992, p.71)

In these early writings, the importance of the relationship between the therapist and child is emphasised. The emergence of the importance of children's stories in their play, and the narrative explanations that they generate about their play in supporting the development of the self, are also evident in these early writings.

The roots of this new model of play therapy are in dramatherapy and other creative arts therapies. This is evident in the emphasis placed on the symbolic and imaginative nature of play, and in the actor/director role of the child and actor/observer role of the therapist in the development of the relationship. This is also evident in the role of creativity and imagination in the development of sense of self, and the valuing of this by recording the child's creations or imaginings.

These core concepts have been expanded on and added to, over the evolution of Narrative Play Therapy. Play remains central to the process. The therapist in Narrative Play Therapy enters the child's play at the direction of the child. This is understood as respecting the child's world and entering that world with the aim of valuing and respecting the child. In playing with the child we learn what feelings and thoughts the child has, and we learn the perspectives of the child (Cattanach 2008).

The developmental nature of play and the need for children to have opportunities to move along a developmental continuum of play has been influenced by the work of Sue Jennings and her conceptualisation of the embodiment, projection and role (EPR) developmental paradigm. This has influenced both the materials chosen in the practice of Narrative Play Therapy, and the therapist's understanding of the developmental play level at which the child is choosing, or indeed, is driven to play.

Imaginative and pretend play allow for the development of 'as if'. The child can try out familiar and unfamiliar worlds with a sense of security, knowing that he or she is only pretending and the consequences of the real world do not apply in play. Narrative Play Therapy has developed to understand this as the process of externalising the problem. It also affords the child the opportunity to consider alternative endings to the story without having to experience any consequences of such endings. This in turn has developed to reflect a similar process in narrative therapy, where the client is supported in reaching his or her unique outcome.

The concept of the therapeutic space, the space between the therapist and the child in which the two people play and in which the relationship develops, had evolved to include the space in the middle between the teller and the listener in which stories are created. In this space, the story provides the structure for the negotiation of shared meaning between the listener and the teller, and acts as a container for the experience (Cattanach 1997).

This introduces the elements that have been added to 'this new model' to create the construct of Narrative Play Therapy, namely the conceptualisation of narrative as a function of the psychology of the self, the developmental research on narrative and play, and the use of story to co-construct a shared meaning (Cattanach 1997, 1999). Bruner's work on narrative has been added to increase our understanding of the role of narrative, how we story our experience to organise our experience, how the way we story these experiences guides our memory and our experience of what has happened, and influences what will happen in the future (Bruner 1990, 1991; Bruner and Luciarello 1989; Cattanach 1997). The stories that are communicated in Narrative Play Therapy include a sense of identity, intentionality and subjectivity. They express the elements of 'who' the child is at that moment in time and what stories the child chooses to tell about his or her play or within his or her play. The story is supported and co-constructed with the therapist in the therapeutic space, scaffolding the child to bring order, sequence and a sense of completion, as the story is structured with a beginning, a middle and an end. The structure of the story allows the child to problem solve by providing a causal explanation for something that has happened in the story. The co-construction can help to place the story within a bigger story, thus allowing the child to gain a broader perspective. This broader perspective can also be facilitated by the consideration of alternative endings, and the clarification of confusions in the telling and the retelling of the story (McLeod 1997). Bruner (1991) identified four key elements of story as an instrument of the mind in the construction of reality. These are that stories are sequential, communicate subjectivity, communicate ambiguity and account for the departure from the ordinary. Developmental research on play and narrative suggest that narrative is developed through play in the context of interactions with another (Engel 2005; Nicolopoulou 2005; Trevarthen 1995). The traditional concept of the self as an isolated, contained unit is challenged and a concept of the self not as an objective entity but an intersubjective, social construction is proposed in the evolving model of Narrative Play Therapy (Cattanach 1997).

In conclusion, Narrative Play Therapy has its origins in a model of play therapy which was influenced by dramatherapy and other arts therapies. It focuses on the centrality of play to the child and the importance of valuing the child by entering his or her world of play and by recording his or her stories and narratives. This has evolved over time to be understood in the context of emerging theories of social construction, narrative therapy and developmental research on narrative and play. The stories and narratives generated within the child's play and co-constructed with the therapist remain the core elements of the therapeutic process and the agent for change.

Neurodevelopment and Narrative Play Therapy

The advances in brain research and the technology that allows for the imaging of the brain are beginning to open new doors to our understanding of child development and the impact of early experience on the development and structure of the brain. This has implications for our understanding of the role of experience in development and how we provide intervention.

The brain

A lower, middle and higher brain have evolved over time, each with different functions, but each developing on the previous base, resulting in a hierarchical development of brain structures. The three parts of the brain are the reptilian brain (the brain stem and spinal cord), the mammalian brain (the limbic system) and the human brain (frontal lobe and neocortex) (Sunderland 2006).

The reptilian brain or primitive brain is instinctive in nature and controls body functions required for survival and to sustain life. These include hunger, digestion and elimination, breathing, circulation, temperature, movement, balance and posture, territorial instincts and flight, fight or freeze instincts.

The mammalian brain or the emotional brain controls social behaviour such as giving and receiving care, playfulness and bonding. It controls strong emotions that are triggered by the reptilian brain. It also helps to control the flight, fight or freeze instinct triggered in the lower brain. The emotions it helps to control include rage, fear, separation, distress, care and nurturing, social bonding, playfulness, exploratory behaviour and lust in adults.

The human brain or rational brain controls higher order functions including creativity and imagination, problem solving, reasoning and reflection, self-awareness, kindness, empathy and concern (Sunderland 2006).

Brain research and child development

Shore, in *Rethinking the Brain* (1997), identifies five areas where new research has informed and changed thinking about child development. These are as follows:

1. Brain research over the last four decades has led to changes in our understanding of the interplay between nature and nurture. Findings suggest that a stimulating environment increases the

number and variety of synaptic connections in the brain. Other changes in thinking on this debate indicate that:

○ Brain development hinges on a complex interplay between the experiences we have and the genes with which we are born.

○ Early experiences shape the architecture of the brain.

○ Early experiences directly affect the way the brain develops.

○ Brain development is non-linear, therefore there are prime times (sensitive periods) for the development of different kinds of knowledge and skills throughout life.

(Shore 1997, p.18)

The child's interaction with the environment and the people in that environment influence the way the brain is 'wired'. Children who are exposed to consistent, predictable, nurturing and enriching experiences are neurobiologically capable of thriving as happy, productive and creative human beings (Perry 2009). When the child experiences feelings of safety, being loved and calm caregiving, oxytocin and opioids are the chemicals that dominate the brain. These in turn make the child feel safe, calm and warm. When the child is feeling this way, he or she is more able to savour experiences, develop a capacity to linger in the moment and enjoys the capacity to let go and drift (Sunderland 2006).

When the child feels fear and rage due to his or her environmental experiences or interaction with adults, the level of opioids and oxytocin is reduced and levels of cortisol increase. Epinephrine and norephinephrine levels also increase in times of stress (Perry and Hambrick 2008; Sunderland 2006). High levels of these chemicals can leave the child feeling threatened and unsafe, overwhelmed, fearful and miserable. These chemicals also put the body into flight or fight mode, leaving the child feeling anxious and/or angry (Sunderland 2006). Perry has identified that trauma-invoked stress and associated release of cortisol can result in the child's stress responses becoming oversensitive, overactive and dysfunctional over time, due to the overuse of the brain stem in driving reactions to the situation (Perry and Hambrick 2008).

2. Early care has a decisive and long lasting impact on how people develop, their ability to learn and their capacity to regulate their emotions (Shore 1997, p.x). An enriched environment and caring

responsive adult interactions support the development of the brain. The responsiveness of the carer to the child's emotions helps the child to regulate their emotions. It supports the movement of functioning in the survival role of the brain stem, to the control and regulation of emotions in the middle brain, and ultimately to the higher functioning controls of the upper brain. Enriched environments and play (including physical play) help to support the development of neural networks in the frontal lobe and neocortex. Exploratory and imaginative play allow the lower brain (reptilian brain)'s 'seeking system' to work together with the higher brain (human brain), supporting the development of synaptic connections and neural networks in the human brain. Enriched environments lower the stress chemicals and allow people to better deal with stressful situations (Sunderland 2006, p.96). The emotional regulation area of the brain is stimulated by physical interactive play, thus helping the child to manage feelings better (p.104). Play and an enriched environment act as a natural de-stressor for the brain. Brain research indicates that 'warm and responsive relationships are key to children's positive development' (Shore 1997, p. xiii).

3. The human brain has a remarkable capacity to change. Children have many more synaptic connections than adults, with the greater density of these synapses remaining for the first decade of life. The principle of 'use it or lose it' is observed in the synaptic connections in the brain. Repeated activity increases the strength of the signal in these networks. Once they reach a level of activation they won't be eliminated. In this way repeated positive or negative experiences shape the brain architecture. Raised cortical levels, associated with stress, destroy neurons and reduce the number of synapses (Shore 1997).

4. There are times when negative experiences or the absence of appropriate stimulation are more likely to have an effect on the developing brain. Babies whose mothers become severely depressed when the baby is older are at greater risk (Shore 1997). Traumatic events that are experienced repeatedly and early in life leave the child more vulnerable in the future (Perry 2009).

5. The wisdom and efficacy of prevention and early intervention is identified. Perry in his Neurosequential Model of Therapeutics proposed a 'more developmentally sensitive, neurobiology guided

approach to clinical work'. He suggests a sequenced application of intervention that 'reflects the child's specific developmental needs in a variety of key domains and is sensitive to the core principles of neurodevelopment' (Perry 2009, p.249).

In practising as a Narrative Play Therapist an awareness of the research on the developing brain can support an understanding of:

- the progressive and hierarchical nature of the development of the brain

- the importance of a relationship that is caring, warm and consistent in supporting the child's progression from instinctive responses to higher order reasoning skills

- the neurobiological nature of stress, the value of play in reducing stress, and the value of playful relationship in supporting and developing a sense of self-awareness and wellbeing.

Narrative Play Therapy
The foundations of Narrative Play Therapy

Narrative Play Therapy is a branch of play therapy that draws on the developmental potential of play and narrative to support the child in developing a coherent narrative of his or her experiences and how these have impacted on the child. It is child-led as the child chooses the materials and toys with which he or she wishes to play. In play, the child's real and imagined worlds come together. Real objects can be used imaginatively, and imaginary objects can be used to create real worlds. Starting points for the creation of stories come from the child's play. The therapist adopts a curious or 'not knowing' stance and facilitates the creation of an open, safe and fear-free space for the child to explore, play, create and make stories. The therapist supports the co-construction of stories through skilled questioning and through facilitating the exchange of ideas and thoughts about the story. The child is supported in creating alternative endings and in generating a range of different stories within his or her play. This supports the creation of cognitive and emotional flexibility, which can then be utilised and accessed by the child in his or her lived world.

The underlying assumptions of the functions of narratives and stories in play and Narrative Play Therapy have been identified:

- Narrative Play Therapy is a way of controlling our world. In Narrative Play Therapy the telling and playing of stories offers the child an opportunity to control his or her world. The child can decide what roles the players will take and the development of the storyline, the events, obstacles to be overcome and the outcomes of the story or play. This can be done at a distance through pretending, and can support the child in trying out behaviours without consequence in the real world.

- It helps children to make sense of their lives and to develop empathy. In play and story making the events don't have to be real but the themes that emerge are similar themes to those in the child's life. In playing different roles or imagining what it is like for the other character, the child begins to develop empathy for the other.

- In working collaboratively, stories and narrative play are co-constructed between the therapist and the child. In this co-construction the relationship is explored and developed.

- The theoretical framework of social construction theory and narrative therapy informs the understanding of the development of identity. It describes the development of identity as being based on the stories we tell about ourselves and the stories others tell about us.

- In play and creating stories we can explore ways of shifting and expanding and changing stories, knowing that we do not have to bring these into our 'lived' life.

- This approach recognises that children live in an ecosystem, in a culture and at a specific period in time, all of which influence the way we see things.

- This collaborative work is child-led in the context of a relationship. The child chooses to play with small world toys, draw or make things. As they play they tell a story about what they are doing. The role of the adult is to listen and ask questions about the story. Sometimes the adult might tell stories that are congruent with the child's play. The relationship is deepened by sharing experiences of telling and listening.

These assumptions place Narrative Play Therapy within the new post-modern context of play therapy. Within this framework the concept of 'the self' and 'the problem' are seen as socially constructed.

The self

From a post-modern perspective, the self is seen as socially constructed in the context of relationships with others and systems in the environment. The person is seen as an active agent, actively constructing their identity in the stories they choose to tell and the stories that others tell about them. According to Cattanach, Malone (1997) stated 'that each person's life is lived as a series of conversations. It is in the flowing reciprocal exchange of conversation, that the self becomes real' (Cattanach 1999, p.81). Conversation becomes the symbolic medium for self-presentation. Engel, in her work on children's narratives, stated that 'every story that a child tells contributes to a self-portrait that the child can look at, refer to, think about and change'. The self-portrait is also 'used by others to understand the person who tells the story' (Engel 1995, as cited in Cattanach 2006, p.83). In Narrative Play Therapy, the self and identity emerges in the stories that the child chooses to tell and in the open space between the therapist and the child, where the child is storyteller and the therapist is the empathic listening audience. The co-constructed nature of the story-making process supports reciprocal conversations and the symbolic representation of possible selves in play and story.

The problem

Within Narrative Play Therapy, the problem or reason that brings the child to therapy is socially constructed and defined. It is rooted in cultural, interpersonal and individual conditions. As can be seen from the brain research discussed above, the child's individual genetic make-up may play some part in the developing difficulties. However, these difficulties can be ameliorated or exacerbated by the environment, including the interpersonal environment in which the child finds him- or herself being brought up and also the experiences they have. For example, in the culture of the school which four-year-old Jack was attending, the expectation was to sit down, remain on task, even when they were bored, and complete the learning task within a certain time frame. When Jack was unable to comply with this cultural requirement he was identified as distracted and unfocused and parents and staff queried attention type difficulties. Thus his behaviour was socially constructed and culturally defined. From a post-modern perspective, problems are framed as a lack of opportunity, capacity or permission to story experiences in a satisfactory manner. In Narrative Play Therapy problem saturated stories bring the child to therapy. This blinds the child to other stories and other resources (Cattanach 2006). Narrative Play Therapy offers opportunities for externalising the problem by placing it within the play and the narratives created. It offers opportunities to try out different stories and alternative endings. In creating stories and playing, the child has an opportunity to explore possible selves, until a story emerges that is satisfactory to the child at that time.

Setting the scene – the environment

In considering the materials to be chosen for therapy, the Narrative Play Therapist considers the developmental needs of the child and the need within the play therapy process to be able to move along this developmental continuum. The EPR developmental paradigm is a useful framework for the consideration of the materials for the play therapy environment (Cattanach 1994; Jennings 1993). A range of suggested materials within this framework are presented. Case studies are used to illustrate how children have used these materials. This section concludes by considering the creation of the therapeutic space.

Sensory and embodiment materials can include slime, sand, gloop, clay, play dough, finger paints and other such materials. Blankets and pieces of different textured materials allow for the creation of cubbies and other enclosed spaces. The child can also be rolled up in them or swung in them. A large square of lycra material can prove useful on both counts. Objects such as smooth marble and semiprecious stones, sponge and brushes add to the richness of the sensory and embodiment materials made available to the child. Joe was five years old when he first started play therapy. He had been placed with a foster family as an infant and had regular access visits with his mother. However, he was taken by his parents from the foster family without permission when he was a year old and remained with them for six weeks. He had then been taken into care and placed with another foster family where he was currently placed. When he started play therapy he created chaos, emptying everything on the floor. His ability to settle in the play therapy sessions was facilitated by offering him sensory materials as he played in the tent. These include slime and gloop which he explored in a very sensory manner. He noticed a duvet in the room and queried why it was there. The therapist suggested that some children liked to be wrapped up in this or swung in it. Joe requested to be wrapped up in this and was gently rocked back and forth.

The therapist narrated stories about the baby being safe and wrapped up and sang/hummed different lullabies. This sensory embodiment play was observed for another six sessions and was reflective of his developmental needs. Joe was then ready to move on and explore and play with other toys in the room.

Art materials, clay, small world characters and architectural structures, as well as wild, domestic, prehistoric and mythical creatures, form part of the play therapy toys and materials made available to the child to support projective play. Sometimes children choose to play with these, making stories with the different characters and creating scenes with the different materials provided. Others use the miniatures to create a picture in the sand. Art materials are used to create picture and stories. David was three years old when he attended for play therapy. His parents had separated following ongoing domestic violence. When David first entered the playroom, he noticed the boxes of animals. He spent several sessions exploring the animals in these boxes, finding family groups of animals with two larger animals and two to three smaller animals. Each group was placed on a different floor tile and, where there was a moveable join in the toy animal's head, it was lowered as if grazing. As the sessions progressed David was able to add more and more objects to the floor tile, 'as if' creating a living environment for the family of animals. The need to have two big animals in each group appeared to diminish over time, though he continued to group similar animals together.

Role play and dramatic play is supported by the presence of some props such as phones, microphones, hats, glasses, shoes and the different lengths of materials. Some equipment such as syringes, breathing masks, foam swords, home corner equipment and hand and finger puppets are also made available. In role play the child takes on the role of actor/director while the therapist acts as an actor, looking for direction from the child. Children will often use the furniture in the room to create the space for the event to happen. Jessica was six years old when she first began to role play and use the dramatic play props. She was adopted abroad, so little was known about her first 18 months of life. She was referred to play therapy due to ongoing difficulties with making a secure attachment with her adopted mother, and the family was having problems managing Jessica's behaviour. After several play therapy sessions, Jessica noticed the doctor's kit and became curious about the objects in the kit. Having explored the function of each item, Jessica asked if she could play doctors. She directed the play therapist to be the doctor and she was the patient. She used a couch in the room as her sick bed and became a very demanding patient, always unsure of what was wrong with her, 'I just don't feel good', and making the doctor carry out a large range of investigations and do some detective work to figure out what was wrong with the patient. The pain would be alleviated for a short time only to return somewhere else. When the therapist said she wanted to be the patient, she was only allowed to have 'simple' things wrong with her, which could be fixed with a pill or a plaster. Jessica could only tolerate being the doctor for a short time before requesting a change of roles back to being the patient.

Narrative Play Therapy is practised in a number of contexts and environments. Some therapists have a dedicated playroom with a range of toys and materials, access to sand and water, space for large physical play and drama. Others have to practise in confined, small spaces and often have to provide a portable means of converting bedrooms, family rooms or principal's offices into a safe, contained environment in which the child can explore, play and create. Cattanach (1992, 1994) proposed the use of a play mat that can provide a contained space for the therapist and child to play. This can be constructed at the beginning of therapy and de-constructed at the end of the session allowing the themes, play and stories to be contained within the play space. The mat also demarcates the playing and 'not-playing' space (Cattanach 1999). It is important to create these two spaces to construct imaginative play. This contributes to the 'me' and 'not me' dramatic distancing that the play therapy intervention offers. It allows for a special 'as if' play world to be created where imaginary stories, places, people and events can be played out. The 'not-playing' space allows for information to be shared and the rules and boundaries to be revisited if required, thus keeping the play space intact. The concept of two spaces has proved very useful for children who have difficulties in complying with rules and boundaries when they become totally absorbed in their play. In this portable framework of creating a play therapy environment, a large blue oilcloth mat is used to outline the boundaries of the play therapy space. A wide range of materials, discussed above, is made available to the child.

Natalie was seven years old when she first came to therapy. She became so engaged in her play themes of chaos and destruction that she was unable to hear the rules of 'not hurting each other and not damaging the toys'. Disruptions were seen as an invasion of her special time. When the concept of the playing/not-playing space was introduced to Natalie, she was better able to hear the rules and any requirement to remind her of these rules was done by moving into the not-playing space. This reduced the negative impact of this type of disruption, while helping her to feel safe and to continue to explore her experiences in the play and stories.

In conclusion, the range of toys and materials provided within this developmental framework allow the child to move along the continuum of play and narrative, supporting exploration and symbolic expression. The open, fear-free play space allows the child to explore real and imagined worlds in the company of an attentive adult. Stories and narratives are generated with complex plots, actions and characters which portray thoughts, motive and belief within the child's play. The facilitation of this open fear-free environment allows for the developmental potential of play and narrative to emerge in the context of the relationship with the therapist. The therapist meets the child in their world by participating in their pretend play under the child's direction, and in co-constructing stories with the child. In this therapeutic space and through the relationship with the therapist, the child can begin to explore, test and define his or her possible selves (Cattanach 1999).

Meet the characters: the role of the therapist and the other main players

The role of the Narrative Play Therapist, as with other therapists, is to begin to develop a relationship with the child and the significant adults in his or her life. The therapist and the child enter into a relationship that is mediated through play. The purpose of the relationship and the play is to make sense of the child's world through the narratives and stories which emerge (Cattanach 1999). This is achieved initially by creating a safe, fear-free environment. Rules and boundaries are established to create a predictable environment and help the child feel safe. The Narrative Play Therapist adopts a curious but 'not-knowing' stance. He or she enters the world of the child and their play with curiosity and wonder, and meets the child with genuineness, shedding preconceptions of the child or professional interpretations of what the child's stories and play might symbolise for the child. Instead, the therapist enters the child's play, as a player directed by the child, or as a scribe for their stories. The child's play, narrative and stories are then co-constructed through active listening and questioning to understand the child's understanding and interpretation of his or her stories, play or narrative explanation.

This then sets the atmosphere in the play therapy room for safe, fear-free exploration of emerging play and narrative.

In meeting with the child's parents or caregivers, the Narrative Play Therapist's role is to listen to the stories that they bring about the child's difficulties and what brings them to seek help at this time. It is important to identify if there is 'good enough' care available to the child within his or her ecosystem to support the child as he or she explores their stories. On occasions, the environment is not sufficiently fear-free or inadequate supports are available to the child to progress with intervention. On these occasions, it is the role of the therapist to support the family and the system in identifying the supports needed before therapy with the child can begin.

In setting the scene for Narrative Play Therapy to begin, the child is introduced to the therapist and the play therapy environment. This is another key element in the process of creating this open, fear-free environment. The initial meeting may take place in the presence of a significant carer. The therapist shares with the child his or her awareness that something has happened to the child and/or his or her family that might be sad or scary (or maybe even happy). It is acknowledged that the child might need some help in sorting out feelings about what has happened. It is explained to the child that he or she will be invited to play and make stories to sort out these feelings. The child is introduced to the idea that the stories don't have to be about him or her but that sometimes things happen in stories that are similar to the child's experience: 'the stories and play we do together are "not about you but I bet you that the same things have happened to people in stories that have happened to you"' (Cattanach 1997, p.36). The child is introduced to the toys and materials that are available in the playroom. The child is introduced to the idea that 'in here' he or she can play what and how he or she wants, and that if there is a story the therapist can write it down. This introduces the child-led nature of Narrative Play Therapy. The general rules and boundaries are introduced to the child. These are similar to other models of play therapy and include that the toys need to stay in the room, respect for each other and respect for the toys and that if the child chooses to leave the room (without good reason) he or she chooses to end the session. In explaining the roles and responsibilities, and rules and boundaries of Narrative Play Therapy, the therapist communicates his or her ability to enter the child's play world and help him or her sort out and make sense of confusions and feelings (Cattanach 1999).

During the play therapy sessions it is the role of the Narrative Play Therapist to play with the child under the direction of the child, and to record their stories as they emerge. The therapist mediates the social and cultural world which the child inhabits by asking questions about the stories and the narratives brought into the therapy space. The aim of questioning for the therapist is to gain an understanding of what is happening in the play from the child's perspective and generally to keep up with the rapid shift in roles and events that happen in the child's play and narratives. This facilitates the co-construction of stories and play sequences. At the beginning of play and story making with children in therapy, there is often confusion. In playing with the child, the therapist may use questions to clarify the role, the behaviour and motivations of the character, and the sequence of events that he or she is to enact, so that the therapist can play the role from the child's perspective. In co-constructing stories, clarification on the sequencing of events, the introduction of new characters and the changing motivations of the characters form the bases for questioning. Questioning therefore helps to sort out confusion and supports the child in developing a coherent narrative with a beginning, middle and end. The child and therapist negotiate a shared meaning that is congruent with the child's lived-in world (Cattanach 1999). The therapist listens to the story and acts as scribe for the story. The child has permission to explore and experiment with alternative stories and alternative endings. Cattanach (2006) recounts the story four-year-old Mary told about the wicked witch and the wicked dragon. In the first version the witch died. In discussing what it meant to be dead with Mary, she generated four more endings for the story, namely, that the witch could die forever, die and come back, go to prison or become a good witch. The child can play around with elements of the story such as time, space, characters and roles. Sometimes the end of the session does not coincide with the end of the story but the end of the chapter, with the story continuing over several weeks. Thinking about stories as chapters can offer support to the child in being able to end his or her play/story at the end of a session. It also provides a bridge into the next session and assigns the role to the therapist of the 'keeper of the story'. The child is then held in mind by the therapist, thus supporting the child's sense of identity as separate, but in the context of a relationship.

In bridging the gap between sessions, the therapist, as 'keeper of the story', becomes the storyteller, telling the story so far. The therapist reads or recalls the stories dictated by the child, both in the words used and the tone and atmosphere of the story. In the role of storyteller, the therapist also chooses stories for the child that are congruent to the child's experiences or feelings and/or what the child has invented (Cattanach 2006). Myths, legends and other published stories can be identified that convey the sources of dread and fear in the child's life and can offer new hope. George was four years old when he began therapy. Due to a number of difficulties within the family and the absence of his dad, George was not able to be cared for on a full time basis by his mother. He regularly received respite care organised by the local social services. He found the transition to respite care difficult and his behaviour in school deteriorated following periods of respite care. The story that came to mind when playing with George was the story of Hansel and Gretel. I read this story to George and he requested that it was read on several more occasions. George questioned the fairness of the children being left in the woods and struggled with the idea of the witch's house and the concept of 'all not being as it seems'.

Supporting the experience of endings through the co-construction of the ending of therapy is another role for the play therapist. In the same way as stories have a beginning, middle and end, the ending of therapy is introduced to the child. The number of sessions available for therapy and thus the end is often dictated by the money available for the intervention, whether dictated by insurance companies or the pressure on statutory and voluntary organisations due to waiting lists. The child is supported in co-constructing how the therapy ends, whether or not the ending is dictated or negotiated within the system that the therapist is working. Through questioning the child is supported in identifying what ritual or celebration he or she would like to participate in to signal the ending of therapy. Children's ideas are sought on what they would like to happen to their stories, art work and digital art created in the sessions. Some children want to make a book of their stories created in therapy. Others request that the therapist continues to be the 'keeper of the stories'. In deciding what to do about the stories, the therapist and child need to consider how the stories and other work created in therapy may be received by significant people in the child's life. If the child chooses to make a storybook, the therapist can discuss with the child who he or she wishes to show the book to, the timing of when it might be shown, and where the child might store the book for safe keeping when 'it moves in' to the child's lived world. The book is then co-constructed. Stories and pictures for inclusion are identified. Annamarie chose to spend her second last session making the cover for her book. She created a cover of leaves using coloured paper and gold markers. She included only the stories about trees that had been co-constructed during therapy. (Annamarie has continued the story-making process at home between sessions and brought in a new story each week.) The book was to 'move in' under her bed and she decided that she could take it out at night and read it to herself if she had had a 'bad day'.

Avenues into story

Stories and storied play are the main tools used in Narrative Play Therapy. These are used to establish a relationship, to understand the child's world and to facilitate change. The themes that children present in their social world also appear in the imagined stories they express (Cattanach 2006). This begins the process of externalising the difficulties. In therapy the stories that children present in play are explored, and an exchange of thoughts and ideas about these stories is facilitated. Together the child and the therapist work to co-construct the stories, expanding the themes, changing and shifting meaning and exploring alternative plots and solutions until a new and more satisfying story emerges and a new way of being develops. The story acts as a container, a space between the therapist and the child in which shared meaning is negotiated between the two in the context of the relationship of the storyteller and the attentive audience, and as a container for experience (Cattanach 2006).

A number of avenues to stories have emerged over the development of Narrative Play Therapy and are explored further in the case studies in Part II of this book. In this section I will outline the four main avenues to story based on the writings of Ann Cattanach and the experience of practitioners who trained with her. These are adult-directed, child-led play based, storytelling and meta-storying of children's play.

Adult-directed

When children and young people come to therapy their anxiety level may be raised for a number of reasons, including anxiety about what is expected of them, and how they are expected to conduct themselves. Therapy is not usually something you can find out about from your friends or siblings, in the same way as you might find out about your new school or transferring to secondary school. An adult-directed activity to support the child into the process of co-constructed story making and to begin building the relationship is often useful. It helps to reduce some of these initial anxieties and to begin to create a safe, fear-free space. A number of techniques that are adult-led are laid out in more detail in Chapter 3.

They include variations on the House-Tree-Person Drawing, the Squiggle Game and the 6-PSM and BASIC Ph. The following story was created by Jasmine, aged 11. She was attending therapy due to ongoing concerns about her emotional wellbeing. School was particularly difficult for her and it was felt that she was not achieving her full academic potential. To support Jasmine in developing a relationship with the therapist and to reduce her anxiety about attending therapy, Jasmine was invited to draw a picture of a tree and the following story was co-constructed.

The Tree

This is a big colourful tree. It's old, about 200 years old. It is in the woods – on its own. It is very rare.

Lots of people are coming to see it because it is rare and so old. In this part of the wood there are all the non-colourful trees. All the colourful ones have been cut down except for this one.

This theme of two different worlds became apparent throughout her therapy in the numerous stories that she then created from her pictures and play in the sand.

Another adult-directed approach to story is based on the story-making approach developed by Alida Gersie and Nancy King. In this approach, traditional and folk stories are explored in a structured manner. The belief is that hearing and telling stories stimulates the imagination. The storyteller and listener begin a journey together and through a process of connecting with the story's content and themes the listener can discover personal meanings that the content has for them (Gersie and King 1990). Cattanach (1994) gives an example of this approach. She tells the story 'The Witch and the Rainbow Cat' based on one of Terry Jones' tales in his collection *Fairy Tales* (1983). The child is invited to imagine what the witch sees in the mirror currently and in the future. The child is also invited to continue the story from different points and to give the story an ending as a way of exploring the themes of the story. In this story the theme of what the future might hold for the main protagonist and paradoxically for the child can be explored. I have used this approach with a range of stories for children. *Badger's Parting Gift* (Varley 1984) is an example of a story that I have used with children who have been bereaved. By using the themes and the experiences of the characters in the story, children have begun to explore their own bereavements and the feelings they have about their loss. This approach is also linked to the therapist as the storyteller approach described further below.

CHILD-LED PLAY-BASED

In travelling down this avenue to stories, the therapist uses the child's play and stories. In play the child may provide a running commentary on the actions, events and motivations of the characters in his or her play. The therapist offers to write these down as it sounds like a story the child is telling. The therapist may use questioning to support the structure and sequence of the story and to clarify the meaning of actions for different characters in the story. For instance, children may create stories about the pictures they create in the sand. The following is another of Jasmine's stories that she told following the creation of a picture in the sand.

Two Worlds – Water and Land

The different worlds of the land and sea.

On the Land

One day the dinosaur eggs hatched. The T-Rex and the triceratops hatched. Everyone came to the party from the landside.

Over to the Sea

The crocodile was fighting with the red-eyed blue crocodile over the snake. They wanted to eat the snake. The red and orange frog was enjoying the fight. The other two brothers were not interested. The tortoise began to sing and the seals began to dance. It was very crazy. The hippo came to break up the fight between the seals.

On the Land

The rhinoceros and the three tigers and black tiger and the pigs began to fight. The camel was watching them. Everybody, all the animals are clapping and cheering for the rhinoceros. (It's like humans really, except animals.) The two-headed dinosaur (mum and dad) watched their egg and the triceratops dad was minding his egg too. The two-headed purple man with a stick and bandage came to the party.

On the Sea

The big beetle came to dance but he was too big so he couldn't get in.

The End.

Storytelling

The therapist as storyteller and a 'keeper of stories' is a theme throughout Narrative Play Therapy. In this role the therapist holds a wide range of stories, from the stories children tell, to published stories, to myths and legends passed down in the oral tradition of many cultures. The aim of storytelling is to find a story that has meaning for the child, whether in the themes of the story, or in its similarity to the struggles of the child or the imagined world the child has created. Cattanach gives many examples of the store of traditional myths and legends that she held as a keeper of the story. Sometimes children bring the stories from their culture, such as traditions of the 'boogie' man and ghosts or the banshee. Children may also bring published stories that have a resonance for them. Louise was a young girl who came to therapy with a story in mind. The story she brought was *Bye, Bye Baby*, a sad story with a happy ending by Janet and Allan Ahlberg (1991). She immediately identified with this story and spent several sessions acting out the story. She set up obstacle courses that the baby had to travel over before being found by the mother. The mother had to be nurturing and pleased and excited to have found this beautiful baby and the baby succumbed to this nurturing. This play sequence was followed with a request for the story to be read.

The storyteller can create a story for the child. In Chapter 10, Carol Platteuw describes the process of creating a story, with an adoptive mother, for her child. She shared this story as a model of storytelling.

Meta-storying

In meta-storying the therapist engages in a process of storying the child's play over the course of play therapy. This can include placing individual sessions in the contained structure of a story or using different elements of the child's play to story his or her experience and create a story with many episodes, characters, plots and subplots. As the child plays he or she is asked if this is an episode that the child would like added to the story. As the child becomes familiar with this process, he or she begins to request that particular elements, play sequences or plots are added to the story. The story becomes the child's overarching story of therapy. In Chapter 4 Kate Kirk uses the structure of meta-storying to support the child in this externalising process. The following is an example of the meta-storying of an episode of play.

Moving Day

Once upon a time two people were moving into a new house and decided to have a few friends over for dinner.

First one person went shopping to buy food and other things for the house. This person found a very helpful shopkeeper who had lots of 'two for one' offers. He also threw in a few things for free and helped to pack up the shopping as he chatted to the customer. He then helped by delivering the goods to the new house.

When the shopping arrived there were lots of things to put away. One person did a lot of the sorting out, figuring out where things would go in the new house, where the pots and pans would go, working out how the oven worked and sorting out the fridge. This person was also a very good cook and made lovely pizzas and chicken for the dinner and a tasty cake with fresh fruit. He worked out who would come to dinner and at what time. He was very independent and organised. The other person helped with some jobs like setting the table and making some calls.

All was ready and it was 6 pm.

The therapist offers to tell the story in the following session. This can give the child a sense of being held in mind, between sessions. The child is invited to make changes or amendments so that the story is a satisfying account of what happened. Meta-storying also provides a record to the child's play and the evolving themes that emerge.

Conclusion

Narrative Play Therapy is a form of play therapy that supports the child through playing and stories to reach a satisfactory understanding of their situation. This understanding is negotiated through the co-construction of stories. The therapist's curious but 'not-knowing' stance, and his or her participation in the child's world of play, helps to create an open, safe and fear-free environment and supports the development of the relationship. This allows the child to explore and try out new stories and new endings. The developmental range of toys and materials made available to the child act as a medium for the generation of stories. A range of avenues into stories are identified. The story acts as a container or a space between the therapist and the child in which shared meaning can be negotiated through questioning and talking. The child is supported in creating a range of possible stories and possible endings in the imaginary world that can transfer into the lived world of the child.

References

Ahlberg, J. and Ahlberg, A. (1991) *Bye Bye Baby: A Sad Story with a Happy Ending.* London: Mammoth.

Bruner, J. (1990) *Acts of Meaning.* Cambridge, MA: Harvard University Press.

Bruner, J. (1991) 'The narrative construction of reality.' *Critical Inquiry 18*, 1–21.

Bruner, J.S. and Luciarello, J. (1989) 'Monologue as Narrative Recreation of the World.' In K. Nelson (ed.) *Narratives from the Crib.* Cambridge, MA: Harvard University Press.

Cattanach, A. (1992) *Play Therapy with Abused Children.* London: Jessica Kingsley Publishers.

Cattanach, A. (1994) *Play Therapy. Where the Sky Meets the Underworld.* London: Jessica Kingsley Publishers.

Cattanach, A. (1997) *Children's Stories in Play Therapy.* London: Jessica Kingsley Publishers.

Cattanach, A. (1999) 'Co-Construction in Play Therapy.' In A. Cattanach (ed.) *Process in the Arts Therapies.* London: Jessica Kingsley Publishers.

Cattanach, A. (2006) 'Narrative Play Therapy.' In C.E. Schaefer and H.G Kaduson (eds) *Contemporary Play Therapy. Theory, Research and Practice.* New York: Guilford Press.

Cattanach, A. (2008) *Narrative Approaches in Play with Children.* London: Jessica Kingsley Publishers.

Engel, S. (2005) 'The narrative worlds of what is and what if.' *Cognitive Psychology 20*, 514–525.

Gersie, A. and King, N. (1990) *Storymaking in Education and Therapy.* London: Jessica Kingsley Publishers.

Jennings, S. (1993) *Playtherapy with Children. A Practitioner's Guide.* Oxford: Blackwell Scientific Publications.

Jones, T. (1983) *Fairy Tales.* London: Penguin Books.

McLeod, J. (1997) *Narrative and Psychotherapy.* London: SAGE Publications.

Nicolopoulou, A. (2005) 'Play and narrative in the process of development: Commonalities, differences and interrelations.' *Cognitive Psychology 20*, 495–502.

Perry, B. and Hambrick, E. (2008) 'The neurosequential model.' *Reclaiming Children and Youth 17*, 3, 38–43.

Perry, B. (2009) 'Examining child maltreatment through a neurodevelopmental lens: Clinical applications of the neurosequential model of therapeutics.' *Journal of Loss and Trauma 14*, 240–255.

Shore, R. (1997) *Rethinking the Brain: New Insights into Early Development.* New York: Families and Work Institute.

Sunderland, M. (2006) *The Science of Parenting: How Today's Brain Research Can Help You Raise Happy, Emotionally Balanced Children.* London: DK Publishing.

Trevarthen, C. (1995) 'The child's need to learn a culture.' *Culture and Society 9*, 2, 5–19.

Varley, S. (1984) *Badger's Parting Gift.* London: Random Century.

Chapter 3

Assessment, Record Keeping and Evaluation in Narrative Play Therapy

Aideen Taylor de Faoite

Introduction

Assessment, record keeping and evaluation are all important elements of any professional stance. Professionals are required to be accountable for their actions and decisions. In play therapy, as in other professions, these are often dictated by the requirement of the organisation or the contexts in which the therapist works. There may be statutory requirement and practice procedures that are related to professional licensing of the therapist. Quality assurance and inspection systems such as Ofsted (Office for Standards in Education, Children's Services and Skills) in the UK will also require the professional to maintain records in a certain manner to ensure the safety of the client. The following methods of assessment, record keeping and evaluation have been developed to support the Narrative Play Therapist in meeting these requirements while reflecting the theoretical framework and practice of Narrative Play Therapy.

Assessment

Three main contexts for assessment can be identified in Narrative Play Therapy. These are the context of the parent/caregiver relationship with the child, the context of the child–therapist relationship and the context of the child in their environment.

Assessment within the context of the parent/caregiver relationship

The aims of assessment within the context of the parent/caregiver relationship are to:

1. identify the 'problem saturated' stories that the family tells about the child

2. listen to the stories of the family and stories that the parents are told about their child by other elements of the child's ecosystem, e.g. schools, childcare, other professionals

3. begin to identify the stories of hope and resilience that can be shared about the child, e.g. Was there a time when things were different? Can you remember a positive experience with your child?

The initial meeting with the parents/caregivers and referrer offers an opportunity to hear the stories that bring the child to therapy. Sometimes families have their own 'problem saturated' story to tell. This can often be extensive but added to by the burdens of the other 'problem saturated' stories about their child. Parents/carers may have been on a waiting list for some time. This will also have had an impact on the story being told by the time the therapist hears it for the first time.

CASE STUDY

A family requested referral to an intervention service due to ongoing concerns about their child's behaviour. He was described as a very active four-year-old who could not settle to class work and his teacher was having significant difficulties managing his behaviour in the context of a large class size. Parents were experiencing similar difficulties at home in trying to get him to remain on task both for school activities and activities of his choosing.

The child and family were offered an assessment six months after the initial referral. Based on the referral story the assessment team had prepared a large space for movement and activity before settling to a play-based developmental assessment.

When the child and parents arrived for the initial assessment, the child presented as a calm, interested young boy. The problem saturated story had changed. While he still has some difficulties with settling to activities and remaining on task, his behaviour was manageable in school and at home. The six months from the initial reference coincided with the end of the school year and the beginning of a new school year.

Time for maturation and change in the child's environment can change the reason for referral. The majority of stories are more burdened by an extended waiting time. The focus of the family and referrer can also have changed but the difficulties remain.

The initial assessment with the parents/caregiver is also a time to identify how long the difficulties have been present, the magnitude of the difficulties from the different adults' perspective and the priorities of the parent. Stories of hope and resilience need to be sought and acknowledged. These can include finding the stories of when times were different before the problem arose, remembering positive events and experiences with the child and identifying the behaviours that are positive throughout the day. Parents can become so overwhelmed, by the pressure from others or due to their own mental health difficulties, that they find it difficult to identify such glimpses of hope or resilience.

Following the initial meeting with the parents/caregiver, a joint session with the child can be helpful to witness how the child and parents respond to playful tasks presented. In supporting this playful interaction and to reduce the pressure on the parent to play in the presence of the therapist, the Squiggle Game has proved useful. This game is adapted from the game developed by Derek Winnicott in his work with children as a psychoanalyst and child psychiatrist (Winnicott 1991, p.16).

THE SQUIGGLE GAME WITH FAMILIES

Pencils, crayons, markers and a range of paper sizes and colours are made available to the family, who are invited to learn a new game called the Squiggle Game. One person is invited to choose a page and a colour and to make a scribble on the page. The next person is then invited to make something out of it. Then the second person is invited to make a mark on a piece of paper so that something can be made out of it in return. If there is more than one parent/carer and the child present, this can become a 'round robin' game, where the squiggly line is passed onto the next person in the circle to make something of it. The direction may need to be changed to ensure that everyone starts and everyone has a chance to finish a picture.

Variations: The squiggly line can go around and be added to for a number of agreed turns before someone has to make something of it. Another variation is to stick the pictures on the wall and to have the adult and child pretend they are in an art gallery and they have to put a title on each of the paintings. The therapist acts as the gallery curator recording the title and any commentary that the person chooses to put with the title.

CASE STUDY

A father and son attended a joint session as part of an assessment. The Squiggle Game was introduced first with the therapist and child modelling it to the dad. The dad was then invited to play the game and the therapist stepped back. They had a discussion to decide who would go first and the dad went first. He drew a vertical line that continued horizontally at a right angle. He then invited the child to guess what he had started so that the child could finish the picture. It became a guessing game, with the dad giving hints on request, including that it was something they had seen on the way into the session, the colour of the 'object', and finally the conversation that they had had about it on the journey. The child eventually guessed what it was and completed the drawing. While this proved challenging for the child, as his dad wouldn't give him the answer, the child persisted in the interaction. The atmosphere was friendly and playful with an edge of competitiveness.

The Squiggle Game was followed by a very positive father and son play session in the sand. This was familiar territory for the child. The child constructed a scene in the sand while the dad asked pertinent questions to show interest in the emerging scene, made comments linking the scene to familiar places to the child and offered technical support on some construction issues. It was a privilege to witness this session, bearing in mind that I held the role of assessor for the court.

The father and child had made the game their own and had demonstrated their communication style. They were able to move between each other's worlds, the dad in the sand with the child, the child playing the guessing game with the dad. Experiences they had shared together emerged as part of their playful interaction, both in guessing the object, and recalling similar scenes that they had visited. It offered a richness of information that had not been evident from individual conversations with each person about the other, thus thickening the narrative plot. The Squiggle Game can therefore be used as a valuable assessment tool in Narrative Play Therapy to observe the parent/caregiver relationship in a structured way.

Assessing the child in his or her natural environment

Where possible, it is recommended that the child is observed within the natural environment and in the context where difficulties arise. When observing the child the following points should be borne in mind:

- What strategies is the child using to connect with others in the ecosystem?

- What is the problem with the behaviour? And whose problem is it?

- What might the behaviour be communicating?

- Begin to identify the goals of misbehaviour.

- When is the problem behaviour not occurring?

When observing children in their environments, and beginning discussions with the adults supporting children in those environments, I have found the Adlerian constructs of the Crucial Cs and Goals of Misbehaviour useful. The assumption is that behaviour is goal directed and communicates the goals of the child. The Crucial Cs have been identified as Connect, Capable, Count and Courage (Lew and Bettner 1998). When children feel connected, they will have a sense of belonging and their behaviour will be co-operative in nature. When children feel capable they feel they can do things and their goal of behaviour is self-reliance. When children feel they count, they feel they can make a difference and their goal of behaviour is to contribute. When children have courage, they can manage things that come their way, both expected and unexpected, and the goal of their behaviour is resilience (p.63). In this construct of behaviour, the Crucial Cs are the goals that children strive for and their behaviour will reflect their striving for these goals. The goals of misbehaviour are construed as misguided attempts to achieve these goals. The four categories of misbehaviour first identified by Dreikurs and Soltz (1964) are attention, power, revenge and proven inadequacy (later changed to avoidance; Lew and Bettner 1998). Each goal of misbehaviour has been linked to a Crucial C. Children who are seeking connection, acceptance and a sense of belonging will use attention to achieve this goal (Kottman 1995). Children who use power as a goal of behaviour may mistakenly assume that they only feel capable when they are in control (Lew and Bettner 1998). Revenge as a goal of misbehaviour is often used by children who want to feel capable as they feel unacceptable and unwanted (Kottman 1995). Children who use a misguided goal of avoidance often feel discouraged, that they will not succeed and therefore they give up trying. The three elements of information that help the therapist in understanding the child's misguided goals of behaviour are the child's behaviour and feelings, the feelings and reactions of the adults who interact with the child and the child's reaction to criticism or punishment (Kottman 1995, p.107).

CASE STUDY

Jane was seven years old when she was referred for assessment and intervention. She had ongoing behavioural difficulties at home and was very disruptive in school. In observing the child in the classroom it was noted that Jane used a range of strategies to gain the attention of the teacher. Some were constructive, such as putting up her hand to respond to a question. Others were destructive, such as giving silly and rude replies when she did put up her hand and wait her turn or shouting at the teacher across the class or walking around the room disrupting other children. The teacher tried to ignore some behaviours. Her feelings and reactions ranged from mildly irritated to annoyed by Jane's constant attempts to gain her attention. This behaviour was then considered in the context of the Crucial Cs construct and a new narrative emerged: that child needs to feel connected to the group and have a sense of belonging within the classroom. Working on these elements identified in the assessment became the focus of intervention.

Assessment in the context of the child–therapist relationship

The aims of initial assessment within the context of the child–therapist relationship are:

1. to begin to develop a therapeutic relationship

2. to identify the child's ability to engage in the medium of play and to be playful in the context of the therapeutic relationship

3. to begin to create and co-construct narratives and stories in the context of the therapeutic relationship

4. to identify themes as they emerge in the assessment.

At the beginning of the assessment process it is helpful to get to know the child's perception of him- or herself as the therapist will have heard others' stories of the child. Cattanach developed the 'shield' as a projective technique that can act as 'an ice breaker and an initial assessment of how the child perceives him/herself at the moment of the drawing' (1994, p.84).

THE SHIELD

Method:

- Draw a shield and divide it in six.

- Get the child to draw the outline of his or her shield similar to yours.

- Introduce the shield by saying 'I am going to ask you some questions and you are to draw the answer to the question in the shield. Draw the first thing that comes into your head. You can use as many colours as you like. When the shield is complete it will tell a story.'

- When the child has finished drawing ask the child to explain what he or she has drawn.

- Write down the answers in the original shield, explaining to the child that it is going to help us remember what each picture means.

- Offer possibilities to the child if he or she is finding it difficult to generate ideas. Lots of encouragement and reinforcement of the child's ideas is suggested as children coming to therapy carry failure and 'not good enough' stories of themselves and may have little experience of encouragement.

Table 3.1 represents the sections of the shield and the questions related to each section of the shield.

Table 3.1: The shield

1st section What is the best thing that has ever happened to you?	2nd section What is the best thing that has ever happened to you in your family – any family? (Children in care may have experienced many families)
3rd section What is the worst thing that has happened to you?	4th section What do you want from other people, not your family, but people your own age?
5th section If you only had a year to live and all the money you want, what would you do for the year?	6th section Now people are at your funeral and remembering you – what three things would you like people to say about you? They don't have to be true. (The therapist can offer to write the words.)

Source: Adapted from Cattanach 1994, p.83

In Chapter 7 Sharon Pearce presents a case study and research in the use of another version of the shield, both in assessing a child who has experienced parental separation and in evaluating the progress made in play therapy. In Chapter 9 Ann Marie John presents her adaptation of The Shield as an assessment tool for narrative family play therapy and described how families have used the shield in therapy.

Another variation of the shield that I have used only has four sections. The sections are:

- me as a baby or small child
- me now
- me when I'm older
- three things that I would like to happen if I was granted three wishes.

CASE STUDY

In working with a group of young people with chronic and life shortening illnesses, this assessment tool proved very interesting. The group initially worked individually on their shields and then shared their thoughts on the pictures drawn for each element. Some members of the group struggled to draw 'me when I'm older'. Older was often only their next birthday. As they were in hospital at the time of the group, all drew 'me now' in different states of unwellness, reflecting their current health difficulties. The 'me as a baby' was often an idealised picture of a bonny baby, while the three wishes were full of hope and idealism about finding a cure for not only their own illness but lots of illnesses that they had become familiar with over their times in hospital. One group member, whose mood was very low at the beginning of the group, initially could not think of three wishes. However she gradually became infected by the other group members' passions for what a cure would look like and how it might work for different children whose conditions they were familiar with.

STORY STEMS

Story stems can be useful when the assessment period is time limited or when the child is having difficulties engaging in narrative work. The child is given the beginning of a story and invited to complete the story by playing or dramatising the end of the story. A range of story stems assessment procedures have been developed over the last half a century. Initially they were developed to assess feeling and fantasies (see Moore and Ucko 1961). More recently the Story Stem Assessment Profile has been developed to assess the child's 'perceptions and expectations of family roles, attachments and relationships without asking the child direct questions about their family', which might cause stress or anxiety (Steele *et al.* 2007, p.168). The child is presented with the beginning of a story, highlighting familiar everyday events with an inherent dilemma. The child is asked to 'show me and tell me what happens next'. The therapist observes how the child responds verbally and non-verbally to the story stem, and, using a standardised rating scale, scores what the child says and does to complete the emotionally charged story beginning (Steele *et al.* 2007).

The Story Stem Assessment Profile, the Manchester Children Attachment Story Task (MCAST) (Goldwyn *et al.* 2000) and CMCAST (a computerised version of the MCAST; Minnis *et al.* 2008) offer a standardised assessment tool to assess children's attachment and understanding of relationships. These also offer the Narrative Play

Therapist a valuable structure to address the assessment aims identified above.

THE SQUIGGLE GAME WITH CHILDREN

The Squiggle Game is a valuable tool in supporting the development of the child–therapist relationship. I find it particularly helpful in beginning work with older children and young people who are very self conscious about 'playing'. It offers an interactional structure, a physical 'holding' environment and a useful communication tool. The game is played in a similar way to the one described above in work with parents and children. The child and I will draw pictures for each other based on the squiggle provided. We give the picture a title and occasionally we will use the picture as the basis of a story that we co-construct. The game offers a framework for co-construction, initially as the picture is co-constructed and in conclusion as a title is created or a story completed.

THE HOUSE-TREE-PERSON DRAWING

The House-Tree-Person Drawing was first developed by Buck (1948) and grew out of Goodenough's Draw-A-Person Test which was used to assess intelligence functioning (Deffenbaugh 2003). However, Buck's aim was to assess the personality of the child, not his or her cognitive skills, and the items were chosen to be familiar items to the child which therefore could be drawn and discussed by the child. In Narrative Play Therapy at the beginning of therapy I have adapted this as a tool to support the development of a therapeutic relationship between the child and therapist and as an avenue into story making and storytelling. The child is invited to draw a house or a tree or a person. I usually start with the tree but, for younger children, I may start with the house as a more familiar object to draw. A range of paper sizes and colours are made available to the child as are a range of art materials such as pencils, crayons, markers, glue, glitter and collage material.

The child is invited to draw a picture of a house. Then they are asked to tell me about the house. I write down their responses. The story of the house begins to emerge. Questions are asked to facilitate the co-construction of the story. Common questions include:

1. How old is the house?

2. Where is it located?

3. What is around it? Or is it alone?

4. Is there anyone inside the house?

5. What do they think/feel about the house?

6. What does the house think/feel about the people?

7. What do passersby think of the house, e.g. is it a nice house, a scary house, an angry house, a happy house, a haunted house, etc.?

8. What does the house say about itself?

9. How did it get to be that kind of a house?

As the questions are responded to, a detailed biography of the house begins to emerge and the story begins to be written. The story always begins with 'Once upon a time there was a house, a...house' (very old/young) depending on the age of the house and the words or tone used when describing the house the child had drawn. The story continues to be co-constructed between the therapist and the child with the therapist recording the story.

The story and the picture are often then kept by the therapist until the end of therapy, when the child can decide, in discussion with the therapist, what will happen to the story. Sometimes children want the story and picture to become part of their storybook of therapy. Deciding what happens to the story and making books become part of the ending of therapy. Some children request that the stories are kept in a safe place by the therapist.

The 'tree' and the 'person' drawings are administered in a similar manner, though often, I don't follow them in consecutive sessions but intersperse them throughout the therapy process. The themes within each story and across stories begin to emerge. These can include loneliness: the house lives all alone in the middle of nowhere with no one living in it and no one passing by; destruction: the tree got blown down in a strong wind; nurturing and reparation: an old man who had experienced many carefree, fun days playing with his friends in the tree as a child passed by; he was sad to think of the old tree dying, but then he noticed a sapling growing by the tree and realised that now the sapling would be able to access the light and could grow big and strong. The stories are read back to the child and any corrections needed are made so that the story is satisfying to the storyteller and the listener. Again it provides a contained activity for beginning therapeutic conversations and co-constructing a story. The themes are recorded and tracked across stories and play sequences within the therapy. Themes that have emerged in these assessment sessions then become the work of therapy, thus providing useful concrete information to parents, carers and referrers.

BASIC PH AND SIX PART STORY MAKING

This is another useful assessment tool in Narrative Play Therapy. The BASIC Ph was developed by Dr Mooli Lahad 'as a quick assessment of coping modes with the objective of helping the therapist reach an understanding and develop contact with the client based on the therapist's understanding of the client's language'. The assumption underlying the BASIC Ph is that 'to tell a projected story based on the elements of a fairy tale and myth, we will see the way the self projects itself in an organised reality in order to meet the world' (Lahad 1993, p.11).

The BASIC Ph represents the redefining and classifying of factors and mechanisms important 'to the development of resilient person-environment relationship' (p.7). It is a multi-modal approach to help identify the range of coping mechanisms and resilience of the person in times of stress. BASIC Ph is an acronym and the elements are as follows:

- *Belief*: What are your beliefs about the situation? – 'It is God's will'; 'It is fate.'

- *Affect*: How do you feel about the situation? – Overwhelmed, out of control, in control, angry, surprised, shocked?

- *Social*: What are your support networks and can you draw on these? – Who is there to help you?

- *Imagination*: What do you imagine will happen? – Can you imagine alternative endings or solutions?

- *Cognitive*: What do you know? – What skills/information do you have?

- *Physical*: What can you do? – Can you actively do something? – Can you relax, can you do this for others or yourself?

The Six Part Story Making (6-PSM) was developed based on Alida Gersies's methods (Meldrum 1994) to support the child in creating a story. The analysis of the story, using the framework of the BASIC Ph, helps the therapist assess the child's dominant coping mode and supports the therapist in making connections with the child through these modes.

The child is invited to draw a picture for the six pieces of the story. I usually provide a cartoon template with six boxes for the drawings and space underneath to write the text/script. These story elements have been identified in fairytales from around the world (von Franz 1987). Table 3.2 indicates the sections of the story to be filled in each of the six boxes.

Table 3.2: Six Part Story Making

1. Main character: hero, or heroine. They can be real or imagined. Where does he/she/it live?	2. The task or mission of the main character. What is the mission the character is assigned?	3. Who or what can help the main character if anything at all?
4. Who or what obstacle stands in the way of the character carrying out his/her/ its task or mission?	5. How will the hero/ character cope with the task/mission?	6. Then what happens? Does it end? Or does it continue?

Source: Adapted from Lahad 1993, pp.11–12

The child then tells the story that goes with his or her pictures and this is recorded verbatim. Lahad suggests that the therapist listens to the story on several levels, including the tone used to tell the story, the context of the story and its messages, and identifying the dominant coping modes of the story (which of the elements of the BASIC Ph are present in the story as it is told by the child). This is how the assessment is used in times of stress to identify coping mechanisms. The structure of the 6-PSM and the BASIC Ph can be used to assess and to understand other stories created in the context of the playroom, whether the story is created with characters in the sand, puppets or in role play. The themes of the stories created can be analysed to identify the dominant mode/modes of the child. Knowing the child's dominant themes and modes of coping can facilitate the therapist in communicating with the child using his or her preferred mode. The information can be shared with parents/carers to increase their understanding of the child and the language needed to support the child in times of distress. For example if the child's dominant mode is physical, doing some relaxation exercises before going to bed may help the child in times of distress and support the relationship between the child and parent/carer.

The BASIC Ph and the 6-PSM therefore offer the Narrative Play Therapist an assessment tool, which is contained, supports the child in communicating their sense of self and which offers a framework for assessment themes that emerge in therapy. In Chapter 6 Alison Webster describes the use of the 6-PSM in her work with children in schools.

Record keeping

Narrative Play Therapy focuses on two main elements in the play therapy process, namely the stories created and the developmental modes of play used to create these stories. Record keeping therefore reflects these two main elements. Therapists record the stories in different ways and using different media. The scenes of play created in the sand or using other sensory material and/or small world materials are often photographed and these photographs become a digital record of the themes and stories in play therapy. The therapist offers to write the story as the child dictates it or as the story is co-constructed between the storyteller and listener. Some therapists like to have a special book to write these stories in and the book becomes part of the materials of the therapy and part of the record keeping process. I often write the story as the child constructs, dictates and edits the story and type it up, making it available for the following session. This is then stored with the photographs and any art work created in therapy. The modes of play namely, Embodiment, Projection, Role Play and Games with Rules (Jennings 1993) are also identified in the record keeping process. The nature of the play engaged in using these materials can also be recorded. For example, was the nature of the engagement with the materials exploratory, playful, pretend or imaginative? Feelings expressed, explored or enacted are recorded.

The risk/ritual observation of the nature of the child's play can also be recorded. Jennings identified ritual in play as 'known, safe and repetitive rituals that the child has already established' (Jennings 1993, p.138). The following questions help to identify where the child is on the risk/ritual continuum.

- What does the child initially go to play with in the playroom?

- Does he or she begin with the same play materials each week?

- Does he or she play with them in the same way each time?

- Does he or she always want to play the same character in the dramatic play?

- Does he or she always arrange the furniture in the house the same way?

The pattern of ritual will emerge over a number of sessions. Risk observations include trying out new things, beginning with something new or general changes in the routine with which the child approaches his or her play in the play therapy room. Does the child try out new toys, create new scenes and play sequences, use new textures in sensory play, try out new roles in dramatic play or create new pictures in the sand? Children will engage in both risk and ritual for different reasons. Some children will remain at the ritual ends of the continuum for a long time, needing the security and comfort of doing things in a certain order. When children's play is on the ritual end of the continuum, the therapist may also need to consider if this is traumatic play. The child's inclusion of and tolerance for change or variation in the play and presence or absence of joy or relief from the play also need to be recorded. On the risk end of the continuum the child may feel a sense of safety to explore, try out new toys and roles, and begin to think about and take new perspectives – all elements of the recording process. A child's ability to explore, persistence at a task and curiosity can be reflective of the child's attachment experience (Creasey and Jarvis 2007). In a mixed group of developmentally delayed and typically developing children, a little four-year-old with Down Syndrome was observed to play the role of baby assigned to him by two caring girls who wanted to play mother. He was happy to play baby until he tired of this role and then said 'no – I mammy' and proceeded 'to cook the dinner'.

Figure 3.1 is a suggested recording sheet that reflects the elements identified for recording the play therapy process in Narrative Play Therapy.

Narrative Play Therapy Record Form
Child: . . . . Date:. . . . .
Session no. . . . .
Separation from parent/guardian:

Embodiment play
Materials used: (list)

Story co-constructed:

Feelings observed: (list)

Ritual   I   2   3   4   5   Risk (circle as appropriate)

Comments:

Themes: Exploratory, Constructive, Nurturing, Aggressive, Protective
(circle as appropriate)
Other: . . . .

Projective play
Materials used: (list)

Story co-constructed:

Feelings observed: (list)

Ritual   I   2   3   4   5   Risk (circle as appropriate)

Comments:

Themes: Exploratory, Constructive, Nurturing, Aggressive, Protective
(circle as appropriate)
Other: . . . .

Child: . . . . Date:. . . . .
Session no. . . . .

Role play
Materials used: (list)

Story co-constructed:

Feelings observed: (list)

Ritual   I   2   3   4   5   Risk (circle as appropriate)

Comments:

Themes: Exploratory, Constructive, Nurturing, Aggressive, Protective
(circle as appropriate)
Other: . . . .

Games with rules
Materials used: (list)

Feelings observed: (list)

Ritual   I   2   3   4   5   Risk (circle as appropriate)

Comments:

Themes: Exploratory, Constructive, Nurturing, Aggressive, Protective
(circle as appropriate)
Other: . . . .

Figure 3.1 Narrative Play Therapy record form

Evaluation

The evaluation of Narrative Play Therapy aims to identify the themes that have emerged, and the resolution in those themes, the ability of the child to identify and explore a range of endings and to identify the changing narrative that adults hold about the child.

Revisiting some of the projective techniques identified in the assessment section can be helpful in identifying the changing stories and the child's sense of self as the therapy comes to an end. For example revisiting the shield activity and reviewing the current responses with previous responses can support an understanding of the journey the child has travelled and help in the evaluation of the intervention.

Reviewing the story themes and tracking the changes in these themes supports the therapist in tracking changes. Often what the therapist is observing in these changes is the wider range of stories being told, the wider range of endings being proposed and the range of perspectives that the child is now able to take.

Children may also begin to evaluate therapy as they come to the end of the process. Children will often begin to recall things that they did during therapy as the therapy comes to an end: 'Do you remember when we made that with the slime and you wrote down my story?' Children may ask for stories to be re-read to them, enjoying them as a listener. Deciding what to do with the material created including stories, art work and photographs of sand tray work can become part of the child's evaluation of the therapy process. The child assimilates the stories that are part of their sense of self in the present and rejects the stories that are no longer stories they hold about themselves.

An evaluation of risk/ritual observations over time will often provide an indicator for the ending of play therapy. The child begins to move between risk and ritual and a balance is achieved. The outside begins to be brought into the therapy and children recount stories of their daily life experiences in a tone that is more relaxed and less 'problem' focused.

In sharing the themes and the changing stories with the carers/parents and referrers, their stories also become less problem focused and more resilient focused. Some stories remain but their intensity and the all pervading nature of the difficulties seems to lessen.

Conclusion

Assessment, record keeping and evaluation are key elements of any professional practice. This chapter presents a range of strategies that can be used to support the professional framework for Narrative Play Therapy while reflecting its theory and practice at this time. They reflect the range of practice reported in this volume and how practitioners have adapted others' approaches to reflect their needs as a Narrative Play Therapy practitioner. These are offered as a range of possibilities to be adapted and amended to suit the social and cultural context in which the therapist works.

References

Buck, J.N. (1948) 'The H-T-P Test.' *Journal of Clinical Psychology 4*, 151–159.

Cattanach, A. (1994) *Play Therapy: Where the Sky Meets the Underworld.* London: Jessica Kingsley Publishers.

Creasey, G. and Jarvis, P. (2007) 'Attachment in the Preschool Years.' In O. Saracho and B. Spodek (eds) *Contemporary Perspectives on Socialisation and Social Development.* Charlotte, NC: Information Age Publishing.

Deffenbaugh, A.M. (2003) 'The House-Tree-Person Test with kids who have been sexually abused.' Available at www.eric.ed.gov/PDFS/ED482760.pdf, accessed 13 February 2011.

Dreikurs, R. and Soltz, V. (1964) *Children: The Challenge.* New York: Penguin Books.

Goldwyn, R., Stanley, C., Smith, V. and Green, J. (2000) 'The Manchester Child Attachment Story Task: Relationship with parental AAI, SAT and child behaviour.' *Attachment and Human Development 2*, 1, 71–84.

Jennings, S. (1993) *Playtherapy with Children: A Practitioner's Guide.* Oxford: Blackwell Scientific Publications.

Kottman, T. (1995) *Partners in Play: An Adlerian Approach to Play Therapy.* Alexandria, VA: American Counseling Association.

Lahad, M. (1993) 'Basic Ph – The Story of Coping Resources.' In M. Lahad and A. Cohen (eds) *Community Stress Prevention* (vol. 2). Kiryat Shmona: Community Stress Prevention Centre.

Lew, A. and Bettner, B.L. (1998) *Responsibility in the Classroom: A Teacher's Guide to Understanding and Motivating Students.* Newton Centre, MA: Connexions Press.

Meldrum, B. (1994) 'Evaluation and Assessment in Dramatherapy.' In S. Jennings, A. Cattanach, S. Mitchell, A. Chesner and B. Meldrum (eds) *The Handbook of Dramatherapy.* London: Routledge.

Minnis, H, Putter, S., Read, W., Green, J. and Schumm, T.-S. (2008) 'The Computerised Manchester Child Attachment Story Task: a novel medium for a measure of attachment patterns.' Available at www.scss.tcd.ie/conferences/TIMH/12-Minnis.pdf, accessed 2 October 2010.

Moore, T. and Ucko, L.G. (1961) 'Four to six: Constructiveness and conflict in meeting doll play problems.' *Journal of Child Psychology and Psychiatry 3*, 21–47.

Steele, M., Henderson, K., Hodges, J., Kankuik, J., Hillman, S. and Steele, H. (2007) 'In the Best Interest of the Late-placed Child: A Report from the Attachment Representations and Adoption Outcomes Study.' In L. Hayes, P. Fonagy and M. Target (eds) *Developmental Science and Psychoanalysis Integration and Innovation.* London: Karnac Books.

von Franz, M. (1987) *Shadow and Evil in Fairy Tales.* Dallas, TX: Spring.

Winnicott, D.W. (1991) *Playing and Reality.* London: Routledge. (Original work published 1971)

Chapter 4

Story as an Externalising Process

Kate Kirk

Introduction

Narrative Play Therapy is about listening and witnessing as a child's story unfolds. According to Parry and Doan (1994, p.1):

> Once upon a time everything was understood through stories. Stories were always called upon to make things understandable. Stories always dealt with the why questions. The answers did not have to be literally true; they only had to satisfy people's curiosity by providing the answer, less for the mind than for the soul. For the soul they were true, but probably no one bothered to ask whether that truth was factual or 'merely' metaphorical. That question came much later.

Byng Hall (1999, p.132) suggests that actions can tell a story: 'one of the delights of working with children is that they can tell their story so vividly through their symbolic play with toys and drawings'. It is through the medium of children's play that I witness them externalising their fears, anxieties and worries through their poignant stories. Children create stories which can be re-authored, discarded or new meanings added to enable the child to find a resolution to hurts and troubles for him- or herself.

According to Roberts (1999), 'Cox and Theilgaard (1987, p.252) underline the way in which individuals each see the world from their perspective and therefore each lives in a "perspectival world"' (p.6). Roberts continues:

Here, we are for the most part, concerned about life stories or stories about lives, those basic configurations of meaning that we live in and through. However, few, perhaps none present or experience their life story in a manner that could be considered objectively or historically accurate. What we possess is an interpretation of our life experience which we may tell quite differently at different stages of life, seeking to provoke or evoke different responses in our listeners according to our varying needs. (pp.6–7)

This chapter is based on my work with two children from two different backgrounds. The stories they created in play helped them to move forward in their lives and to lessen the grip the past had on them. I have chosen these two case studies to look at Narrative Play Therapy in action. I chose a female sibling pair aged six and eight and a boy of ten. I followed these children through a therapeutic process of a one year period. In the study of the siblings I chose to open with a joint session knowing that I would have to see the children individually. I was curious to see if their relationship had changed since I had carried out an earlier court assessment during care proceedings. All the children were on full Care Orders. Subsequently the siblings were successfully adopted and Paul is managing very well in his long term foster home. The identities of all the children and the families used in these case studies have been changed in order to protect their confidentiality.

What is Narrative Play Therapy? According to Freeman, Epston and Lobovits (1997) the term narrative implies listening to and telling or retelling stories about people and problems. Narrative Play Therapy is made up of the stories children tell about themselves and their families through their projection in sand tray play and using toys and puppets to facilitate the telling of their story.

Cattanach (2008) writes that one of the functions of Narrative Play Therapy is to give the child a way of controlling his or her world and what happens in that world. For a child who lacks power this can be both an enriching and an empowering experience. The use of narrative and stories help us make sense of our lives and experiences. The stories of children who are in the care system are often told and recorded in ways that are not always helpful to them and if these dominant problem saturated stories are repeated often enough they can deprive the child of hope for the future.

Freeman *et al.* (1997) state that narrative therapy employs a linguistic device called externalisation which separates the person from the problem. Greenburg *et al.* (1997) say the term externalising has been used generally to summarise a core set of negativistic, defiant and hostile behaviours including noncompliance, aggression, tantrums and other intense or immature emotional responses to limits. However, when this technique is used therapeutically Freeman *et al.* (1997) suggest that the therapist's main job is to help the child and the family get in touch with the times they have outwitted the problems and this is described as finding unique outcomes that contradict the dominance of the problems in their lives.

The children I see are children whose lives are often compromised by trauma through exposure to domestic violence and abuse of all forms including neglect of their needs. Using the technique of externalisation empowers children and enables them to master the trauma through play. James (1989, p.1) describes trauma 'as an emotional shock that has the potential to cause lasting damage to an individual's psychological development'. She goes on to say that 'trauma also refers to overwhelming, uncontrollable experiences that psychologically impact victims by creating in them feelings of helplessness, vulnerability, loss of safety and loss of control'. These symptoms are vividly portrayed in my first case study when the child uses the technique of externalisation and brings the trauma to the surface. All the children in this study showed they had knowledge of the trauma at a perceptual and sensory level. In Penny's study we see this by the vivid imagery she created by copying her father's words and mirroring the images of him with his gun. Similarly, in the second study, Paul who had no significant attachment to anyone vividly remembered some of the things that had been done to him. Memory plays a very significant role in mastering trauma and changing how we feel about it.

In my work with children in play therapy externalisation happens easily through the use of toys, puppets and the sand tray. Through these objects the child is able to create a space between him- or herself and the problem. The therapist is then able through playful interaction, curiosity and wondering to help the child construct a more helpful story about their lives through their dramatic play, art, sand play or puppet play. Anderson and Goolishian (in Cattanach 2008, p.22) state that a therapist allows the story to unfold until a coherent theme or new meaning emerges from the dialogue.

Case study 1

I met Penny, a brave eight-year-old whilst undertaking a court assessment through play. Penny and her six-year-old sister Frances were in a foster home. Penny was described as a child who was prone to temper tantrums and these could just erupt out of nowhere. There were fears at those early stages that she was not adoptable whereas Frances her younger sister was a child with an easy temperament, a placid nature and therefore more likely to be adopted. Both children had come from a comfortable rural background. They had suffered neglect and had witnessed domestic violence as their father's mental health had declined and their mother sought solace in alcohol. After both children witnessed their father threatening to kill their mother with a rifle they were removed on an Emergency Protection Order under the Children Act 1989 and were placed in foster care.

The rural lifestyle of hunting, shooting and fishing was a normal part of their father's daily life. He often took Penny shooting rabbits and had skinned and gutted them in her presence.

In the foster home Penny's behaviour was a cause for concern and it was clear she had been severely affected by her father's violent and bizarre behaviour. However, there was a part of her that missed him because no one ever said no to him and it seemed she was attracted to him and yet frightened of him. Frances, the younger sister, had spent a great deal of time with her maternal grandmother away from the family home and her behaviour did not show the same signs of trauma that Penny's did.

Penny had witnessed her father's violence on a number of occasions. When she could not get her own way in the foster home she would use the aggressive language she had heard her father use when he ordered her mother around in the home. My assumption was that this was a learned behaviour from her experiences in the family home.

The court proceedings were delayed whilst other family members were assessed as long term carers for the children. This was unsuccessful.

Play therapy intervention

I met the children in my room and outlined the rules that would keep us safe while we played. I stated that there would be no hitting or breaking of toys and with that Penny broke the head off a small doll. I suggested she help me mend the doll five minutes before the session ended and she neither agreed nor disagreed with this proposal.

Frances was keen to play lost and found in the sand tray and set about creating a scene in the sand. Her play behaviour using sand, water and toys to tell her story could be said to follow what Jennings (1999) describes as embodiment play. Frances smelled the wet sand and commented that it was 'yucky but nice'.

Frances' stories in the sand centred on being lost and found. She buried some Duplo dolls and some sparkly jewels. She wanted me to find the jewels whilst she found a mummy doll in the sand. Frances was not overtly distressed but simply said 'I miss my mummy. My daddy was naughty.' I echoed her phrase and we paused. The jewels might be the split off idealised part of herself and which had to be found by the therapist and kept safe.

Meanwhile Penny had been exploring the room and found a puppet box. She took out a fierce looking dinosaur and she pushed this straight into my face. I stopped her and reminded her that we needed to be safe and that we do not hurt each other during our play together.

Penny discarded the puppets and joined her sister at the sand tray. Penny got a medium sized snake and again pushed this towards my face. Again I stopped her and reminded her of the limits. She said 'I've come to see you because my dad got his gun out' and she made a shooting action with her arm outstretched. She then found a large hippopotamus with a gaping mouth and again she tried to push this into my face, yelling as she did, 'Shut your gob up.' She looked at me, smiled and played with the sand until almost the end of the session. She brought the broken doll to me and together we tried to get the head back on. There was a calmness about her. I spoke softly and told her that broken things could often be mended and nothing more was said. I wanted her to feel able to re-author her own narrative to one of hope and this seemed to be the start of such a journey. I told both girls I would write their stories down in my book. They neither agreed nor disagreed.

My first impression of Frances was that her play behaviour was sensory development play; Jennings (1999, p.51) describes this type of play as embodiment and projection. The embodiment is the physicalised play expressed mainly through the senses and projection where the child relates to the external world beyond the body. The hide and seek games in the sand might have been symbolic of being lost and found and needing to be safe. They were also relational in as much as she drew me into her play space almost immediately and although there was sadness expressed for the loss of her mother I considered her play in the session to be relatively normal for her age and stage of development. At this stage there was no mention of her grandmother. Her overall presentation was one of quiet compliance and wanting to please. Among attachment theorists Crittenden (1997) says that children whose caregivers punish affective display dare not and need not use a coercive strategy. Nevertheless, they need to elicit caregiver support. The use of coy behaviour quickly demonstrates that the caregiver likes smiles and sweetness. Consequently many children with rejecting and intrusive caregivers learn to act happy when they are actually frightened and angry. They learn to falsify the display of affect to obtain the nurturing response they desire from the attachment figures.

Both strategies of compliance and smiles could have been protective factors for Frances and having a more placid temperament could have helped her to survive in her family home. Frances' persona remained the same throughout the therapy whereas Penny was stressed and uncooperative and a bed-wetter in the foster home and she presented differently from her sister for the first 12 weeks of therapy. I was surprised by Penny's level of aggression towards me and I understood why the carer was concerned about her. I was very aware that Penny had a rather different story to tell from her sister. Piaget's theories (discussed in Cattanach 2008) of how children incorporate and digest their experiences into existing mental frameworks were pertinent now and continued to be relevant in the months ahead. Cattanach also notes another view, that of constructivism, where the child builds up mental pictures of his or her world which serve as the basis for her beliefs and actions in other learned experiences.

At this early stage it seemed that this little girl had seen and heard more than her fragile state of mind could bear. Penny's trauma was evident and already unfolding in a narrative of violence and aggression. Children's repetitive play themes can reflect their entrenched feelings of powerlessness (James 1989).

Session 2

When Penny joined me for her first individual session she told me 'I didn't want to come but Anna [carer] made me.' She wandered around the room and spoke aloud, 'These men are angry', and she threw them roughly into the sand. Penny found a small gun, aimed it directly at me and said 'I'm going to kill you. You're dead. My daddy shoots foxes and pheasants.' Penny dropped the gun and asked to go to the toilet. On her return she ignored the gun and set about making a scene in the sand.

The scene had connecting tunnels and a lot of trees. Penny then arranged three knights around the tray. I commented that this seemed like where she used to live before. She said 'Shut your gob.' The knights fought each other on horseback until they were dead. Penny became animated and shouted 'Kill you, kill you' bashing the knights together with some force.

Penny left the sand tray abruptly and found some puppets and the dinosaurs she had used in the first session. As before she tried pushing them into my face. I stopped her and reminded her that we did not hurt each other and that she would be safe here. The rules were there to keep her safe. I then commented on her stories to date, 'Once upon a time there was a large wood and the soldiers wore beautiful coloured clothes. They fought each other and many of them did not understand what the fight was about.' Penny interrupted and said 'Put in that they did know but they had forgotten.' I carefully wrote this down. I asked her to remember a time when the soldiers did not fight. She told me 'They are bloody now but they can be mended but not yet.'

Again Penny showed an understanding of the technique of externalisation: 'They are bloody now but they can be mended.' Penny's new narrative contained hope that there was something better and more wholesome ahead. Penny's dominant mood in the session was one of fear, distress and anger. The story she portrayed so far was all about death and the play distressed her to the point of needing to leave the room which could be described as a play disruption in order to manage the anxiety the play evoked. Penny knew better than anyone that her father shot foxes and pheasants. This was stored both in her semantic and episodic memory and she needed to play this through. The play at the beginning of the session did not satisfy her but as she worked through her fears she relaxed a little and in this session she contributed the idea that the soldiers, like the doll in the first session, could be mended. She created chaos by throwing things around her, by threatening the therapist and by expressing her murderous rage in the sand. I suspected that Penny's fear of annihilation was at the root of her traumatic experiences and perhaps this episodic recall re-awakened her anger and fear.

Crittenden (1997, p.61) examines how among the

> new cortical abilities available to preoperational children is the ability to encode information that is more sophisticated than preconscious sensorimotor schema, that is procedural memory. One type of information (that probably appears in infancy) is tied closely to contexts that elicit feelings of anxiety (including

desire for comfort, anger and fear) and comfort. This information exists in the form of perceptual sensory images. Another, more sophisticated sort of information, labelled semantic memory, contains verbal generalisations (i.e. propositions that facilitate prediction of how people or situations will be in the future).

Crittenden (1997, p.61) states that 'semantic memory is cognitive in nature and regulates problem-solving behaviour. Episodic memory, on the other hand, refers to information about specific events. Both affective and cognitive information are integrated such that events unfold in memory in temporal order and with sensory information from multiple modalities.' What Penny was externalising was strong in affect and was also set in a temporal frame.

Session 3

Prior to this session I had the opportunity to speak to the foster carer and to the social worker. Both of them commented that Penny seemed a little less aggressive in the foster home. Penny had told the foster mother not to worry when things got broken because they could be mended. I believed this suggested Penny had taken on the new story of hope that broken things could be mended.

Penny was wetting the bed every night and Anna, her carer, was finding this extremely hard to manage. I introduced her to 'Sneaky Pee and Sneaky Poo' (from White and Epston 1990). I used my own term 'Pee the Bed'. This is the externalisation of the problem, which can give the child the confidence to outwit it. She told me she would try it. I also advised that as well as reducing Penny's fluid intake before bed that she lift her out to the toilet before she went to bed herself as this might help.

Penny entered my room. I thought I saw a smile, 'I didn't want to come today.' I wondered why this was. 'Because you have no good toys here. I don't like these things. When did you buy them?'

Penny became interested in some farm animals and asked me to lift the box down for her. She investigated the contents and found some turkeys. She told me, 'Turkeys live on the farm.' She then found chickens, rabbits and a fox. She lined them up and then ignored them.

She lifted some horses out and made some jumps for them. She told me, 'My mum used to ride horses and she jumped too.' I said her mother must have been very clever to ride horses and do jumps. I made a point of writing this in the story we were compiling. I then asked her if she could ride and jump. She seemed annoyed and left the play. She went to the puppets and found the fierce looking dinosaur. She was about to push it into my face when I stopped her. She made a growling noise and said, 'Shut your gob.'

I conspicuously wrote down that the girl in the story sometimes got bothered by Miss Mad. I wondered why the girl lets Miss Mad get inside her and spoil things for her. Penny ignored my comments and went back to the farm. She found some vultures and eagles and lined them up with the other animals. She made the horse riders jump over the prepared jumps. Two of the riders were successful in clearing two of the jumps and one rider did not manage any of the jumps.

Penny found the rifle and went back to the farm. She shot all of the animals. She then told me, 'My dad tried to shoot me' and with that she pulled the trigger and said, 'You're dead.' She left the room to use the toilet. It is possible she goes to the toilet because she is overwhelmed by anxiety and her narrative breaks down. At this point I was aware that I needed to build a new image of her and to acknowledge her fear and her bravery in outwitting these fears.

On her return she ignored the rifle and played with the sand, humming quietly to herself. I read her the story so far and then asked her if she thought the girl in the story was brave. She shifted the sand from one container to another and she continued to play. I said that I was writing the part of the story, the part where the girl was really, really frightened and even when the girl was frightened she was still being brave. I wondered how this girl managed to be so brave, such a brave girl.

The overall effect of Penny's presentation initially, albeit momentarily, was that she seemed pleased to be in the room but this mood disappeared so rapidly that I wondered if I had really seen it. Her play behaviour showed she needed to be in total control and I suspected this tied in with her avoidant and fearful attachment pattern. I noticed too that she was using coercive strategies and this might have made her believe she could outsmart her father, thereby enabling her to survive. However, the other side of this that was mentioned by the foster carer was that in part Penny identified with her father's strength and his ability to frighten people into submission.

I believe the slaughter of the farm animals seemed to be stored in her memory. This was the first mention that her father had threatened to shoot her. Her real fear was that she too could be slaughtered like the other animals. Penny was frightened for her life. The anger and its intensity suggested that this little girl was terrified for her life. In all of the sessions there was clear evidence of play disruption and not being able to continue the play. Leaving the room to go to the toilet reflected some mounting tension that could not be tolerated by this child so she sought to relieve her tension by leaving the room.

However, what I found reassuring was that Penny had internalised the metaphor that broken things could be mended. She needed to have the hope of renewal and being whole again.

The carer reported her efforts to help Penny externalise her anger appropriately in the home by adopting names for the unwanted emotions, for example Miss Angry, Miss Rude and Miss Fearful. The message I encouraged the carer to give to Penny was clear: you have the right to expect care and attention, love and affection and to be safe. This was really helping Penny to understand that she was not the problem. When Penny got rude, together with the carer she used a wooden spoon to bash Miss Rude well away so that Miss Rude was not spoiling things for her. With Miss Fearful it was more difficult because locking the doors and windows failed to reassure Penny that Miss Fearful could not get in.

I spoke to the foster carer after the session and suggested that she be more vigilant with Penny given the disclosure she had made about her father. This was a historical disclosure and Penny had been through a Memorandum Interview with the Child Protection Team and they believed it had happened. Anna (the carer) told me that Penny had talked to her about it after our last session. She was much less angry but the bed-wetting was worse than ever. She told me she found it hard to manage. She said that Penny was just so exhausting to care for and she wondered if and how adopters would cope with her. She was shocked by Penny's anger as well as her language. She told me that Penny admired her father and especially admired the way he always got what he wanted. This raised the issue of whose story it was. I believe the story emerging was from Penny's perspective.

Session 8

Penny arrived at the session. She smiled momentarily and then told me, 'I didn't want to come but Anna made me. I did not wet my bed last night.' I clapped my hands and asked her how she had managed to outsmart 'Pee the Bed'. She went on to tell me that she got up but she did not drink all the water in the bathroom only little sips and 'I did it.' I clapped again. I went on to tell her that I knew 'Pee the Bed' very well and how she crept up on little girls at night and made them wet their beds. She was not looking at me but was listening intently. I asked her again how she outsmarted 'Pee the Bed'. Penny asked me, 'Have you got your book to write in? Write in I'm cleverer than Pee the Bed and I did.'

Penny wasted no time in finding the rifle and another small hand gun. She told me, 'This is not real. My dad had a small gun in his jeep.' I agreed it was just pretend and that made it safe. Penny took aim, 'You're dead.' She repeated, 'My daddy tried to shoot me.' I said that must have been very scary and she must have been very scared. Penny went on, 'He shoots foxes all the time.' Penny left the room and went to the toilet. On her return she ignored the gun and played with the farm. She found a toy axe in the box and she told me, 'This is for chopping people up, chop, chop, chop.'

She then discarded the axe and concentrated on making all the horse riders successfully clear the jumps. She then told me, 'My dad does jumps at shows and wins rosettes but my mum jumps better and that makes him madder. I don't want to go home to my house. My dad might get me.' I told her that her father was not at home anymore. She then said, 'He has to stay in the hospital doesn't he?' I agreed that her father had to stay in hospital.

I told her I was curious to know if there was a time when her father had been a kind daddy. I wanted her to think about this if she wished and we could add this into her story. She ignored the question. She told me, 'I don't want to go home but Frances misses Mum.' Then for the first time she asked me to join her in the sand. She hid many small objects and I had to find them. Then it was her turn. I was surprised that she felt able to close her eyes and wait for the signal to find the lost objects. To my surprise as she left the session she said quietly, 'I'll see you next time.'

There was clear evidence of a trauma here; 'chop, chop, chop' and using the present tense 'He might get me' involved fear and trauma in imaged, procedural and semantic memory. Re-remembering needs to be done with care as Penny may wish to exclude her father from her life because he behaved abusively and neglectfully to all of them. As she did not answer I assumed that this was not the right time to pursue this question.

There were many short stories over the course of the year and eventually there was a story of hope, knowing that she would not go home and that she and her sister would be safe together in a home without guns. She was able to acknowledge that there had been times when her father had not always been horrid. Nevertheless, she did not want contact with him nor did she want to go home. Her mother had not featured in her therapy and usually the only comments Penny made about her mother was when her mother did not turn up for contact.

When Penny and her sister moved into their adoptive placement I recommended that the adopters attend a Webster Stratton Parenting course and in addition that they have at least 20 sessions of family play therapy from a narrative perspective spread over the first year of placement. The girls were successfully adopted, the placement has its ups and downs and overall the new family have taken a very empathetic stance on Penny's day to day management and so far so good. I believe the new narrative was rich enough for her to let the adopters into her emotional life and they are continuing to enrich her for the future.

Case study 2

Paul is a ten-year-old boy who has a physical disability that interferes with his mobility. He was raised in an institution for the first seven years of his life.

When I met him he had not been long in his new foster home. The foster carers, who were professional people, were finding it hard to manage because Paul had no idea about turn taking and manners were an anathema to him. His behaviour portrayed many of the characteristics of a child raised in an institution. Routines and food meant everything to him. If these things were disrupted in any way Paul would have a major temper tantrum and at these times he could be very destructive.

I asked the carers what they hoped to achieve from the play therapy intervention and wondered what outcome they hoped for. Both carers hoped that Paul might develop a sense of perspective and awareness that sharing and manners were expected in most families.

I did my assessment using narrative stems (Hodges, Steele and Hillman 2004) to get an idea of Paul's working model of attachment. Paul had no idea what mothers did and he had not learned any useful way of getting his needs met appropriately.

The carers had given me a detailed description of Paul's behaviour in their home and towards them and their family. They considered they were walking on eggshells all the time for fear of starting one of Paul's tantrums.

When I eventually met Paul I understood how hard it must have been for him to find himself dealing with the intimacy of family life which for him would have been like visiting a foreign country. He lacked awareness

of the family rules and values. My first job was to engage him in the
process of play therapy.

I asked him why he was seeing me. I could not help but admire his
insight when he described his situation. 'I'm not nice; I am living there
because I couldn't live at The Oaks anymore.' There was a wistfulness
and a sadness around this statement. He told me, 'I had a mother but she
is gone. I had a father but he is gone. I had lots and lots of helpers and
they are gone too.' Immediately a story of loss emerged and I told him I
would write this down as a *Once upon a time story*.

I told him that this seemed to be the story of a very, very brave boy
and I would write that in my book. I asked him what the title of the story
could be. 'It could be The Brave Boy's Story.' I asked if we could give the
boy a name. 'He is called Blackie after Black Beauty.' I said that the story
then would be about a boy called Blackie who is handsome. There was
a glimmer of a smile but no eye contact. Paul turned his back on me and
played with the shop. He was both the shop keeper and the customer.
He only needed me to write the story down and to make sure I got it
all. I learned very quickly that he was an excellent reader and when he
checked my book he was able to tell when I had not understood what he
had said or when he wanted something changed.

The sessions continued like this for the first month, with relational
play through being a shop keeper, but I was not invited in and therefore
I could only witness the story being created.

At this stage to comment on his attachment/relationships would
have been cruel given his life history. I could only see a child who had
survived major invasive surgery and who was still trying to communicate
his feelings. In my view he was doing this the best way he could. It
would have been almost impossible for this little boy to have developed
a secure attachment at the onset of his life. Contact with his parents was
infrequent. Helpers came and went. Although some were more special
than others many were not. Paul's presentation of self in everyday life
made me think of him as unconnected. Rutter (1997, p.26) says that both
Sameroff and Emde (1989) and Dunn (1988)

> have drawn attention to the evidence that children's relationships
> with other people are complex and involve a range of different
> dimensions and functions. These include connectedness, shared
> emotions, balance of control, intimacy and shared positive
> emotions. If we are to understand the interconnectedness between
> relationships it will be necessary for us to take into account the

range of dimensions that seem to be involved. It seems unlikely that these will be reducible to a single process involving attachment, security or any other postulated quality.

On the surface Paul did not appear to have any real connectedness with anyone. The loneliness of his position was unenviable and was being told very clearly in his stories.

The helpers and the social workers tried hard to get a family for this child and this placement was his last hope of living outside of the institution. The family he has are empathetic and desperate to know how to help him. They worked out for themselves that it would be a long hard journey but still they are there encouraging, supporting and cajoling him.

Paul's first four sessions centred on relational play and a theme of self. Then a new theme emerged as Paul made a scene in the sand of two horses nuzzling each other. He told me they were saying goodbye, 'Look, they are grooming.' This scene soon descended into chaos. The horses threatened the people, then a dog came and an eagle flew over and captured the light. He told me 'The dogs and the horses fight because they do not know what else to do.' He said 'Mess, mess, mess, everywhere.'

I reflected that not knowing can be hard and mess can be cleaned. Sometimes not knowing can be messy. I wondered if capturing the light may have been a metaphor for his lack of joy taking the light from his life.

In the first year of therapy his subsequent stories centred on horses and dogs.

Paul told me to write this down:

> Blackie is the best horse. Blackie is short for Black Beauty. The man is fixing the toilet. The dogs and the horses are running down the lanes, trotting, first there is a canter, then they go really fast calling Emergency, Emergency. The man stops fixing the toilet but no one knows what the toilet is for. Blackie bucks and neighs and kicks and he still don't know what the toilet is for. Now they are all sick and the doctor comes. He takes blood. He tells Blackie I am taking a bit of muscle from you. Blackie is nervous. The doctor is listening to Blackie's heart. There, there, good boy. He has to have an injection because he is scared and there is pain inside him. He is having a blood sample taken and the doctor checks to see if the horse has the right blood. Blackie is very nervous and stuff. The horse never has any other horse's blood

otherwise they will be dead. Good boy, good boy, now he feels a heavy weight. The end.

This was a most poignant story of a sick child with literally no one to talk to about the frightening and invasive treatment that he underwent. Paul absolutely loved coming to the therapy sessions. I typed out some of the stories he did and this pleased him greatly. Several sessions on he told me, 'Once upon a time there was a boy called Sam. He liked to create stories and he is going to create one now. Where is your book? The dogs were assembled. Could you get me an ambulance; the two headed dragon has had a baby.' He made the sound of the ambulance siren.

> The dragon flew on top of the ambulance, quickly, quickly where is that baby? Sam screamed, Come where is that baby! Oh, here come the dogs, I hate the horrible dogs, come on, come on, let's get away, but what about the baby?
> We have to get over there but I thought we were meant to save the baby. The dragon said it is just too frightening. Come on, come on, I am frightened of the dogs said the dragon. Well it's your baby said Sam. The paramedic called the dragon Annabelle and she made strange girly, giggly noises. She was trying to get her fire up and she jumped about and called I hate Mum and Dad and Mum and Dad were nowhere to be seen.

I wondered to myself if Paul felt like the baby who was left behind.

Paul's stories continued along the same lines. Some were more poignant than others and as the stories came and were recorded he made progress – not just in the sessions with me but in the foster home as well. He still had trouble making friends in school and loneliness and trust is an issue for him. He described it so well when he said 'I'm top dog and I'm the leader of the pack. There are 21 dogs in my pack and I am the leader of the pack.' Paul has learned to share too and to take turns in the foster home. The carers have been amazing with this child. They have opened up his world. There is still a way to go and now his new narrative reads *I have a family*.

Conclusion

I consider that the stories told by both children in this chapter meets Brunner's (in Engel 1995, p.70) criteria for what determines a narrative: 'A narrative must contain a plot, a high point of tension that meets some kind of resolution. A narrative remains a narrative whether it is true or false. It is indifferent to facts.' Engel (1995) states that children tell stories to organise their experiences and their knowledge and to communicate that knowledge to others just as in the first part of the chapter Penny told stories of her father. She was working through her experiences of being terrified in his company whereas Paul was equally terrified and faced his experiences alone without a connection to anyone. Now he can say, with confidence, 'I am nice', which suggests the narrative is much richer and hopefully will sustain him in the future. Narrative Play Therapy appeared to work well for both these children and is a helpful starting point to the rest of their lives.

References

Byng Hall, J. (1999) 'Creating a Coherent Story in Family Therapy.' In G. Roberts and J. Holmes (eds) *Healing Stories: Narrative in Psychiatry and Psychotherapy*. Oxford: Oxford University Press.

Cattanach, A. (2008) *Narrative Approaches in Play with Children*. London: Jessica Kingsley Publishers.

Cox, M. and Theilgaard, A. (1987) *Mutative Metaphors in Psychotherapy: The Aeolian Mode*. London: Tavistock Publications.

Crittenden, P. 'Patterns of Attachment and Sexual Behaviour.' In L. Atkinson and K. Zucker (eds) (1997) *Attachment and Psychopathology*. New York: Guilford Press.

Dunn, J. (1988) *The Beginnings of Social Understanding*. Oxford: Blackwell.

Engel, S. (1995) *The Stories Children Tell: Making Sense of the Narratives of Childhood*. New York: Freeman.

Freeman, J., Epston, D. and Lobovits, D. (1997) *Playful Approaches to Serious Problems: Narrative Therapy with Children and Their Families*. New York: Norton.

Greenburg, M., De Klyen, M., Speltz, M.L. and Endriga, M.C. (1997) 'The Role of Attachment Processes in Externalising Psychopathology in Young Children.' In L. Atkinson and K. Zucker (eds) *Attachment and Psychopathology*. New York: Guilford Press.

Hodges, J., Steele, M. and Hillman, S. (2004) *Little Piggy: Narrative Stem Coding Manual*. London: Anna Freud Centre, Great Ormond Street.

James, B. (1989) *Treating Traumatised Children: New Insights and Creative Interventions*. New York: Free Press.

Jennings, S. (1999) *Introduction to Developmental Play Therapy Playing and Health*. London: Jessica Kingsley Publishers.

Parry, A. and Doan, R. (eds) (1994) *Story Re-Visions: Narrative Therapy in the Post Modern World*. New York: Guilford Press.

Roberts, G. and Holmes, J. (eds) (1999) *Healing Stories: Narratives in Psychiatry and Psychotherapy.* Oxford: Oxford University Press.

Rutter, M. (1997) 'Clinical Implications of Attachment Concepts.' In L. Atkinson and K. Zucker (eds) (1997) *Attachment and Psychopathology.* New York: Guilford Press.

Sameroff, A.J. and Emde, R.N. (1989) *Relationship Disturbance in Early Childhood: A Developmental Approach.* New York: Basic Books.

White, M. and Epston, D. (1990) *Narrative Means to Therapeutic Ends.* New York: Norton.

Chapter 5

Holding and Being Held

The Narrative Thread of Supervision

David Le Vay and Ann Marie John

As our title suggests, we are interested in the ideas of Hoffman, Anderson, White and others, all of whom have had a major influence on the development of a social construction framework for family therapy. Hoffman (2010) suggests that we look at things through certain lenses, depending on the context from where we are coming. A narrative lens therefore, from our perspective, suggests a commitment to the idea that there is not one truth about how supervision practice should be but a variety of stories that may be more or less useful. This is similar to Hoffman's stance in family therapy in which the client can explore which of the therapist's ideas might be helpful, rather than perceiving them as being simply right or wrong. Of course there is a potential problem with this in the context of supervision, as the supervisor is often viewed as being an 'expert', or at least an authority, and we will explore this idea more in our discussion about ethics.

We are also interested in the idea of how the stories told in therapy can be mirrored or reflected within the dynamic of the supervisory relationship, perhaps explored within an image, sand tray or role-play. We would suggest that this mirroring/parallel process can help supervisees to re-story experience in a way that can contribute to the therapeutic process. In relation to our own process of writing this chapter, we are aware of how we have privileged slightly different stories in our clinical description of the supervisory process, with DLV exploring stories of externalisation and AMJ exploring stories of reflection and transparency. We have also noticed that it is difficult to find written stories of supervision, let alone one of a narrative orientation within the field of play therapy in the UK, unlike other family therapy and associated arts therapies, where the literature within these fields is more extensive, for example Jones and Dokter (2008), Lahad (2000), Shohet (2008) and Tselikas-Portman (1999). We suspect that, like ourselves, other play therapy supervisors have been telling stories of their practice to each other for many years but just haven't got around to writing them down and this chapter to some extent aims to rectify this, both for our benefit and others. Our writing is designed to mirror the process of Narrative Play Therapy and the supervision process in that it has developed out of conversations between people, something of a co-construction in itself. Whilst this has not always been an easy task, it felt like the most congruent approach.

Orientation

In our conversations and writings together, we noticed that the two of us were approaching this chapter from somewhat different places. We are both qualified dramatherapists and play therapists (a narrative model of play therapy), whilst AMJ is also qualified in a constructionist, narrative model of family therapy and DLV in social work. This has meant that to an extent the issue of supervision has been explored from both a family therapy and play therapy perspective, although clearly the latter has been privileged for the purposes of this chapter. The aim of this chapter is to tell stories of our supervision practice that illustrate some of our ideas around how a storied, narrative approach can be helpful to the supervision process and ultimately, of course, the client's own process. We have sought, where possible, to co-construct this process with our supervisees in order to mirror the process of therapy. While we make some reference to the current literature we do so simply to set the context for our work, rather than seeking to create a model of practice.

The ethics of supervision

Supervision, like therapy, takes place in an ethical domain where child protection and professional standards are inevitably part of the story. Supervisor and supervisee are therefore positioned within certain constraints that structure the process. The patterns of how we create supervision practice are therefore influenced by what Harré and van Lengenhove (1999) describe as 'rights, duties and obligations'. The negotiation of power between supervisor and supervisee mirror those of the play therapy process, in that some aspects of the supervisory contract may be negotiable and others non-negotiable. The supervisor may hold a moral framework as to what he or she must include for the supervision to be ethically appropriate and the supervisee may likewise have his or her own ideas, which may or may not meet those of the supervisor. In some respect this may determine the extent to which they can work together.

Much of the research concerning successful outcomes in both supervision and therapy (Holloway and Carroll 1999) suggests that the quality of the supervisory relationship is a primary factor and the manner in which the supervision process is negotiated, within ethical and organisational constraints, is an important element in describing a 'good enough' supervision process. The nature of the supervision process is difficult to measure in quantitative terms (with the inherent ethical problems around control trials) and so instead lends itself to more descriptive, qualitative methods of evaluation, that is, stories told about the impact and experience of supervision upon the supervisee, the client and the wider service. While this chapter is not so concerned with research, it is about 'enquiry' into our own practice. Skills in supervision have often been described as something of a 'helicopter' process; the ability to move between the positions of client, therapist and supervisee. A narrative model takes this one step further, in the sense that we do not see these positions as separate but instead a series of reflexive, connected stories and indeed the task of supervision can be seen as a process of weaving these stories together in a tapestry of meaning. Unlike the story of Penelope who wove by day and unpicked by night, the task of weaving within supervision is seen as something more meaningful and purposeful.

Questions around the tasks of Narrative Play Therapy supervision

The process, or respective tasks, of supervising a trainee therapist and a qualified therapist are, in our view, very different. Within trainee supervision there is a dimension of assessment and training that creates an extra strand to our tapestry and which is more often than not the dominant story in terms of the external expectations and requirements experienced by both parties. Trainees often come to supervision with stories of supervision experiences that have been negative and detrimental to their development and it can take time to deconstruct and make sense of these experiences. Expectations around the notions of judgement and assessment also create complexity because the decisions to privilege stories of competence or incompetence are based on fixed parameters of evidence that are more an empirical way of working rather than a social constructionist position. Because of these issues and the given parameters around trainee supervision, we have both questioned the extent to which a narrative supervision approach fits with the needs of the trainee, training institution and placement. This is a conversation we will continue to have, but it does raise questions regarding other contexts wherein a narrative approach to supervision might not be as helpful as other approaches. Because of this, and due to our aim to approach this material from a perspective of co-construction, the stories we have decided to tell within this chapter therefore come from our practice with qualified practitioners. Issues here around the notion of terminology are also interesting, particularly in the sense of whether one refers to 'supervision' or 'consultation'. The question of power in the supervisory relationship is an important one to explore and it may be that within a process of 'consultation' the supervisee (or indeed consultee) has a greater sense of clinical responsibility for their work. A question for another day perhaps?

Narrative themes in supervision

Within our practice we have noticed that a number of themes emerge repeatedly in the stories our supervisees bring to supervision. The theme of therapist incompetence is one that occurs frequently, when the therapist begins to bring stories that privilege the notion of having got something 'wrong', perhaps feeling disconnected from the process in the playroom or that they might not be doing enough (or indeed doing too much). This resonates somewhat with Cattanach's (1993) ideas of how the child in therapy often brings feelings of shame to therapy, perhaps in the shape of stories about monsters that can be re-played and re-told and moved to a position of resilience and coping. The stories that are told in supervision are often a complex mix of the child and therapist's process. It is important to deconstruct the story the supervisee brings in order to get a sense of the place or position it is coming from. Sometimes this can happen through a process of asking questions but more often than not a creative approach, for example the creation of an image or a narrative around a sand tray, can be invaluable in enabling the supervisee to see the story more clearly within the context of the therapeutic relationship; sometimes looking at an externalised image can show us things we did not see, or realise, previously. As play therapists, we know that the symbolic process of play allows us to work in a safe way and to explore our difficult material in a way that often 'bypasses' our natural defences, which are often constructed through language.

In the following two examples we aim to illustrate how the process of both narrative and playful creativity within supervision can help to uncover untold stories and create new ones. DLV illustrates this by writing about the process of creative supervision and reflecting on the process of narrative sandplay and image making. AMJ reflects with a supervisee about the significance of making a sand tray in supervision and the impact on both the supervisee and the child.

Narrative Play Therapy supervision (David Le Vay)

I often think of supervision as a process of 'holding and being held'. In my work as a play therapist, I sometimes feel like a time traveller, moving back and forth between the fragmented memories and shifting landscapes of children's trauma. We slay monsters together, run, hide, get lost, fight and conquer. Part of this process is about creating a thread that children can hold on to, the construction of internal narratives and stories that provide some sense of coherence and order within their often chaotic lives. And, as therapists, we too need our thread so that we can safely navigate our way through these landscapes and yet hold on to a coherent sense of our own role and identity. The thread is held in many ways; by instinct, theory, training and experience and also of course through supervision. As both a supervisor and supervisee, my experience is that of both 'holding and being held'. It's a reflexive process, each experience informing the other like the entwined, layered stories that are constructed in the space of the play therapy room. Picture a line of rock climbers or cave explorers, roped together to ensure their collective safety; this is the image I sometimes have of the supervision relationship.

Play therapy is a creative process, often non-verbal and often working within the realm of symbolism and metaphor. It seems only congruent that play therapy supervision should reflect this process, that the supervisory relationship becomes something of a mirror to the therapeutic relationship between therapist and child. The languages of therapy are varied and many, although generally these are simply different languages used to describe the same process, different theoretical lenses through which we seek to understand the work we do. But it is important that the therapist and supervisor speak the same language; that too much doesn't get lost in translation, so to speak. And so in the context of Narrative Play Therapy, in which play therapists are working with story structures through the creative process of play, it is important that supervision is able, when necessary, to become a mirror to this process.

I am also aware, through my discussions with Ann Marie, that our understanding of 'narrative supervision' has a somewhat different meaning for each of us, due to our own respective training and experience and the particular window through which we view this material. For example, the term 'externalisation' as I use it within a context of Narrative Play Therapy has something of a different meaning to how it is used within the context of family therapy. Perhaps there are some interesting conversations to be held here about the meeting points between narrative family therapy and Narrative Play Therapy.

Externalisation within narrative family therapy (Freeman, Epston and Lobovits 1997) generally refers to the practice of engaging in conversations or asking questions that invite a family to view a 'problem' from different perspectives or vantage points. When talking about externalisation in Narrative Play Therapy I am essentially talking about a process through which children express and project aspects of themselves through their play and into their stories, role-play, object play. However, whilst there are differences in theory and practice between these approaches, there are also some key similarities. As Freeman *et al.* (1997, p.147) say:

> The very process of drawing, sculpting or dramatising the relationship with a problem naturally evokes a visceral sense of the problem as located for reflection outside of the self…it can be a relief for children to literally express the externalised problem in a symbolic yet physically experienced way. This allows them to 'see' the problem and ponder it more easily.

This concept of externalisation through symbolic play also connects with the notion of 'aesthetic distance'; a term that I believe was first coined by Edward Bullough (1912) when he wrote:

> [Aesthetic distance] is obtained by separating the object and its appeal from one's own self, by putting it out of gear with practical needs and ends. Thereby the 'contemplation' of the object becomes alone possible. But it does not mean that the relation between the self and the object is broken to the extent of becoming 'impersonal.'

This is something that lies at the very heart of the play therapy process, in the sense that children are able to locate otherwise overwhelming feelings outside of themselves by projecting them onto objects, images, roles and stories. Instead of being simply the 'bad bits' of themselves, this process of externalisation allows children to observe and engage with aspects of their felt experience through the safety of symbolic play. In this way, children are able to tolerate the intolerable. This notion of aesthetic distance, drawn also from art and literature, also plays a fundamental role in the supervision process. The notion of engaging with an image or an object, brought by a supervisee, can facilitate valuable reflection and exploration of feelings that might not perhaps be most easily expressed verbally. The challenge of supervision, and one that I experience frequently, is of having the confidence to apply what I know in play therapy to my role as supervisor. Sometimes it is easy to stay within the comfort zone of speech and I am aware that both supervisees and myself at times are resistant to shifting into the use of creative, narrative imagery.

Narrative Play Therapy draws much of course from social construction theory (Burr 1995) but also upon an ecological model of therapy (Bronfenbrenner 1979) that emphasises the systemic context of our lives and interconnected nature of these systems. The social construction approach acknowledges the subjectivity of experience and how a sense of self is developed through interaction with others. Within play therapy, children construct stories about themselves within the context of the therapeutic relationship. In this sense, therapeutic narratives become embedded within the relationship between child and therapist and engage both parties in a process of ordering, sequencing, sorting and making sense of the complexity of the child's experience. Likewise, within a narrative model of play therapy supervision, both supervisor and supervisee bring their stories into a creative space and similarly, meaning is co-constructed through this relationship. This is a key element of the supervisory process. We need to acknowledge what we take into the supervision relationship and the particular 'window' through which we view and seek to understand the clinical material that is presented. Jane Speedy (2000) talks of how a 'narrative world view, a sense of the world as a storied place to live and work, provides a different position from which to explore the very human endeavours of counselling, psychotherapy and supervision' (p.420). In this sense the introduction of explicit narrative terminology can change the way in which we position ourselves within supervision.

Jan, one of my supervisees, is employed as a play therapist for children within a medical setting, managing the overall provision of play services as well as providing clinical play therapy interventions. It is a complex area of work for a play therapist and the children Jan works with have experienced very significant degrees of injury, trauma and loss through sudden accidents and illnesses. She would also, I think, acknowledge that it has been a struggle at times to carve out a place for herself as very much a child-centred play therapist within a setting that is orientated around a medically driven model of treatment goals and indeed this may be the case for many play therapists working within a hospital environment. However she is a committed therapist and willing to fight battles to raise awareness of the child's emotional need for 'witness' and 'mastery' amidst such trauma and loss and has done much to raise the profile of play therapy within the organisation.

One of the issues within supervision that we have touched upon at different times is our tendency to intellectualise emotion, to allow ourselves to slip into a pattern of using words rather than feeling, perhaps as a wall of sorts that we can each hide behind. Jan is an intelligent, articulate woman and the notion of words as a form of defence is a dynamic of supervision that we have both been aware of. Is there some kind of unconscious collusive pattern being acted out here, I have sometimes wondered? What is it we are hoping to avoid? From a narrative perspective this is interesting, in the sense of the respective personal stories that we each have about the role of words as a form of protection. This is something that we touched upon together, and I can certainly make connections with my own experience of growing up with a profoundly bi-polar father. He was an academic, a man of words, and someone who was unable to express himself emotionally on any significant level. There is clearly a personal story here that I carry with me into the supervisory relationship.

At various points during the time of our working together I have introduced the idea of exploring material in a more creative, non-verbal way, for example the use of a sand tray or an image perhaps. At times I wondered if there was a resistance to this, perhaps within Jan or indeed within myself, and when we explored this a little she expressed her fear that if she worked in a more unconscious way she might become distressed and again, in an unsaid way, this might have been something that we were both avoiding. With this in mind, I would like to say a little about how within supervision we manage to begin to 'grasp the nettle' and move into a different and more creative way of working together.

Jan spoke about her work with an eight-year-old boy called Peter. Peter had suffered a brain haemorrhage during the course of routine surgery and was admitted to the hospital for a period of intensive rehabilitation. Part of his treatment involved a complex tracheostomy, with the result being that if the tubing from his throat became dislodged he would be unable to breathe and could die within a matter of minutes. This meant that Peter had to be under constant surveillance in the event of him needing emergency medical treatment. Peter was awaiting an operation, which it was hoped would result in him being able to breathe on his own again without the need for the tracheostomy.

I was struck by a number of issues about this session, partly around the themes of Peter's play, in the context of the clinical material Jan had brought to supervision, but also the nature of his physical condition and its impact upon Jan and the process. I suggested that she use the sand tray to portray 'Peter's world'. She was a little reticent at first but said she would give it a try. I suggested that Jan remain silent during the process and that we could talk afterwards.

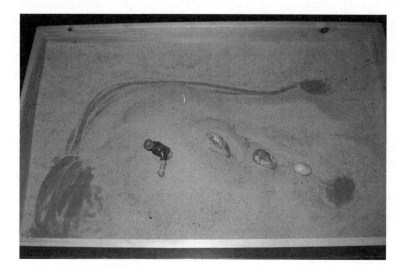

Figure 5.1 Peter's world

I asked Jan to tell the story of Peter's world (Figure 5.1). She said that the small circular area on the bottom right represented her play therapy room. She described it as an oasis. There was a mountain, which was a 'hard place to be' and the three stones represented the play therapy process. As Jan talked she, without realising, began referring to the largest stone as herself. The bigger area of blue on the bottom left, and pathway leading from it, represented the operation Peter was soon to have and the figure itself was Peter making the 'long journey' through recovery and back to the normality of family, friends and school. Jan talked of Peter's vulnerability and her own difficult feelings around 'letting go' and as she talked about her image we noticed together how she had been drawn out of her oasis by Peter, pulled out of the place where she felt comfortable and safe.

As I gazed at the sand tray, I found myself thinking about the visceral quality of the image. It made me think of airways, tubes and holes and the symbolism of the oasis as a place of survival. It also made me think about breathing and suffocating, and how the idea of 'stopping' connected with something terrible happening. I voiced my thoughts to Jan and this led to us to make some connections around her experience of Peter in the session and her own fears around what would happen if she stopped thinking and talking, that is, would she become suffocated by her own emotional responses? Through this conversation Jan began to acknowledge her tendency to intellectualise as a form of emotional protection and we both acknowledged how we had fallen into a supervisory pattern of using words as a defence, perhaps from the impact of her work. I realised that this was something that I had been unhelpfully colluding with, another example of a parallel process, and there was something very poignant in reaching a place where something had begun to be named which in turn gave us a new foothold to our supervisory relationship.

Some weeks after this, I met again with Jan. She spoke about some difficult issues of conflict within her work place and how at times she felt silenced by the bureaucratic and corporate nature of the organisation. Jan said she worried sometimes about saying the wrong thing, that she might be misunderstood and that this left her feeling frustrated. In the midst of all this, Jan also mentioned a girl she was working with who couldn't speak, which meant she had to speak for her and she worried about misinterpreting the girl's feelings.

I felt somewhat overwhelmed by all this and attempted to pull some of the threads together by reflecting upon the difficulty she was having in finding a voice and that when she did it seemed to be around resolving conflict or a fear of getting it wrong. It was as if she felt almost silenced by the organisation, just like the little girl who came to the playroom.

As Jan talked about the current organisational struggles she was experiencing I mentioned the image of an oasis she had created some time ago. She said this didn't fit with how she was feeling currently so I suggested she create a new image.

Figure 5.2 Jan's image

I asked about the story contained within Jan's picture (Figure 5.2) and she talked about the high mountains and the yellow desert, which represented the therapeutic space of the playroom. The small circular area was an oasis but it was far away behind the mountains and difficult to get to. I wondered what Jan's instant emotional response was to her image. She said it felt 'really tough...a hard place to be' and connected this to the feelings of loss that children bring into the playroom. She then went on to talk about how she was aware that she used her language as a defence at times and that she was concerned that she might be at times too controlling as a therapist. Jan said that she felt at times disempowered by the organisation and wondered whether her sessions with children sometimes became a place to exercise her own needs around playfulness and control and in this sense was worried that her own needs could impact upon those of the children.

Jan's sense of being 'done to' and feelings of powerlessness clearly connected with the experiences of the children she worked with and in the sense the playroom may have become a place where they both experienced the need to exercise control. And I wondered about my own process, the meaning that this material held for me in terms of my own life story. I talked with my own supervisor about this and the possible echoes from childhood around how words and intellect can be used as a form of both attack and defence. I was also struck by the complexity of the parallel processes that ran through our work together. Williams (1995, cited in Wosket 1999, p.225) talked of how this process can be 'more of a multi-lane highway than a one-way valve' and Val Wosket (1999, p.225) talks about how the process is 'frequently activated by the supervisor's personal responses' to what is being presented. Wosket also talks about personal disclosure and the benefits of sometimes taking risks within supervision. Indeed, the process of writing about Jan's supervision sessions, and of sharing this with her and having a conversation about what has emerged, has proven to be a powerful exercise from which we have both learned. Certainly, it has made us reflect upon our process together and how mindful we need to be of the respective stories that we bring to the supervisory relationship. Like the relationship between child and therapist, the relationship between supervisor and supervisee is equally a process of co-construction.

But most important, and what I have hoped to illustrate here, is how the use of creative externalisation and the creation of a narrative around symbolic imagery can help to find a way around some of the blocks and obstacles that can exist within supervision relationships. The jazz musician Miles Davis once said 'don't play what's there, play what's not there'. For Davis it was always in the space between the notes that he found his creativity, and as creative therapists and supervisors it is often in the space between the words that we need to focus our attention.

Supervision conversations (Ann Marie John)

I am struck by David's terminology of weaving threads together, a theme we have both used without consulting one another. It is interesting that somehow we have shared this metaphorical notion of supervision as a pulling together and holding of the fragility of the child/therapist/supervisor's internal world. I think in many ways we are using externalisation in the same way: to allow something to be looked at in a different way. Whether through sandplay, role-play or art work, the act of symbolic externalisation can allow something to be processed and a new meaning or story to emerge.

Externalisation in Narrative Family Therapy is often used as a technique to maintain therapeutic neutrality, in other words to find a way of working that does not blame one member of the family. I recently helped a child to create a purple pooh monster from fart putty and we discussed how the monster spoiled things by making him do naughty things when his mum was away. It turned out that the whole family had monsters (Mum and Dad had 'shouty' monsters) and Mum had learned to control her shouty monster and was going to give Dad some lessons. I commented on how crowded their house must be with all these monsters. We agreed it was hard to get rid of the monsters because even if you flushed them down the toilet they hid in the pipes. We agreed that the family would have to work together to outsmart the monsters. This approach is very similar to Michael White's (2007) account of using externalisation with a boy who smeared faeces – the infamous 'sneaky poo' monster.

In my approach to supervision and the example I describe here, I think I am working in a similar way to David, using the non-verbal to find stories that are not accessible by verbal means. The story under discussion is the story of the therapeutic relationship, its history and how it can continue to be useful to the child given that the theme of absent mothers and children has become so poignant. I think what is different in my approach is that I am something of a social constructionist purist in both the way I communicate my account of the work and in the way we use and think about the sand tray that is created within supervision. I have therefore attempted to co-construct the account of the supervision session with my supervisee by recording a conversation and transcribing it. Although it is sometimes like an interview I am attempting to co-create a story of the supervision as one would with a child in Narrative Play Therapy.

The late Michael White (2007) talked about the process of writing accounts of sessions with clients (otherwise the client becomes an object and we become the expert). He also sometimes wrote letters to clients about the session, sharing hypotheses and thoughts. This transparency of approach is one of the reasons I trained in family therapy and it is an important element in my practice.

The following conversation is between me and Sophie, a qualified and experienced play therapist who works with bereaved children. Sally, her client, has lost her mother to an illness. Sophie came to supervision with questions about the meaning of a question Sally had asked her about whether she has children. This had some personal resonance for Sophie at the time and I felt that she felt as if she needed to sort out whose story was whose before answering the question. My question about what it would be like if Sophie showed her sand tray to the child was based on Tom Anderson's ideas of the reflecting team (1987).

Anderson decided to put the family behind the screen and then to ask the family to comment on the therapist's conversation and so was born the 'reflecting team' (now often working in the room rather than behind the screen) with the therapist and family. So the family and team reflect back on one another, almost like a prism creating multiple levels of meaning.

The family can then comment upon whether the team's reflections or hypotheses are helpful or not. This approach requires a certain degree of risk-taking and transparency and I wondered whether a similar process could be applied to the use of a sand tray within supervision, that is, the idea of a sand tray created in supervision being shown to a child. Yet as Sophie recalls this idea stayed with her and she somehow felt that it was a helpful thing to do.

AM   So, I'm trying to think back to the session where we talked about Sally and you did the sand tray and I remember you coming, the sense of anticipation that there was something that it was really important to talk about in a way that perhaps we hadn't talked about in supervision before.

S   I think it was thinking about where Sally was at, really, and what was going on for her. I think I was feeling that something was happening in those sessions but it was hard to define in words...

AM   I guess the question that she asked you (do you have children) is one that comes up quite a lot in play therapy and supervision and I guess that resonates when you said you weren't quite sure what to do with it or how to work with it.

S   Yeah...and needing...to think about how best to respond and how... what would be helpful for her.

AM   Because I had a story about that, and I don't know if you remember in supervision that was something about her putting you in a position where you could take a risk. I guess I'd been thinking... I thought that in the session she had been gradually taking little risks with you and looking back over the session she was gradually opening up a bit. I suppose I was interested that she then put you in that position. So it was really important how you responded to it.

S   Mm.

AM   But I don't know if that's just my story...of making a sort of meaning of it?

S   Yeah, I certainly feel that as you said that she had been taking little risks. Initially when she asked me that question...I suppose I didn't really see it as an invitation to further risk-taking between us.

AM   How did you see it?

S   Well, I suppose I saw it as a sort of risk...yeah I guess risk-taking on her part, she was able to ask me a direct question. I guess at first, I just had this sense that I needed to get it right, I needed to get it right for her...so, yes, certainly on reflection there was a huge element of risk because of that feeling,

AM   For you as a therapist?

S   Yes for me as a therapist because I needed... I wanted to get it right for Sally because I felt it was really crucial for our relationship. But no, I was just going to say, thinking back to what I said earlier, there was the question...that needed to be thought about. It needed a response; it was...it was quite difficult to think about it in words.

AM   I was trying to recall how we came to do a sand tray and I think there was something about it kind of not being a verbal thing.

S   Yeah. I think...also being very unsure what would be right for Sally...what would be the right response and therefore almost words became...inadequate. And I think then...your invitation to try a sand tray seemed to be...yeah, seemed to be the right way to explore things.

AM   So looking at it now do you remember the process? I can remember it being a very thoughtful and quiet and purposeful activity. I don't remember us talking that much about it.

S   No, I think we talked very little while I was actually making it. I recall the process quite clearly and that was...it felt that it was very much led by what I was drawn to and there wasn't... I didn't, I certainly didn't have a preset idea of what I was creating or where I wanted to go with it really...it was happening...it was developing as I explored the different objects and found things to use. And yeah the two figures that I chose to represent Sally and myself I think there was... they seemed to make themselves known to me.

Figure 5.3 Sand tray

AM   It's interesting for me because I've worked in this room for quite a long time and some of those things I hadn't seen before and so it was all…it all felt very new to me as well because somehow I hadn't come across these things.

S   Yeah, and just looking at it again this evening I am… I am struck by… there's something still so much…although it was a number of weeks or months ago now…there's something still very much in looking at it that speaks of Sally. It's almost like…as if there were a whole load of different sand trays, pictures…I would know that that's Sally's or that was done with holding Sally in my arms and, yeah it's…

AM   So what would be the…what words would you use to describe… when you talked of… I guess when you talked about the seahorse finding you in a way it almost felt like a story that was sort of unfolding.

S   Yeah I think that was really how it felt with each…with each object really. It was definitely the objects finding…finding me rather than me looking for something specific or something to…to represent our therapeutic relationship.

AM   I remember us getting to the end of the sand tray and it felt to me like something had been processed really in a non-verbal way and I'm not sure if there was any more clarity after the sand tray…

S   Um…

AM   …I mean what the answer was to the question [laughs].

S   The question was, I'm not sure that there was…there was certainly not, you know, a crystal clear answer to the question. But I certainly remember that Sally's mum was very much around in that sand tray and that felt very significant and very important and remember having the strong feeling of somehow…being entrusted with this little girl and that somehow Mum was around and her kind of… wanting to make sure that her little girl is OK.

AM   Mm, I remember that conversation…

S   Okay.

AM   I remember that part of it and I don't know…it almost felt like you were working in a bit of a different dimension. I wondered if you were sort of exploring who you were to each other and sometimes it was okay to maybe be the mum…because that's certainly what Sally was wanting.

S   Yes.

AM   My feeling was that's why it was poignant…

S   Yeah.

AM   So then we got to the end of the session.

S   Mm.

AM   And I think I've rather [laughingly] off the cuff said something about, 'Oh I wonder what it would be like if you showed the sand tray to Sally', a bit like you would do in a reflecting team as a way of tell the family what you're thinking.

S   And that stayed with me [laughs].

AM   And that stayed with you? [laughs].

S   Yeah and I remember...it stayed at the back of my mind and...well at the forefront and then at the back of my mind for about two or three weeks and...I just kept on wondering what it would be like to share it with Sally and just, I suppose, yeah go back to the risk-taking thing. She risked a question and could I risk showing her...showing her a picture of this sand tray? It was about two or three weeks after that visit and I'd printed out the photos and kept wondering... wondering.

AM   And it kept staying with you.

S   Yeah it certainly did...it was around... I'd acknowledged that...that Sally had asked me a question and I remember the week after and I think the week after that she was just clearly not interested in getting an answer or going...

AM   It went away...

S   ... revisiting it...it went away for a couple of weeks and then, yeah, I think it was about the third week that suddenly it was there again...

S   I'd wanted to acknowledge that she had asked me and that we could...think with her about...that sort of a response and answer but it wasn't until about the third week or fourth, third I think, that it was important for her or meaningful.

AM   Mm. And I'm trying to think back to how you presented it to her the sand tray?

S   Yeah [laughs] so am I.

AM   [laughs]

S   Yeah it...[sighs]... I think it was in relation to what Sally had asked and acknowledging that I hadn't forgotten that she'd asked me and then I think I let her know that while I was thinking about the question I'd done some playing in the sand while I was thinking about it and I remember she'd kind of looked up. She was doing some drawing I think and she looked up when I said I'd done some playing in the sand and I'd sort of reflected on that and I sometimes find it really helpful to play in the sand and think about things…and then I remember I said to her that I'd taken a picture of what I'd done playing and I let her know that it was there and that if she wanted to see it she could if she chose to look at it and she carried on kind of drawing [laughs].

AM   Until she was ready.

S   And then suddenly she looked us and she said 'where is it…where's the picture?' and it was on the other side of the room so I said it was there if she wanted…and she jumped up and went over and got it [laughs].

AM   And I remember it was very live in the room when you came in to supervision and she had…a strong response to the figures. Did she say who was who or was that…?

S   Yeah. She looked at it and she wanted to know what the different… I was quite struck by that, she immediately kind of assumed and attuned to the fact that it was a symbolic representation. I didn't explain anything about it. She just picked it up and she immediately… sort of intuitively took on board the fact that it was a symbolic representation of us. Even now when I'm thinking about it I'm just struck by it again…

AM   It's quite a leap.

S   Yeah. I mean there was nothing in what I said or I did that gave her any sort of…indication or preconception that that's what it was about but she…[laughing] yeah actually I'm really struck by it now as I'm thinking about it.

AM   And she was quite mindful of what you're doing as well as you being mindful of her.

S   Yeah and so she wanted to know what the figures were…who the figures were representing and what the objects meant and she just developed her own sort of response and kind of symbolic interpretation really of what they all meant which, yes it's kind of… I was quite fascinated by it all over again.

AM   What was happening with you when that was kind of going on? Because I guess in terms of your risk-taking…what was interesting really was doing a sand tray as risky as, you know, answering the question or…

S   Mm…

AM   Because I mean it does...it's quite an unknown quantity?

S   I was intrigued. I was really intrigued by her response. I mean she could have looked at it and put it down and...that would also have been okay. I suppose in my thinking about what it might be like to share it with her I just... I thought of...some different scenarios and what that would be like for her and for me and like I said I didn't really kind of think about her...interpreting or wanting to know what they represented, so I was intrigued and just really, really interested in what sense she was making of it.

AM   I was wondering where it took you to really in your relationship and answering the question in a different way to the way people usually answer questions. In a way it felt like you gave her the answer she needed but not in a verbal way.

S   Yeah I...when she was so interested in the symbolic representation of the objects I wondered whether that would be something that Sally might decide to try because she hasn't used the sand and she did... I think the following session or a couple of sessions later she made a little foray into sand play. She just only did it the once but what I feel after this was something about...something about the symbolic representation, something about enabling a different kind of playing because I think what happened shortly after that session, maybe two sessions, three sessions later was that Sally started to use role play and that was something she hadn't...she hadn't used at all and up until then our sessions had been kind of...very art-based where there was some sort of interaction between us but not a lot. I was left with a feeling that it somehow, on some level, gave her permission to use the space a bit differently and to use me differently because she started to involve me very directly in the role-play and giving me clearly a side role. So...she played the same sort of role-play in many, many sessions where she experimented with different relationships and ways of reacting in expression of emotions and so...I don't know... whether that had a direct link to it.

AM   So I don't know if there's anything else you want to say or if there's anything you want to ask me? I guess the other thing I'd thought was I didn't do a sand tray of my supervision...it would have been nice to reflect but somehow that didn't happen...to take the reflection the other way as well and I guess I see it as...to reflect back...because in a way I'm kind of saying...well...you know, even putting the thought into your head, in a way I was taking a bit of a risk as well in terms of practice. Now I'm getting too complicated...but it feels like we're done unless there's anything else?

S   No, I don't think so. I mean I don't know whether…in a way just wondering what your thoughts were as the supervisor?

AM   Well…because I did my research on those sorts of questions [children asking therapists about their family – particularly if they had children] quite a long time ago it was quite interesting for me that it was coming up. And aware of how close it can feel when those questions come up and how difficult it can be really and thinking, kind of feeling, that somehow there needed to be another way. You needed to find another way to answer that question or that it needed to go to a different level. I mean my sense was there was something going on between you… I mean I'd call it risk-taking but…the sense of it being really important, as you say, to not get it right so much but to work with her and stay with her…

S   Yes.

AM   …and I know that doing sand trays for me can help…in supervision can just free things up a bit but I hadn't expected it to have the impact that it had in the room with us and then it felt very important what we were doing. I'm a bit like you and kind of almost felt the presence of her mother in the room with us actually. It was very…quite profound and you know that idea of sort of being entrusted I think. It felt really important and of course I didn't know, I hadn't thought that you would show her [the sand tray] but I was just fascinated really by… I suppose I felt that in a way you'd answered the question that she'd asked about, 'How much can you hold me and think of me?' and that's quite simplistic in a way but there was a sense of mindfulness between you. She's mindful of you making these symbols about her and you're mindful of her while you're making them. And as you say seeing it does bring back the kind of intensity of that.

S   Mm.

AM   I guess it felt as if we…we brought a bit of what was going on into the room in supervision as well.

S   Mm.

In this conversation, Sophie and I attempt to co-construct a meaning of the supervision process during one session and how making a sand tray when Sophie was perhaps stuck with what to do next helped her to process what was going on between them. Her decision to show Sally the sand tray as a way of communicating with her at a different level helped Sally to experience how she was held in Sophie's mind. This allowed Sophie to be a symbolic mother to Sally and act in a way that did not in any way impact on Sally's memories of her own mother. Similarly Sophie could express her own 'mother feelings' towards the child, safely creating a story for Sally that demonstrated she was held in mind.

When Sally began to guess the figures in Sophie's sand tray therapist/client roles were reversed for a short while. Sophie's sand tray allowed her to become vulnerable in the therapeutic relationship in a way that is not usually possible for a therapist and, as Sophie suggests, this opened up new ways of being and playing together in the playroom.

Conclusion

As we wrote this chapter together we wondered about what we might call it and ultimately, the notion of 'holding and being held' seemed to capture what for us what lay at the heart of the supervision process. As the play therapist has to 'hold' the child in the course of the work, so the therapist is 'held' through the process of supervision. The child is present within the supervisory relationship; the supervisor is present within the play therapy relationship. Within the triangular relationship, there is always the presence of the 'unseen third'. It's a reflexive process, a feedback loop if you like, that continually folds back upon itself, one informing the other. This is the thread of supervision, but of course it is also a narrative thread, a complex interweaving of stories.

The metaphor of the narrative thread has in many ways been the fabric that has bound this chapter together. The narrative view holds that we exist within a world of stories; that our reality is constructed and mediated through our interaction with others, as the prevailing winds of circumstance carve out patterns in our understanding of ourselves, our relationships and the world about us. Both supervisors and supervisees carry their personal stories with them, stories that will have a significant impact upon their work, for example, stories about power, authority, perfection, of not being 'good enough'. It can be helpful to acknowledge and explore these stories, to be curious about their meaning and the implications they may have for one's work. Like the flow of a river, one might track the source of these stories and the course of their journey over the years and think about how helpful or unhelpful they have been in the context of the therapeutic relationship. And children of course also bring their stories into the therapeutic space, stories that provide distant (sometimes not so distant) echoes of our own.

Within this chapter, we have sought to convey a sense of how ideas from narrative therapy can be incorporated, integrated into the play therapy supervision process. David talks about the process of creative supervision, using sandplay and image making to externalise and make visible the internalised narratives that we can have about ourselves and our work. The supervisee is invited to explore the stories within the material and reflect upon the possible meanings they may have. Ann Marie reflects upon a conversation with a supervisee about the process of sharing an image created within supervision with a child in therapy and the meaning this has for all of them. It is a process that poignantly integrates ideas from play therapy with the notion of the 'reflecting' team in family therapy. As we said earlier, this is not a model of supervision and there is nothing dramatically new in our approach. Indeed, it is more a synthesis of ideas, drawn from narrative and social construction therapy, family therapy, creative arts therapy and, of course, play therapy. But integral to our approach is the acknowledgement of issues of power and transparency and a challenge to the traditional notions of the supervisor (and therapist) as expert. Indeed, the day when one claims the position of 'expert' is the day when they may as well shut up shop and head for the hills, for it is also the day when they cease to learn. A supervisor is more experienced, may hold a sense of benign authority and a degree of clinical governance, but this is different from an expression of power. Narrative supervision, like Narrative Play Therapy, is a collaborative process, a place of playful curiosity: a place of holding and being held.

References

Anderson, T. (1987) 'The reflecting team: Dialogue and meta-dialogue in clinical work.' *Family Process 26*, 4, 415–428.

Bronfenbrenner, U. (1979) *The Ecology of Human Development.* Cambridge, MA: Harvard University Press.

Bullough, E. (1912) 'Psychical distance as a factor in art and as an aesthetic principle.' *British Journal of Psychology 5*, 87–117.

Burr, V. (1995) *An Introduction to Social Construction.* London: Routledge.

Cattanach, A. (1993) *Play Therapy with Abused Children.* London: Jessica Kingsley Publishers.

Freeman, J., Epston, D. and Lobovits, D. (1997) *Playful Approaches to Serious Problems: Narrative Therapy with Children and Their Families.* New York: Norton.

Harré, R. and van Lengenhove, L. (1999) *Positioning Theory.* Malden, MA: Blackwell Publishers.

Hoffman, L. (2010) 'An art of lenses.' *Family Process 29*, 1, 1–12.

Holloway, E. and Carroll, M. (1999) *Training Counselling Supervisors.* London and New Delhi: SAGE Publishers.

Jones, P. and Dokter, D. (eds) (2008) *Supervision of Dramatherapy.* London and New York: Routledge.

Lahad, M. (2000) *Creative Supervision.* London: Jessica Kingsley Publishers.

Shohet, R. (2008) *Passionate Supervision.* London: Jessica Kingsley Publishers.

Speedy, J. (2000) 'Consulting with gargoyles: Applying narrative ideas and practices in counselling supervision.' *European Journal of Psychotherapy, Counselling and Health 3,* 3, 419–431.

Tselikas-Portman, E. (1999) *Supervision and Dramatherapy.* London: Jessica Kingsley Publishers.

White, M. and Epston, D. (1990) *Narrative Means to Therapeutic Ends.* New York: Norton.

White, M. (2007) *Maps of Narrative Practice.* New York: Norton.

Williams, A. (1995) 'Visual and Active Supervision: Roles, Focus, Technique.' In V. Wosket (1999) *The Therapeutic Use of Self: Counselling Practice, Research and Supervision.* London: Routledge.

Wosket, V. (1999) *The Therapeutic Use of Self: Counselling Practice, Research and Supervision.* London: Routledge.

PART II

Narrative Play Therapy Practice

Chapter 6

Working with Narrative Play Therapy in the Primary School System

Alison Webster

Introduction

> In 2004, 10% of children and young people aged 5–16 [in the UK] had a clinically diagnosed mental disorder (Office for National Statistics 2004). Older children (aged 11–16 years) were more likely than younger children (aged 5–10) to be affected (12% compared with 8%). Mental disorders among young people increased between 1974 and 1999 (Collishaw *et al.* 2004). However, this upward trend was halted during 1999–2004, according to the most recent national survey of young people aged 5–16 years (Office for National Statistics 2004). (National Institute for Clinical Excellence (NICE) 2008.)

I have worked and trained in the field of childhood mental health and well being for over 20 years within health, education and voluntary sectors. Many of the families referred to me for play therapy have had school age children coping with a range of difficulties and challenging situations in their lives. These include depression; bereavement and loss; trauma; abuse; emotional and behavioural concerns; chronic illness and life threatening or limiting conditions; family and parental conflicts; school problems; peer issues; learning difficulties; and physical disabilities.

My experience within schools has given me much food for thought about the many challenges facing my colleagues in education, and what a crucial part schools have to play in the development of our children's mental health and well being. It has been important that the interventions I offer be based on a flexible understanding that, in order to reach the needs of school-aged children and young people, I develop 'narratives of support' reaching out beyond the stereotypical, clinic-based interventions that can contribute to pathologising the child's needs and further disengaging hard-to-reach families.

Working creatively with schools can offer opportunities to access children in a non-clinical environment, thereby providing early intervention, taking the pressure off parents who have issues with clinical settings, and reducing the amount of time needed to attend appointments outside school. Engaging openly with other professionals, such as support staff and teachers, helps them to understand better children's mental health issues and how these might impact on the child's learning and developmental needs. This can provide a much-needed level of gate-keeping and early intervention for children, whose needs, if left unrecognised, could escalate and result in long-term mental health and well being issues extending into adult life. Training on mental health and well being for staff, combined with consultation and support, can help raise competencies in offering appropriate and timely interventions to the children in their care. This can also lead to a better, clearer and more efficient use of referrals to the mental health services available to schools. This is invaluable within a fast-changing professional field, as is the case at the present time.

Use of Narrative Play Therapy within my work

Narrative Play Therapy (NPT) is a central part of my orientation as a practitioner and fits well within the clinical thinking of my CAMHS team regarding systemic interventions. The theory on NPT has informed many of my interactions when working within the multi-agency and multi-professional context of supporting children in schools, particularly when developing my ideas around collaborative and joint working on cases and in developing therapeutic alliances and in understanding a complex arena of work with diffuse discourses, including those around mental health; interagency work; children; families, plus clinical and educative interventions for specific populations. A combination of presentations to my CAMHS colleagues, plus other statutory and voluntary agencies in the borough, about both my wider role in the community and my practice as a play therapist, has been helpful in ensuring transparency, inviting dialogue and in building 'therapeutic bridges'.

Assessment and process tools

I use a range of assessment tools, processes and procedures in my core CAMHS work, some of which are generic tools used by any CAMHS practitioner, some of which are more specific to my practice as a play therapist, such as a version of a write and draw tool called Six Piece Storymaking (6PSM), which I have modified over the years to include a contextual aspect. I may use this technique within a 'write or draw' method, but I also combine it with sand tray work and small-world toys – a '3D' approach – to help children engage with this narrative play. A digital camera is often the medium of choice in capturing and recording these narratives with children, as well as me writing the co-constructed story with the child. These stories are also combined with a themes analysis, tracking play behaviours and the themes contained in these narratives over the therapeutic journey. Themes that are absent are also considered, for example, loss, which may point out an aspect of the child's difficulties or avoidance of painful areas of need.

Who is in the story?	Where are they?	What are they doing?
Is there a problem?	Is there any help?	What happened next?

Figure 6.1 Creative storymaking method

EXAMPLE OF CREATIVE STORYMAKING METHOD

A co-constructed story around a child acknowledging his parent's mental health needs around depression and gang related pressures on their family:

Figure 6.2 The warriors

The Sand Monster lives by himself. There's also a Lizard Monster. Lots of warriors try and attack them. Everyone's getting hurt – they kick and stick each other. The Sand Monster is very scared. Someone tries to bust in – they kick the door in. The Sand Monster is strong and tries to protect his house. The warriors want money. No one's going to rescue him even if he asks for help. The Sand Monster is left to be attacked and put in jail for ever. The Lizard Monster stays in doors all day long. (Boy, age 7)

Examples of themes expressed: the need for protection, powerfulness, powerlessness, fear, anger, violence, hopelessness, withdrawal and isolation, depression, futility and lack of trust in getting help.

Theoretical influences, ideas and orientation around my practice
Collaborative play therapy

If we are to really understand the perspectives of children we should start by entering their world through sharing the processes by which they make sense of their environment... Play is the medium of communication because it is the way children structure their experiences. So let us all learn to play with children to find out what they think and feel. (Cattanach 2007, p.39)

In collaborative play therapy a combination of focused, direct and non-direct approaches are used. These are needs led, taking into account that the developing child is part of an ecological system, not an isolated individual. Collaboration between the child and therapist is developed, where what happens in sessions is co-constructed between the two, that is, the therapist is in an active, responsive, 'here and now' relationship to the child. Both child and play therapist use play as their primary means of communication with each other. Cornerstones of collaborative play therapy are based on social construction theory and narrative therapy. Its core thinking around the development of identity is based on the stories we tell about ourselves and the stories others in our environment tell about us. I also use aspects of attachment theory linked to Narrative Play Therapy in my practice. These help me to develop further understanding of the complexities involved within the dynamics of relationships concerning the child.

Ecosystemic and social constructs theories

The basic systemic unit is seen as being the child. The individual is seen as being separate, autonomous – not just a metaphor for the family system. The child's ecosystem is seen as being made up of interactional social systems, plus an intra-psychic symbolic system.

Ecosystemic Framework

1. Microsystem
2. Mesosystem
3. Exosystem
4. Macrosystem

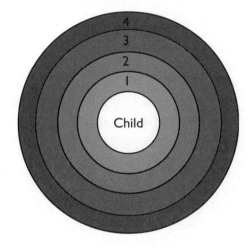

Figure 6.3 Diagram of ecosystemic model

The microsystem is seen as being the immediate setting containing the developing child and their complex interrelations with their environment, for example home or school.

The mesosystem is seen as being the links between the microsystem and the other systems in which the child participates and has relationships with, for example home, school, health services and social services. Relationships with peers, extended family, friends, plus healthcare and social services staff could all be considered as important influences on the child within this system.

The exosystem provides links between systems which may never be entered by the child, but which may have profound effects on them, for example parent's work place, courts, parental mental health clinics, local council and education services.

Finally, the macrosystem holds the cultural beliefs and norms concerning, for instance, family values; market forces; governmental policies, agendas and structures – perhaps particularly relevant at the time of writing, regarding the wide-reaching changes facing many people using and working within public services.

Ecosystemic play therapy does not focus solely on the functioning of the child client. Rather, an important focus centres on optimising the functioning of the child in the context of that child's ecosystem or world.

Developmental and historical phenomena are incorporated as relevant to understanding the child's functioning. Prout and James (1990) discuss that the making and breaking of concepts of childhood is itself affected by social context: that these concepts change with social activities and are part of an ongoing historical process. Many Westernised ideas of childhood are noted as being the likely scaffolding around which daily life experiences of children are determined and controlled, potentially restricted and used to distance childhood from adulthood.

Exploration of children's own individual perceptions of how they get their needs met is seen as essential to help understand their behaviours (which may be dysfunctional) clearly within context. Efforts are made to understand these behaviours without contributing towards pathologising the child. This can be a particularly helpful stance to take when adults see the child as the main problem and, for example, seek a diagnosis without thinking about environmental, trauma or relationship triggers that may be negatively affecting the child.

The play therapist is seen as being an integral, inseparable part of the system connecting with the child's experience. Reality is seen as the result of interaction between the observer and the observed. Thus a co-constructed relationship and reality is developed within the symbolism and containment of play. Treatment may (and should in my view) involve some combination of individual, dyadic, family, consultation and advocacy roles with other systems affecting the child.

Narrative therapy

Narrative therapy is the re-storying of the client's lived experience (Epston and White 1990). Stories are invented by the client and significant others to explain life events. People experience problems when stories do not represent their lived experience. Children are often pathologised as 'needing therapy', their 'story' in danger of being dislocated from the adults around them. Their stories are seen and heard using an 'adult lens' and often not in relationship to how the children understand their lives. With any child referred to me for play therapy, I will predict that the story around the referral will have key differences between what I am told by adults and what the child knows, has been told, overheard or understood about why they need therapy.

In so doing the child can be demonised and the adults involved in supporting the child are not encouraged to take responsibility for their part in the child's circumstances. Children can be further disempowered in such narratives by an abuse of power and a lack of meaningful discourse that prohibits them from being heard or understood in a child-centred context.

Narrative Play Therapy

Use of NPT helps to readdress the balance in favour of the child. Co-constructed as well as deconstructed stories contained within the play therapy assist children in exploring meaning and creating other possibilities in their lives. This partnership between therapist and child can allow children to have a voice in an otherwise difficult, generally adult orientated world, where childhood is often dislocated, demonised, commercialised and sentimentalised. A combination of mindfulness, contribution of the self, acute observation and attuned concentration enables me as a therapist to affiliate with the child and the many aspects of relationships that are shown in their play narratives, and in my relationships around the child.

Because play is the main vehicle of communication used within these stories, a crucial task of the therapist is to build a bridge using these play narratives to help other adults listen to and understand the child – to strengthen a therapeutic alliance around the child, where their views can be considered and taken seriously, not dismissed as being 'just play'.

Some important questions to ask in this process are how do we create a storied therapy that connects accurately with a child's lived experience? What is our responsibility as therapists to help others involved with the child understand this co-constructed story? What is the interaction between the child, the perceived problem and the system – and how might this help or hinder the child in getting their needs met? How might the evolution of therapeutic alliance during play therapy affect children's narratives – especially children with differing attachment styles?

Attachment

When working in schools I have often started a therapeutic intervention by observing the child in class. This can help me to help gain a clearer understanding of a child's behaviour in context and to plan ideas for supporting concerns within a collaborative framework around the child.

Much can begin to make sense when time is taken to think about the relationship behaviours – the attachment behaviours that the child might be using in relationship to staff, family and peers. It is equally as important to assess the attachment behaviours that are being triggered in others as a response towards the child.

PLAY THERAPY CASE EXAMPLE

A six-year-old boy was referred for play therapy by his teacher, due to her concerns about a breakdown in their relationship. She described Kai as being aggressive towards her, very disruptive and unable to cope in many group situations in class. I went into class to observe the situation, and saw a child desperate to gain his teacher's attention. He was eager to answer questions, though often he did not have any answers, but was seeking approval and recognition. I observed the teacher ignoring the child, giving little, if any, eye contact or verbal acknowledgement to him. When I asked her about this, she said that she was worried that other children in the class would think she was favouring Kai if she gave him too much attention. She was also very concerned about Kai's peer relationships, as he often distracted others around him and found it very difficult to cope with transitions in the school day, such as changing from room to room or changes in school staff. Kai attended both the school's 'Breakfast' and 'After School' clubs fairly often, meaning his day at school often started at 8.00 am and finished at 6.00 pm. We started to see a pattern of how this seemed to affect his behaviour, and, importantly, we were able to work together to identify the triggers to some of Kai's hyper-aroused behaviours, many of which could be attributed to noise and light levels to which he proved especially sensitive when tired.

A key piece of background information that had been out of focus for this child was that he had been born very premature, with the likelihood of some developmental difficulties that were only just beginning to surface, but which the teacher had not clearly understood as being probable causes for many of the impulsive and anxious attachment behaviours that she was having to deal with.

Attachment framework

Helpful questions to use that fit within attachment theory, describing relationships using secure, ambivalent, avoidant or disorganised categories, are noted by Bomber (2007) (Table 6.1).

Table 6.1: The use of attachment theories to promote 'good enough' understanding of relationships and needs

Key questions	Common behaviour/beliefs	Anxiety response
Secure attachment		
Is the child confident that they will receive help when they ask for it or need it? Can they be quickly reassured when a parent or caregiver leaves their proximity?	Securely attached children believe that adults are helpful, can be trusted and are reliable. They are often able to calm and soothe themselves to some extent when distressed. Securely attached children exhibit distress when separated from caregivers and are happy when their caregiver returns. These children feel secure and able to depend on their adult caregivers. Such children are usually able to form positive peer relationships and play well with other children of their age.	When such children are anxious, they believe that adults can be trusted to help them and can be reassured quickly. When the adult leaves, these children may be upset, but they feel assured that the parent or caregiver will return and that they will find comfort.
Ambivalent attachment		
How needy is the child in relationships – how fearful are they of being ignored or abandoned?	These children cannot depend on their parent (or caregiver) to be there when they are in need. Ambivalently attached children usually become very distressed when a parent leaves their proximity. There is often a belief that adults are unpredictable, with the child frightened of being ignored or not having their needs recognised – that they are 'forgotten'. They find it particularly difficult to be by themselves, and are often unable to cope well in group situations, as they become distracted easily and often distract others around them. There are often conflicts concerning possessions, games and the need for personal space, i.e. these children do not recognise this need in others, nor do they share easily (toys, activities or people).	Ambivalently attached children are often experienced as being clingy, dependent, whiney, intrusive and disruptive. This is often seen as their way of gaining attention, and sometimes includes over-possessiveness or clinginess in their friendships as well as with adults. There is often a feeling of emotional exhaustion for all concerned, and the children may be deemed over-emotional and highly sensitive.

Table 6.1: The use of attachment theories to promote 'good enough' understanding of relationships and needs *cont.*

Key questions	Common behaviour/beliefs	Anxiety response
Avoidant attachment		
What is really going on with a child who avoids proximity or closeness with others?	Avoidant children may seem very independent, perhaps beyond their years, may be uncurious about new situations or people and may shun or seem indifferent to any other uncertainties. They have learned that depending on parents won't get them the secure feeling they want, so they learn to take care of themselves. Children with an avoidant attachment tend to avoid parents or caregivers. When offered a choice, these children will show no preference between a caregiver and a complete stranger. Children showing such behaviour seem to value achievements much more than being close with others – peers as well as adults. They do not often ask for help but can get frustrated easily. They are often task-oriented and find it difficult to use their own initiative. They can also be very competitive and find it difficult to accept failure. In response to this, they either become aggressive or hostile and uncooperative towards both adults and peers. They often seem to 'punish' a returning caregiver by ignoring them and have difficulty developing warm relationships with adults.	The impression of wishing to be independent is often linked with an anxiety around intimacy and contact, that is, it could be considered as a defensive response to limit intimacy. You may see simultaneous but contradictory impulses in a child to approach and to withdraw. Such children may suffer social isolation, hostility both to and from peers and disconnection from adults, in part due to poorly developed social skills.
Disorganised attachment		
How do we understand children who are described as unpredictable, confusing in the support they need from adults, making no sense, chaotic (perhaps in their demands and needs), unable to show empathy or remorse and often hostile towards others, including their peers?	Children who demonstrate such confusing behaviour may also give conflicting, unpredictable responses to others, with a level of risk or an absence of safety for them. There may be an element of them seeming not to understand how to respond – a 'numbness' or 'freeze up' in social or conflict situations. Their play skills can be very limited and stilted, or repetitious in nature. It is essential to consider this as a possible result of children having experienced hostile, neglectful or helpless care in their early years. N.B. Sometimes a child can show such behaviours due to particular circumstances in the family, e.g. bereavement or divorce. However, it is usually for a shorter period of time that lasts as long as the situation in the family does.	When anxious, behaviours with a shock or risk element to them may often be seen. One minute they are loudly demanding your attention, the next seeming to be fearful of you and shouting at you to 'stay away'. There is little consistency, if any, in what helps them to calm down. Nothing these children do seems able to stop their anxiety from increasing. Sometimes help offered by others is seen as a threat, especially if a positive touch is attempted – it actually seems to escalate their distress. Containing their distress seems very challenging for both these

Play, trauma and the use of narratives

Relatively recent research findings in the field of neuroscience would seem to suggest that play choices enhance synaptic growth in the early years, and pruning in later years, and that brain development seems to parallel the development of play in children. Attunement, not excessive stimulation, seems to be the key, with the uplifting theory that growth might be possible at any age (Panksepp 1998; Schaefer 2003).

Crucially, a child's play behaviours may show aspects of trauma, with the child replaying the situation repeatedly – seeming to be stuck within the experience without being able to find a resolution. Traumatic memories are often not coherent stories. They might be considered as 'hauntings' – with constant retriggering from, for example, a facial expression, tone of voice, gesture or external noise. As Gil (2006, p.162) says, 'It is critical to remember that if the play does not help resolve the traumatic concerns, questions, or conflicts, it is likely to become stagnant and lose its reparative potential.'

The use of therapeutic stories or narratives can help guard against this. They provide time for conscious reflection on feelings, not just for discharging them. Such emotional exploration can be safely contained through the distance of metaphor, providing the child with the opportunity to connect without retriggering – helping them to process their experience of feelings (Sunderland 2001).

PLAY THERAPY CASE EXAMPLE

A 12-year-old girl was referred to me via a therapeutic foster care service. After an initial assessment stage, where a tentative therapeutic alliance had been formed between Chloe and myself, I noted from tracking the play narratives over a number of sessions that there had been an absence of themes around loss – a key traumatic aspect of this child's life. A theme around 'stuckness' had featured in our sessions for many weeks, combined with a repetitive narrative around 'things getting broken and needing fixing', but never being resolved. I introduced a new narrative arising from animal puppets in the playroom.

I developed a therapeutic story around pets, which led into a story around the loss of such pets, with me volunteering a story around a much loved cat who became unwell and had to be 'put to sleep' after I recounted various stories of life with this cat. Suddenly Chloe volunteered her own narrative around a family pet being abandoned and needing rescue – a step forward in acknowledging both an aspect of personal loss within the safety and emotional containment of the therapeutic story, plus a trust in the therapeutic relationship, which had started with this child challenging me as to why they should trust me. My answer had been to say that they were quite right – that I had to earn such trust, in so doing recognising the need for the child to be given their own say in how this relationship was to be built, and to respect the defences they needed to use in order to attend therapy.

POTENTIAL EFFECTS OF TRAUMA

The effects of childhood trauma vary greatly, depending on the type and severity of the traumatic experience. These effects can include severe anxiety; extreme anger and hostility; self-harming; phobias; depression; substance misuse; risk-taking; promiscuity; suicidal thoughts and/or attempts on own life; eating problems and disorders.

In some cases, trauma is not immediately evident. Sometimes trauma does not show up until much later in life or until it is triggered by certain circumstances. Other meanings or diagnosis may be given to the child, masking the trauma – which may be post traumatic stress disorder. An example of this could be a child who has suffered a trauma, but is diagnosed with attention-deficit hyperactivity disorder (ADHD) – behaviours such as lack of concentration, disruptiveness, restlessness, aggression and irritability, immaturity and regression, plus compulsiveness causing difficulties in the child getting their needs met – actually masking the real problem and cause for many of these behaviours.

It can also be a reason behind a parent's seeming lack of attunement. I have supported such a situation during a parenting class, where a parent privately disclosed childhood abuse to me, which surfaced around discussions concerning bereavement within the main group. For many years this parent had been suffering from difficulties in her attachment and care of her children and was on the verge of having her two youngest children taken into care. The abuse and loss suffered in her own childhood had never clearly surfaced until this point, but the new narrative I was able to construct with this parent in the form of a therapeutic letter helped to change the perceptions of other professionals and served to point out another important direction of support crucial in enabling this family to move on.

TRAUMA AND BRAIN DEVELOPMENT

Build, reorganize and strengthen new brain circuitry through experiences that generate new ways of thinking, feeling and behaving. (Gil 2006, p.59)

Batmangehelidjh (2005) in a video interview expressed her views around neuroscience, saying that the quality of the attachment relationship that is provided for children sculpts their ability to control their behaviour, to plan and to be prosocial. She talks about how shocked she is to see how children are being demonised and turned into monsters by adult narratives, that by so doing, we are cheating on childhood, seeing childhood as a failure to be left behind in shame as we grow up:

> Children end up in custody or in court being punished for crime, when they're not only carrying the misdeed they committed, but they are also carrying an enormous amount of misdeeds that were perpetrated against them by adults who should have stepped in to protect them. (transcribed from video recording, Batmangehelidjh 2005)

A recurring theme in Batmangehelidjh's thinking is 'emotional thermostats'. Children, in her view, who have suffered from trauma have often lost their capacity to feel. How often, I wonder, do we receive referrals of children for therapeutic support who are described as being unfeeling, unable to show remorse or take responsibility for their actions; who are angry and unable to empathise with others? Assessing this 'emotional thermostat' is crucial, as it is only by doing so that we can gain a sense of the damage, but also the resilience available to each child we work with. I am also mindful of how painful any changes can be to unlock this 'thermostat' that has been put in place for a reason, to help a child survive – and that in traumatised children this work can be slow, full of fear for all concerned, and take much longer than resources might allow for.

Dramatherapy

Jones (1995) describes key core processes at the heart of dramatherapy. These include projective identification and dramatic distancing. Projective identification is the process whereby a person identifies with a character in a story. Dramatic distancing refers to the way that emotional and psychological problems can be accessed through metaphor. For children the use of such metaphor can free them from anxiety or fears of being judged and can make problems easier to explore and tolerate. The group process is also an important consideration when offering therapeutic support in schools. Dramatherapy ideas around this can help children externalise issues and concerns, harnessing both creative arts processes and the inherent qualities of groups around modelling, social skills, identity, self-esteem and peer relationships.

Hybrid learning styles

An interesting and comparatively under-researched model, hybrid learning theory offers an integrated continuum of constructs around biological, social–cognitive and experiential models of personality. It may be helpful to consider regarding aspects of how personality develops and also to help make some sense of some of the stress responses and behaviour used by children, for example sensation seeking in traumatised children (Brom, Pat-Horenczyk and Ford 2009; Jackson 2008).

Sensory integration

Sensory integration is used by some occupational therapists, physio-therapists and speech and language therapists who incorporate it into their practice. It works on the principle that children who do not experience touch, movement, body awareness, sight, sound, gravity and other sensory experiences in the normal way will experience dysfunction in information processing, development and behaviour (Stephens 1997). The child is assessed and then taught to seek out the sensory experiences they need in tactile, vestibular and proprioceptive areas. I have found it to be an interesting area to help think about resources for alleviating stress within school children, for working with traumatised children, and it has links with some aspects of play therapy theory around embodiment play.

Stress, coping and resilience in childhood

Understanding stress

Stress can be understood as being either internal or external influences that disrupt an individual's normal state of well being. As discussed by Middlebrooks and Audage (2008), these influences are capable of affecting health by causing emotional distress and leading to a variety of physiological changes. These changes can include increased heart rate, elevated blood pressure and a dramatic rise in hormone levels. They go on to say that stress can be considered as being an inevitable part of life, but that it is important we differentiate children's experiences of stress, knowing when to offer help and understanding how children cope with stress. Childhood experiences of stress are described as fitting into the following categories (Table 6.2).

Table 6.2: Childhood experiences of stress

Positive stress	Tolerable stress	Toxic stress
Adverse experiences that are short-lived/ minor	Adverse experiences that are more intense but still of fairly short duration	Sustained, intense, adverse experiences
Considered to be a normal part of development	Can usually be overcome if help is there	Children unable to cope by themselves
With attuned help, children can learn to cope with it	Can become positive stress with such help	Appropriate support can help the stress response back to its normal baseline
	Can become toxic if such help is not there	Can compromise biological systems plus brain development
		Can lead to long-term health problems

Source: Compiled from Middlebrooks and Audage 2008

In the UK a three-year research study tracked the emotional well being of a sample of children and young people between 2004 and 2007. It suggests that children who experience three or more stressful life events, such as family bereavement, divorce or serious illness, are significantly more likely to develop emotional and behavioural disorders. The study also considered factors which may protect against the onset of, or help children recover from, emotional and behavioural disorders. 'Social capital' factors such as networks of family and friends, participation in clubs and groups and perceived safety in the neighbourhood were strongly linked with emotional well being. The school setting and its influence on children's emotional well being was also considered in depth. The study suggests that the persistence and onset of a mental disorder can be linked to factors such as school exclusions, absenteeism and achievement at school, as well as the existence of special educational needs (Office for National Statistics (ONS) 2008).

Resilience and coping

Luther (1993) points out that there seem to be many conceptual problems in the area of resilience. Risk research needs to focus on specifics that can affect adjustment, bearing in mind the wide variations children may show in using successful coping behaviours across differing environments and stressors. It is also highlighted that even when children show apparently adaptive coping behaviours in stressful situations it does not necessarily mean they are emotionally healthy, that is, it has been recognised that emotional distress can often underlie impressive overt competence of such children (1993, p.442).

Rutter's work talks of children's resilience in the face of adversity and the importance of acknowledging the changes in their perceptions of fear as they grow older – that they are more likely to worry about their personal adequacy and the future than younger children, which may have implications for how they appraise and respond to different kinds of stress and adversity (Rutter 1985, p.607). May (2008, p.294) notes that a resilient child will be able to 'integrate his or her experiences on a cognitive and emotional level and cope with the stresses of life's adversities without his or her normal development being impaired'. She discusses Rutter's advice that children should be seen within a developmental context with the understanding that there is a predisposition for some (but not all) to naturally develop resilience factors as they age (p.295). These include:

- the cognitive ability to appraise and attach meaning to an experience

- a coping strategy of being proactive or reactive

- a child's self-esteem and feelings of self-efficacy as well as a range of problem solving skills

- a child's cognitive set, influenced by secure relationships and positive experiences as well as temperamental attributes

- a child's ability to adapt to and influence interactions

- the accumulation of positive experiences of encountering stress competently and appropriately.

There has been limited research into how children build both their understanding of stressful events and their coping repertoires at different ages and stages (Bossert 1994; Rossman and Gamble 1997). Another important area to consider is the problems faced by many children who may want to cope more actively with stressors, but do not have the personal resources to do so, or indeed the personal efficacy. This may be further affected, as already noted, by the inequalities of power inherent within adult–child interactions. Wertlieb, Weigel and Feldstein (1987, p.558) say that 'an appreciation of and immersion in the child's own construction of a stress and coping process is likely to be crucial to therapeutic engagement'.

Emotional and mental well being within the primary school system

> Don't ignore us when we are young – we are your future. Every child matters and teachers need to notice when we are distressed at primary school. We need help and support early on – not when it's too late. (Young Minds 2009)

In its health guidance for promoting children's social and emotional well being at the primary stage, the National Institute for Health and Clinical Excellence (NICE 2008, p.5), discusses children's social and emotional well being as being very important, with potential to affect their physical health (both as a child and as an adult) and can determine how well they do at school. It is suggested that good social, emotional and psychological health helps protect children against emotional and behavioural problems, violence and crime, teenage pregnancy and the misuse of drugs and alcohol.

In considering the public health need and practice in this area, it is noted by NICE that:

> In 2004, boys were generally more likely to have a mental disorder than girls, and the prevalence of mental illness was greater among children living:
>
> • within disrupted families (lone parent, reconstituted)
>
> • with parents who have no educational qualifications
>
> • within poorer families and in disadvantaged areas (Office for National Statistics 2004).
>
> (NICE 2008, p.11)

There is variation by ethnicity. Children aged 5–10 who are white, Pakistani or Bangladeshi appear more likely to have a mental disorder than black children. Indian children are least likely to have such problems. Looked after children aged 5–10 were at least five times more likely than average to have a mental disorder (42% versus 8%) (Office for National Statistics 2004, p.11).

Issues of transition and attunement

Geddes (2006) discusses the long history of children with emotional and behavioural difficulties within the school context and how their disengagement and underachievement within their education sets up the dynamics of problems that can have far reaching consequences into adulthood and within society as a whole. She also notes the burden of stress this places on teachers and feelings around guilt and persecution for families (2006, p.2). In such a challenging situation is it any wonder that there can be diminished mental health and well being for everyone concerned? Policies around inclusion and shrinking budgets continue to challenge professionals to respond effectively to addressing these children's needs.

I have heard increasing concerns expressed from primary school staff about the number of children who seem to be starting school without having had early years' experiences, such as at nursery school or within playgroups. Staff have observed to me that many such children seem ill equipped to begin their school life, with poor social and communication skills and difficult attachment behaviours, resulting in a great deal of time being needed to attune to these children as a way of helping them to adjust to the transition to school.

This issue around transition is a recurring theme in my clinical work, and it is common to find that school aged children continue to find problems coping with transitions throughout their school years. The transitions most often thought to cause distress for children are on first entering formal school and on transferring to secondary school. Undoubtedly these transitions bring with them challenges for children vulnerable for a variety of reasons to transition, such as having experienced trauma; having a learning or physical difficulty; having social and communication difficulties, which might also include English as an additional language; having family conflicts, etc. But there are other types of transition that can adversely affect children struggling to make sense of an environment they are anxious within. Bomber (2007, p.113) discusses these as being changes in the school day and environment which are considered as being normal, for example within the curriculum, working and playing environments, structure of work, patterns of relating to other people, and, in some cases, staff. However, she notes how these transitions can cause enormous anxiety for children who may have attachment difficulties, especially when these changes are unexpected or unpredictable, for example interruptions to the classroom.

PLAY THERAPY CASE EXAMPLE

I met a young boy of six within a series of workshops I was running for a group of boys in Key Stage I (children between the ages of five and seven) around stress awareness. Tyrell came from a background of aggression, neglect and difficulties in his home life, with lots of fighting with his siblings – one of whom had autism. An older sibling was serving a jail sentence for robbery. He had been described to me as being one of those 'naughty boys', with various areas of delay in his development and learning. His play behaviour showed similar lags, with Tyrell seeming to operate on a much younger level than might be expected for his age and stage. It soon became clear to me that this was a child who was worried by transitions, even affecting his ability to come into and leave the sessions. It would have been all too easy to interpret his initial behaviour as non-compliance with wanting to attend the workshops. I put in place a strategy whereby Tyrell was collected by one of the teaching staff working with me in good time to attend the session. The teaching assistant (TA) was armed with one of the sensory toys from the workshop as a 'visual bridge' to help calm him on his way into session. This, combined with a strategy around giving Tyrell a 'job' on coming into the room, for example handing out name badges, soothed Tyrell enough that he was able to engage with the sessions. His behaviour on leaving the room showed a range of delaying strategies, this being an expression of his difficulties in finding his way back into the next part of his day. Again, the security of having the same TA help him back into class did much to reassure Tyrell, and also built up a rapport between the two. On one particular day, the TA and I observed Tyrell making his way to an outdoor session in the playground. He accidentally bumped himself on the knee walking past a bench. Instead of seeking comfort by saying what had happened and why he was upset, Tyrell lashed out at a nearby child. This started a fight, for which Tyrell understandably got into trouble with the teacher. The TA observing was able to see 'in action' just how difficult it was for Tyrell to get the help he needed when distressed. We were able to generalise our observations back to Tyrell's teacher, who had not considered these aspects of difficulties, but seemed to have termed his behaviour as purely oppositional.

Attunement

Attunement is an active stance that allows a child to be brought into a harmonious or responsive relationship. We need to be able to empathise with children, to see beyond the behaviour whilst providing containment for this and, in so doing, adjust our responses appropriately to meet the needs of a child. Historically it is often boys who are noticed first for such issues, their distress often being voluble, noticeable and with a teacher response that is often driven by 'naughtiness'. Quieter, but equally distressed, troubled or anxious children, often – but not always, girls, are likely to remain invisible for longer. Geddes (2006, p.9) asks 'I wonder again why we don't prioritise vulnerable young girls who may one day be the mothers of troubled boys?'

Early intervention and emotional / mental health and well being

> Lack of investment in mental health promotion in primary schools is likely to lead to significant costs for society. (NICE 2008, p.15)

Much work has been done over recent years to try and provide a cohesiveness around early intervention and emotional and mental well being, with initiatives such as SEAL[1]; Parent Support Services; National Healthy Schools and Extended Schools programmes. It is helpful to consider these as being within a paradigm of integrated, comprehensive programmes offering both universal and targeted support, and working in partnership with children and their families, but not forgetting support and training for teaching staff.

This latter is an area that I view as being under-developed generally in schools in the UK, partly perhaps due to a lack of awareness of the need for staff to be offered formal supervision to enable them to reflect on and cope with the pressures inherent in the many challenging aspects of their work with children. A teaching assistant once wrote in a card to me, 'Who am I going to talk to now?' as I was leaving my post in a school counselling team. I had offered a reflective space once a month for TAs in the school to come to discuss particular children, and although not

---

1   Social and Emotional Aspects of Learning (SEAL): This curriculum resource is used in schools and aims to develop the underpinning qualities and skills that help promote positive behaviour and effective learning. It focuses on five social and emotional aspects of learning: self-awareness, managing feelings, motivation, empathy and social skills.

offered as being formal supervision, but rather a consultation process, it became increasingly apparent to me how little time is made available for this generally in our schools, with staff often seeming to rely on staff-room conversations for their main support.

Therapeutic alliance, safeguarding and accountability

I consider the development of therapeutic alliances to be one aspect of helping to safeguard children, promoting clarity around the child's needs – their voice being heard clearly within this alliance. There have been concerted efforts in recent years, with variable success, in promoting effective interagency work. There can be many aspects of 'fragmented stories' around children, caused in part by a lack of clarity over therapeutic aims that are obvious to all involved with the child. Therapy could be termed as being effective to the extent that it can be characterised by a strong positive emotional alliance. There need to be negotiated, reasonably clear goals, accepted and understood by all relevant parties – including the child. Multi-agency services around the child need to be aware of these goals, with meaningful dialogues and commitment to tasks that have relevance to the goals, and vice versa. These therapeutic goals need to be mindful of the wider context of work around the child, and not in my view cut off from being discussed, scrutinised or part of how the therapist accounts for their input. It is also important to help develop a reflexive discourse over how other agencies respond to this work, and perhaps adapt their own response to working with the child in the light of such input. A key issue here can be that of confidentiality. I absolutely accept the need for clear, boundaried privacy around the child regarding therapeutic processes, with a clear understanding by all involved, including the child, around my responsibility as a therapist to pass on information if I'm concerned the child is being harmed or is hurting others. But I also think that confidentiality can sometimes be used to shield the therapeutic intervention (and therapist) from scrutiny. Appropriate transparency can be a tricky balance to achieve, but one which can offer unexpected and rewarding aspects of therapeutic alliance and, not least, positive ways of maintaining engagement with hard to reach children and their families.

Understanding roles, power and status between children, families and staff

A systemic approach is particularly helpful in enabling me to think very creatively around how to reach out and further therapeutic engagement and also puts me into the position of 'narrative humility', thinking as a life-long learner endeavouring to develop my ability to join others seeking to help the child, rather than yet another 'expert' who contributes to disempowering the child, their family and perhaps other colleagues who are involved with the child. I write this with a wry smile on my face, as both working within a CAMHS team and having experience outside of this statutory service, I am well aware of the stereotypes often held of those of us working within mental health services. And some of you reading this may well be 'bristling' at this moment, but this is the narrative that I have heard and am responding to. I invite discussion!

PLAY THERAPY CASE EXAMPLE

Within the school system, it is important to acknowledge how power and status can affect relationships. I remember one mother, whose five-year-old child was giving great cause for concern within her school, to the extent of being on the point of permanent exclusion. At a parent review meeting this mum looked startled when I commented on some positive aspects of her daughter's behaviour, becoming upset and telling me, 'All I ever hear about is the bad stuff – nothing good is ever told me.'

Previous experience

Some parents have a difficult history themselves within the education system, and taking their own children back into a school can bring many painful memories to the fore. No wonder some parents can come across as being disinterested in their children's school career. All those old feelings around disempowerment and lack of status surface and can be difficult to overcome without some attunement from staff. I am struck by how many parents I've met who struggle to establish a positive relationship with the child's teacher. Some of this seems to be around feelings that their 'naughty child' is being poorly parented, which may be the case, but is it helpful to feel judged and criticised for this, without support being offered?

Beliefs around childhood and parenting within a social constructs model

There are some helpful issues to think about regarding the value placed on multiculturalism in clinical practice. It is the existence of alternative world views that can enable optimal problem solving, but only if this is a perspective which respects both our own and others' views. The development of our own self-identity in relationship with a wide variety of groups and a stable world view and self knowledge from which to compare and understand others' views is essential in helping us to recognise, address and celebrate diversity with children and their families (O'Connor and Ammen 1997). Three key areas of cultural beliefs can be categorised as shown in the list below:

1. Cultural deviance: the idea that anything that is different from your own culture is bad or threatening. Children can show this prejudice through their learnt behaviour, e.g. a three-year-old using racist or homophobic name-calling. It might also be argued that there are aspects of gang culture that show such intolerance to difference.

2. Cultural relativism: the idea that 'anything goes', i.e. no matter how destructive behaviour is, it is tolerated because it is attributed to cultural difference. Overly permissive parenting styles can show aspects of this, as can reluctance from staff to challenge these types of cultural beliefs. Discipline is one such discourse that can present difficulties around what is acceptable in one culture and what is not tolerated in another. Another such example that has received attention in recent years is female genital mutilation (FGM).

3. Cultural differentiation: the idea that cultural beliefs can be evaluated, i.e. not just accepted or rejected, within a context that allows a variety of perspectives, whilst also endeavouring to ensure that these differing ideas have a minimum negative impact on others.

(O'Connor and Ammen 1997)

It is important to ask ourselves how we learn about the cultural backgrounds from which children and their families come – and how our own backgrounds may affect what we learn. It is also important to consider how complicated this can be within a single family, who may have a transcultural background, with many beliefs being held around parenting, education and children.

Challenges for school age children – being heard and understood!

Developmental literature looks at middle childhood in a number of ways. It is suggested that children's fears will change with age – as does their ability to articulate these fears, that is, a greater level of cognitive functioning. An assumption might be made that it will be easier for children at this stage to articulate their experiences of stress, anxiety and trauma. Hagglof (1999), in discussing school age children's abilities to cope with illness and hospitalisation, notes that this is a social period of time when children widen their contacts with people, and compare themselves, for example with peers. It is also suggested that there is a 'psychological crisis' period for children around the age of nine, with an increase in worries and psychological symptoms: these children are able to ask questions on existential issues such as death, disease and war but do not yet have a well-developed capacity to cope with such issues. Stressful situations for this age of child can cause more variety of reactions than with younger children:

• anxiety problems

• depressive symptoms

• stomach-ache

• headache

• hyperactivity

• attention deficit symptoms

• secondary enuresis, incontinence or encopresis.

Developmental risks potentially affecting emotional and mental well being include: bereavement; loss; disability (learning and physical) and illness, including potential effects on siblings; being in care; family conflict (including separation and divorce); parental mental health; abuse; domestic violence; peer conflict and bullying; self-esteem.

PLAY THERAPY CASE EXAMPLE

A nine-year-old girl was referred for initial assessment having been involved in a traumatic accident at school, resulting in surgery. Now fully recovered from the surgery, the child's behaviour had deteriorated over the subsequent six months, both towards her mother and at school. Over the following couple of terms we explored aspects of this trauma, but contained within a narrative play structure that captured the child's feelings around her mother, who had had a baby shortly after the child's accident. The child's natural feelings about becoming a sister for the first time had been skewed due to the aftermath of her accident, and her mother's emotional availability to her had understandably been diluted. As the therapy developed, so the 'onion layers' of understanding peeled back to reveal how this child had been trying to get her needs met, a key response being the efforts made by the child to take control of her mother. I also knew that there was likely to be a secondary trauma around the child's accident, the first being the incident at school, followed by the emergency treatment. This trauma only started to surface clearly much later in the child's therapy, and was first observed in her hypervigilence regarding ambulance sirens. The mother eventually felt able to engage with the school, supported by me, as there were some ongoing dynamics around the original accident and the effect it had also had on the child who caused it, which had never been explored or understood by the school.

From her first session, the child seemed exuberant to be able at last to talk about her feelings in a way that connected and made sense to her, making immediate and ongoing use of the medical play on offer to her. Her mother noticed this relief and told me that 'it was like having my daughter come back to me' after these initial sessions. It was only the beginning of a therapeutic journey that covered much emotional territory. Another emerging theme arose about half way through this child's therapy, whereby she explored aspects of her feelings towards an absent father, who was serving a jail sentence. With my help, the child wrote some therapeutic letters, which she wanted to show to her mother. Through this medium she was enabled to talk with her mother about her fantasies and wishes to have a relationship with her father, even though he was in jail. It was really important that the child's mother also received support with another colleague during this time, as her daughter's behaviour was sometimes not easy to manage. This is what I call the 'Pandora's Box' of therapy, that is, that you can never be sure what is going to emerge once that lid is lifted. This parent was enabled to explore aspects of her own mental health and well being and also completed a parenting programme.

Figure 6.4 Boy of 11 depicting his concerns about pain and being unable to eat due to medical treatment[2]

Challenges for families – balancing it all!

There can be many diverse and sometimes conflicting needs within families. As a working parent myself, it is all too common to find myself wondering just how many 'plates I can keep spinning'. Ecosystemic pressures can tip the balance in how resilient a family remains, especially when further unexpected events are thrown into the equation, such as illness or bereavement, or a change in environments, such as redundancy. A robust assessment of risks and resilience factors are crucial at both onset of therapeutic support, but also as part of the review process and as part of ending input.

Parenting styles

This is an area that needs careful consideration, as, being a parent myself, I bring my own perspective and upbringing with me, which may well be different to those of the families I meet. It is all too easy to leap to assumptions and make judgements – something I hear sometimes within

---

2   This child expressed his feelings around the intrusive nature of medical interventions and pain, that he had experienced as being traumatic in nature on top of the actual health concerns. Medical treatment can be experienced as being a 'secondary' trauma additional to illness and injury. This is often not fully appreciated or understood by the adults around the child.

the school system, as a response to the frustrations many staff can feel when trying to engage with parents.

Two key areas of possible parenting diversity that O'Connor and Ammen (1997) note, and that I find useful to think about, include:

INDIVIDUALISM

Children are seen as connected to and dependent on the caregiver, but their parent wishes for them to develop self-autonomy. There is encouragement for children to develop their independence, for example by doing things for themselves such as dressing, making choices and expressing their feelings. Confidence and self-assurance is encouraged, and a sense of being considered special is deemed important within this parenting style.

CONNECTEDNESS

Within this parenting style the family is paramount and independence is seen as being less important than, or as potentially getting in the way of, close, life-long family relationships. I wonder how many of us might consider our judgements when we say things such as 'she's too old for that' or 'they should be doing that for themselves' within such a worldview. A connected style of parenting focuses on interdependence fostered between parent and child. Humility and humbleness are encouraged; feelings of worthiness are connected to fitting in, belonging and putting others first. Self-help skills may be delayed, compared to the other group where independence is a primary goal. The expression of individual feelings may not be encouraged as the need for harmony and a lack of conflict is valued more highly.

Other aspects of child rearing diversity worth considering

When thinking about other aspects of child rearing it is worth considering diversity issues that may affect what parents expect of their children at different ages and stages. How might gender affect this? How is play valued, for example in relationship to education and learning? This may have a profound implication on how play therapy is understood and supported by parents. What are the views held around discipline? This is often a particularly difficult area within families, who may hold a variety of perspectives based on their own individual upbringings and cultures. What is expected from the child in terms of roles and responsibilities within the family? How are children talked to and included in decision making within the family? Thinking about the nature of the parent–child attachment, it is worth asking what diversity issues might be affecting responses to children's distress and displays of affection. What issues might there be around expectations of behaviour, for example at mealtimes. How are children expected to dress? What is the possible impact on the child who has members of the family other than parents who are expected to take on a caregiving role? What is the possible impact on the child who is expected to be a caregiver to younger members of the family?

PLAY THERAPY CASE EXAMPLE

A ten-year-old boy, Jamal, was referred to me when I worked as part of a school counselling service. His teacher was concerned over his peer conflicts and escalating disruptive behaviour, especially when in the playground. Jamal came from a strict Muslim background, living with a devout father, who was very concerned that his eldest son adhered to a religious path acceptable to the family. This required that he follow a code of conduct, and much friction had been created when Jamal had outbursts both at home and at school. There was also concern that Jamal wanted more independence, that is, to go out to play more on the estate where the family lived, but where known gangs recruited youngsters. The child I met was initially very unengaged, seeing play as babyish and not for boys. Slowly he began to express an interest in the many sensory games and toys I had on offer – particularly the more disgusting stress balls, farting putty and slime so beloved by many play therapists! He then gravitated to the sand and water boxes always available, and narrative play scenes began to emerge using small-world play figures.

There was one particular occasion when Jamal stormed into the playroom, having had a difficult time in class with a supply teacher (often a difficult transition or change in the anxious or ambivalently attached child's day, as already noted). I thought that I'd try to co-construct what had actually happened in class with Jamal, and invited him to create a 'picture' of what had happened using sand tray work. As we worked together it became clear to me that something wasn't working – Jamal was getting increasingly more upset and angry, not calmer. I asked him to create a story of his choosing, instead of insisting that we concentrate on the classroom issues.

This immediately defused his frustration, and Jamal spent the rest of the session constructing a water and sand world story with themes expressed around betrayal, loss of a treasure, kidnap and revenge. What surfaced through this session were the unexpressed feelings Jamal had towards his biological mother, who had divorced from his father when he was aged five, and had been just starting school. The unpredictable visits from his mother, who lived abroad, and the subsequent attachment problems he had had towards his father and his stepmother, who'd had a new baby, had put pressure onto Jamal and his family. He struggled with accepting a situation that he'd never been able to express any grief about, either in the aftermath of such changes to his family life, and later as he grew. Being on the cusp of another transition into secondary school combined with trying to cope with a new teacher had reactivated previous feelings around loss and trauma for Jamal. It was essential that his father was helped to understand the impact of such loss and the need for his son to be supported in at last expressing his grief.

Figure 6.5 The use of small-world play to help children explore their thoughts and feelings about the world

6PSM: Co-constructed story around loss and separation caused by a parental divorce – 'The Mermaid's Story'

Once upon a time there was a mermaid. She was friendly but didn't have lots of friends. There was an evil man – a human who lived under the sea with the mermaid in a shell. They were enemies. One day the man took the mermaid and hid her – because someone wanted to marry her. He got the army involved and ran and ran until he buried her under the sand so no one could ever find her again. The mermaid was sad as she had gone away from the water and her shell was lost too. She said that she didn't care. The man had sharp knives on his hands and feet and legs. He tried to be good but he just couldn't. This made everyone angry. (Boy aged ten)

Examples of themes expressed: friendship, conflict, loneliness, isolation, good and bad, the need for protection, lack of protection, fantasy and reality, secrecy, theft, revenge, betrayal, separation and loss, need for nurture, attunement, confusion, fantasy, worry, anger and fear.

Figure 6.6 shows how Jamal evaluated his own degree of problems throughout his therapy (A, B, C = beginning, middle and end). There is a marked shift in how this child became more congruent in using this self-report tool and the play themes that emerged from his play and stories. By the second report he was acknowledging and exploring through his play the particular issues he had at that time in class with relationships with staff, friends in the playground and at home with siblings. There was another key positive shift in his self-reporting of problems by the final use of this tool, as is clearly seen here in Report C. This change seemed to be reflected in the other evaluation scores obtained at the end of intervention. Jamal also commented in his evaluation form that he thought the play therapy support 'very fun and help me control my behaviour...I liked it a lot.'

Challenges for staff – keeping children in mind

I'm including some therapeutic group work around stress awareness workshops, which I've been running as a coaching model to facilitate primary school staff into using play-based strategies to help support children struggling to cope within peer relationships, specifically when out in the playground. I'm not asking these staff to use play therapy, but I am asking them to better understand how meaningful narratives around stress awareness between adults and children can be elicited using such an approach. It has thrown up many questions for staff around why play is not used more within the curriculum to help children with stress in general and challenged some perceptions over the depth involved in the thinking that should be underpinning our interactions with children through play.

Report	A			B			C		
Degree of problems	None	Some	Lots	None	Some	Lots	None	Some	Lots
Teachers		✓			✓		✓		
Friends		✓			✓		✓		
Classroom	✓					✓	✓		
Playground	✓				✓		✓		
Parents	✓			✓			✓		
Siblings	✓			✓	✓		✓	✓	
Other		✓			✓			✓	

Figure 6.6 Jamal's evaluation of his problems – child's self-rating tool

Sort Out Stress Project (SOS Club!)

Figure 6.7 Examples of stress reduction/embodiment play resources

This was run as a lunchtime club of stress awareness workshops for up to eight children in Key Stage 2 (children aged between 8 and 11 years). These children had been identified as finding particular difficulties around playground interactions, including being aggressive; peer conflicts; not wanting to go out and play; social difficulties; issues around separation, loss and parental conflicts. One child had a sibling diagnosed with autism spectrum disorder (ASD), who had been permanently excluded from the school the previous year; another boy had cerebral palsy. The group consisted of four boys and four girls between Years 3 and 6. Each session lasted up to 30 minutes. Use of a digital camera was helpful to record the process and provide presentation and teaching materials using a visual narrative. The project was evaluated by the children who had attended the sessions. Two teaching staff observed and participated in the five sessions with a view to further developing the project within their school, both as a club format and also within class as part of support strategies for individual children.

Aims of project

- To help play ground staff identify stressed children and offer a positive strategy of time-out.

- To give children a chance to calm down before end of play…ready for learning.

- To use a range of sensory based activities to support 'left–right' brain switches, that is, to help children regulate from emotional states to thinking states.

- To offer an opportunity for individual and small group nurturing through creative and therapeutic play.

- To help individual children recognise and reduce stress levels within a play therapy group based process.

Dragon story narrative

A two-headed dragon puppet was introduced as part of a narrative task to get the children to think about games, toys and activities focused on stress recognition and stress relief:

> Once upon a time there lived two very rare water dragons called Slurp and Gluggle – they're twins joined at the tail – look, can you see? This happens only once in a thousand years – so we probably won't see this again in our lifetime! These dragons live in a beautiful garden with a large lake in it. Well actually it's a volcano with a lake in the middle of it. The only way to get to this lake is up a very steep mountain – the volcano itself. At the very top there is only one way to get into the lake for a swim – by diving in! Now Slurp likes diving and Gluggle likes swimming, but guess what… Slurp thinks swimming is boring and Gluggle hates diving because she doesn't like heights! The water dragons have been fighting and arguing so much that they've forgotten how to have fun and how to play together. They were once really good friends, but now they just shout and cry at each other. They are both feeling very angry and upset by all this. They haven't been able to enjoy the lake for weeks now. They heard about SOS Club and wondered if we could help? (Webster 2010)

Figure 6.8 Two-headed dragon puppet

Each week we explored a variety of games, toys and art activities focusing on emotional language; stress awareness; distraction and calming skills; problem solving and conflict resolution. Additional support was developed linked to a Restorative Justice Coordinator working with Youth Offending Services, who ran a training programme for playground staff alongside the play coaching sessions.

Examples of key observations and narratives developed with the children

Issues surfaced about personal space and recognising accidents, that is, being pushed or shoved by accident or on purpose. Many of the children seemed to find this a difficult area to understand and a recommendation that emerged was the need to help them to understand key concepts around personal space. Another key area worth further exploration could be how children recognise stress in others, for example other children and also staff, siblings and parents/carers. Turntaking and sharing were common themes coming out in the workshops, combined with listening to others and being heard. Feeling left out or lonely was also a theme in the group as evidenced by a couple of the girls who seemed to find it difficult to fit into the group process. One girl was able to express her feelings about why she needed to come to the group, 'Why do I need to come – I don't get angry or upset?' It was observed that this particular child seemed to come to the group unwilling to connect with peers, and preferring activities that did not invite others' participation in her play choices. For such a child, finding inclusive ways of helping her identify with peers whilst respecting possible cultural differences in how she might value play was important to consider. It is also important to understand how some children use over-distancing as a coping method, that they push their feelings away, which can be due to overt emotions not being encouraged by family or their wider community. It is not just those children who act out using aggression who may need the help of peer group work.

A child fed back at the end of one workshop that 'the thing that makes me calm down is the smelly thing[3] and when I'm alone just for a bit and when I play my toys from the SOS Club!!!'

Examples of observations and key narratives developed with staff

Staff struggled to adapt to some new ideas and approaches at first during these coaching sessions. Much of this focused on how they perceived differences in their classroom roles and what I was asking them to consider by using a play-based intervention in relationship to these children. Taking the time to observe the group dynamics – starting where the children are at as they come into *each* session and being ready to change ideas for the session if not suitable for the need of the group after these observations – was a key element of its success. It was crucial to help staff acknowledge just how important it was to resist over controlling the children's behaviour and response to the play environment – and how this can also be in conflict to traditional teaching staff roles.

It was important that I educated staff into trusting how play-based activities can be harnessed by children to help find healing and support, however old they are. Ideas promoting the use of play activities to help contain emotions; redirect aggression; challenge behaviour; offer safe risks to help children explore their ideas; promote relaxation and fun; encourage self-expression and creativity were central messages that staff needed to hear.

I also actively modelled within sessions how as adults we can encourage self-esteem and social skills – modelling aspects of behaviour you want to see in the group, for example promoting sharing, noticing

---

3   Aroma oil drops on a tissue are used as part of the ending ritual of each session to provide a reminder to use a deep breathing technique if the child feels upset or angry later in the day.

others in the group who use behaviour or skills you want to see, and pointing this out to the group. The provision of active and specific praise to help enhance self-esteem and self-identity within the group was crucial to how this message was heard by the children.

Summary

Narrative therapy acknowledges social constraints around an individual's understanding of their life and, importantly, what aspects of individual agency and power are possible within these constraints. Narrative Play Therapy supports the process of helping to explore the dominant social discourse within a child's stories, and has to be seen in the context of what is also known about other systems, and perhaps most importantly, the relationships affecting the child. It is important that we recognise the impact of power on vulnerable children and their particular difficulties to find more helpful stories around understanding their lives. Bruner (1986) writes about considering narratives as being structures that are about power as well as meaning. But the child needs advocates in order to ensure that these stories are shared appropriately and heard clearly.

In summary, I may use a combination of treatment roles, interventions and theories with a changing 'lens' or narrative focus possible throughout each therapeutic journey – and indeed this 'lens' may change and adapt in each and every session offered to the child. Using a combination of direct and non-direct approaches, focus and techniques, means that I have to remain aware of the context and often changing circumstances of each individual referral. The child's voice, which should be at the heart of this process, can be swamped by adult agendas, which may include coerciveness and pathologising of the child's needs as a reason for therapy. I also need to consider whether the goals and expectations from the various systems around the child are realistic and achievable within the scope of my role and available timeframe for therapeutic intervention.

The therapeutic alliance is thus a co-constructed reality and, indeed, narrative with the child. It needs to take into account these many contextual factors – primarily aiming to develop a responsive, child-centred, attuned and prescriptive approach. This can help the child explore, understand and resolve presenting issues and concerns, whilst strengthening resilience within a collaborative framework of play therapy. Such support needs to be linked to as many of the other important relationships and systems around the child as is possible.

It is surely the case that schooling is only one small part of how a culture inducts the young into its canonical ways. Indeed, schooling may even be at odds with a culture's other ways of inducting the young into the requirements of communal living... What has become increasingly clear...is that education is not just about conventional school matters like curriculum or standards or testing. What we resolve to do in school only makes sense when considered in the broader context of what the society intends to accomplish through its educational investment in the young. How one conceives of education, we have finally come to recognise, is a function of how one conceives of culture and its aims, professed and otherwise. (Bruner 1996, pp.ix–x)

References

Batmangehelidjh, C. (2005) *No Child is Born a Criminal.* Hay Festival Video. Available at www.guardian.co.uk/commentisfree/video/2010/jun/05/child-criminal-camila-batmanghelidjh, accessed 1 March 2011.

Bomber, L. (2007) *Inside I'm Hurting – Practical Strategies for Supporting Children with Attachment Difficulties in Schools.* London: Worth Publishing.

Bossert, E. (1994) 'Stress appraisals of hospitalised school age children.' *Children's Health Care 23,* 1, 33–49.

Brom, D., Pat-Horenczyk, R. and Ford, J.D. (eds) (2009) *Treating Traumatized Children: Risk, Resilience and Recovery.* New York: Routledge.

Bruner, J. (1986) *Actual Minds, Possible Worlds.* Cambridge, MA: Harvard University Press.

Bruner, J. (1996) *The Culture of Education.* Cambridge, MA: Harvard University Press.

Cattanach, A. (2007) *Narrative Approaches in Play with Children.* London: Jessica Kingsley Publishers.

Collishaw, S., Maughan, B., Goodman, R. and Pickles, A. (2004) 'Time trends in adolescent mental health.' *Journal of Child Psychology and Psychiatry 45,* 8, 1350–1360.

Epston, D. and White, M. (1990) *Narrative Means to Therapeutic Ends.* New York: W. W. Norton.

Geddes, H. (2006) *Attachment in the Classroom – The Links Between Children's Early Experience Emotional Well-Being and Performance in School.* London: Worth Publishing.

Gil, E. (2006) *Helping Abused and Traumatized Children – Integrating Directive and Nondirective Approaches.* New York: Guilford Press.

Hagglof, B. (1999) 'Psychological reaction by children of various ages to hospital care and invasive procedures.' *Acta Paediatrica Suppl 88,* 431, 72–78.

Jackson, C.J. (2008) 'Learning to be saints or sinners: The indirect pathway from sensation seeking to behaviour through mastery orientation.' *Journal of Personality 76,* 4, 733–752.

Jones, P. (1995) *Drama as Therapy, Theatre as Living.* New York: Routledge.

Luther, S.S. (1993) 'Annotation: Methodological and conceptual issues in research on childhood resilience.' *Journal of Child Psychology and Psychiatry 34,* 4, 441–453.

May, D. (2008) 'Contemporary Play Therapy: Time-Limited Play Therapy to Enhance Resiliency in Children.' In C.E. Schaefer and H.G. Quadroon (eds) *Contemporary Play Therapy – Theory, Research and Practice.* New York and London: Guilford Press.

Middlebrooks, J.S and Audage, N.C. (2008) *The Effects of Childhood Stress on Health across the Lifespan.* Atlanta, GA: Centers for Disease Control and Prevention, National Center for Injury Prevention and Control.

National Institute for Clinical Excellence (NICE) (2008) *Promoting Children's Social and Emotional Wellbeing in Primary Education.* London: NICE Publications.

O'Connor, K. and Ammen, S. (1997) *Play Therapy Treatment Planning and Interventions: The Ecosystemic Model and Workbook (Practical Resources for the Mental Health Professional).* San Diego, CA: Academic Press.

Office for National Statistics (ONS) (2004) *The Health of Children and Young People.* London: Office for National Statistics.

Office for National Statistics (ONS) (2008) 'Three years on: A survey of the emotional development and wellbeing of children and young people.' Available at www.statistics.gov.uk/articles/nojournal/child_development_mental_health.pdf, accessed 1 March 2011.

Panksepp, J. (1998) *Affective Neuroscience: The Foundations of Human and Animal Emotions.* Oxford and New York: Oxford University Press.

Prout, A. and James, A. (1990) 'A New Paradigm for the Sociology of Childhood.' In A. James and A. Prout (eds) *Constructing and Reconstructing Childhood.* Basingstoke: Falmer Press.

Rossman, B.B.R. and Gamble, W.C. (1997) 'Preschooler's understanding of physical injury: Stressor, affect and coping appraisals.' *Children's Health Care 26,* 2, 77–96.

Rutter, M. (1985) 'Resilience in the face of adversity: Protective factors and resistance to psychiatric disorder.' *British Journal of Psychiatry 147,* 598–611.

Schaefer, C.E. (2003) *Play Therapy with Adults.* Hoboken, NJ: John Wiley and Sons.

Stephens, L.C. (1997) 'Sensory integrative dysfunction in young children.' *AAHBEI News Exchange 2,* 1.

Sunderland, M. (2001) *Using Story Telling as a Therapeutic Tool with Children.* Milton Keynes: Speechmark Publishing.

Webster, A.J. (2010) 'Sort Out Stress Project.' Unpublished ms.

Wertlieb, D., Weigel, C. and Feldstein, M. (1987) 'Measuring children's coping.' *American Journal of Orthopsychiatric Association 57,* 4, 548–560.

Young Minds (2009) *The YoungMinds Children and Young People's Manifesto.* Available at www.youngminds.org.uk/campaigns-policy/manifesto/youngminds-manifesto, accessed 4 August 2010.

Chapter 7

Narrative Play Therapy with Children Experiencing Parental Separation or Divorce

Sharon Pearce

Divorce and children's services

The divorce rate has risen rapidly in Western societies. Statistics suggest that one in two new marriages in the USA will end in divorce. In the UK the figure is one in three. The proportion of children involved in these marriage breakdowns has also risen. Annually in the UK over 100,000 children can expect their parents to divorce (Office for National Statistics 2010). In the UK in 2008 120,000 couples divorced. These marriages involved 106,000 children under the age of 16; 22,000 were under the age of four (Office for National Statistics 2010).

The literature in this field has burgeoned as professionals have begun to acknowledge the grief of separation and loss faced by children in relationship breakdowns. In one of the classic studies of the 1990s, the Joseph Rowntree Foundation (Rodgers and Pryor 1998) concluded that children from divorced families experienced negative outcomes, including poverty, behavioural problems, educational difficulties, leaving home early, becoming sexually active early, depressive symptoms, etc. at roughly twice the rate of those from intact families. Stevenson and Black (1995), more recently supported by Rodgers and Pryor (1998), however cast doubt upon this stark conclusion, pointing out that these disadvantages occurred to only a minority of children whose parents separated.

Children whose parents divorce experience a wide range of emotions in the surrounding trauma. Children's losses in divorce include the loss of familiar family patterns and the separation and anxiety involved with losing a parental attachment figure. Divorce may involve conflict and hostility between the parents thus compounding the emotional situation for the children (Sarrazin and Cyr 2007). There may be a change in the family's economic circumstances or a move away from familiar areas and from family and friends.

Children's reactions to separation and loss are documented in the work of John Bowlby (1969, 1973, 1979, 1980). They are likely to experience shock, disbelief, confusion, fear and anxiety about who will look after them, anger and sadness. Many children, unable to understand why their parents are divorcing, feel guilty and blame themselves for the divorce. Children may feel that they have to become involved in their parents' marriage, trying to blame, rescue or placate one or both parents to prevent the marriage breakdown. Parents involved in the height of conflict may not appreciate their children's feelings, and may underestimate their distress (Sandler, Kim-Bae and MacKinnon 2000; Taylor and Andrews 2009).

Continuing inter-parental conflict is the biggest factor in those children referred for mental health intervention (Emery 1992, 1999). Pre-existing marital conflict is the highest disposing factor in the small group of children who are deemed to have serious externalising problems following parental separation (Block, Block and Gjerde 1986; Emery 1982).

Intervention

In the 1990s it became clear that an increasing number of referrals for children, young people and their families to their local health authorities involved problems that were related to parental separation. By the time of referral to an agency the 'problem' was often perceived as intractable and was well camouflaged by a myriad of intervening issues.

Among professionals, in both the public and voluntary sectors, a perspective emerged: resources were being used on a problem, which if recognised and acknowledged could benefit from an earlier intervention. The result was a project designed specifically to offer counselling support to children who experienced distress following parental separation. A decision was taken to base part of the service in a school, as it was considered that a number of benefits would flow from its involvement:

1. The adult(s) suggesting play therapy would be those most likely to be aware of the children's distress on a daily basis.

2. School referral could only be made with parental consent.

3. Children and parents viewed school as a safe and containing environment.

The project concentrated on one school where there was a high rate of unemployment, with an increase in marriage breakdown. The area was poorly resourced, receiving its social services, health and psychiatric support from another town. The school worked hard to provide support for parents. The teachers involved made it a consistent element of their teaching responsibility to actively assist pupils attempting to cope with distress.

Adaptation

The concept of 'adaptive tasks' has been promoted as a framework for organising thinking about children's divorce adjustment. Wallerstein (1983) defined six adjustment tasks:

1. Acknowledging the reality of the divorce.

2. Resuming customary developmentally appropriate activities.

3. Dealing with feelings of loss and rejection.

4. Resolving feelings of anger and forgiving parents.

5. Accepting the permanence of divorce.

6. Achieving realistic hope for future loving relationships.

Progress through the adaptive tasks hierarchy is not necessarily linear. According to Wallerstein the adaptive or maladaptive outcomes of divorce on children are the results of the kinds of mastery children achieve over these tasks. Children can either maintain or resolve feelings of anger or rejection; the outcome of children's adjustment to parental separation and divorce determines their long-term view of themselves and their world.

Children's ability to achieve these tasks is mediated by their levels of understanding, and there are parallel developments between children's social cognition and their reactions to divorce. Children's reactions to divorce is influenced by the way they co-ordinate social perspectives and reason about social relationships. Younger children's perspectives are influenced strongly by their families. Adolescent children are beginning to test out family boundaries and have loyalties to peer networks that, while they may be seen as challenging to the family, are a source of support to the young people themselves. Latency aged children fall between these two categories; however, they are also influenced by their peers and the school environment is particularly important to them.

School

The role of school and peers is particularly important for children experiencing parental marital frustrations. Research carried out by Hetherington (1989) showed that the social and cognitive development of young children from divorced families was enhanced if children were attending schools with explicitly defined schedules, rules and regulations, consistent warm discipline and expectations of mature behaviour. Schools play a buffering role for children undergoing stress, affording them security in a structured, safe, predictive environment. The protective factor of authoritative schools is most marked for boys, for children with difficult temperaments and for children exposed to multiple stressful events.

Peers

Peer relationships became more influential with age; children who were actively rejected by their peer group or who did not have a single close friend showed increased long-term problems in adjustment. However, a supportive relationship with a single friend could moderate the adverse consequences of marital transitions and the effects of rejection by other children.

Attachment

Children respond differently to parental separation and divorce; some are profoundly relieved by the end of their parents' marriage, particularly if it has been a marriage punctuated by conflict and violence, others are deeply distressed. Some children are more 'resilient' (Hetherington and Stanley-Hagan 1999; Rutter 1981) than others, so that differing reactions can occur within the same family. The work of John Bowlby on attachment theory shows that whether a child's attachment is secure or insecure illuminates potential responses to the process of parental separation/divorce (Bowlby 1979, 1980). Attachment is defined as the emotional bond that develops between children and their care-givers.

Attachment behaviour refers to any of the various forms of behaviour that the person engages in to obtain or maintain a desired proximity (Bowlby 1988). Threats of abandonment by the attachment figure at *any* age can cause intense emotional reactions such as anger, anxiety, rage, etc. In children and adolescents these emotions can lead to dysfunctional behaviours. Mary Ainsworth (1982; Ainsworth *et al.* 1979), Bowlby's colleague, coined the term 'secure base'. The secure base allows the child to venture forth and explore the world, returning when necessary to be comforted, supported and cared for. Without a secure base the individual will resort to defensive strategies, for example splitting off anger, protest, despair and detachment in order to minimise the pain of separation. Bowlby states that the nature of the original parent/child relationship remains stable and consistent in later life relationships. However, he also states that traumatic or significant events in the original parent/child relationship may alter the security of the base, subsequently altering their experience of relationships. This was confirmed in a study by Woodward, Ferguson and Belsky (2000) which shows that divorce decreases security attachment styles between parents and children.

Ainsworth *et al.* (1978) observed that attachment theory emphasises 'the bond that ties' and the physical proximity of child and carer. However, as Cattanach observes (1997, p.119), 'attachment theory emphasises the carer/child relationship in terms of functional adaptation to the environment without much emphasis on the construction of meaning between the child and carer', which influences a child's development and without which an understanding of the full picture of the child's inner and outer world cannot be gained.

Social construction

Social construction, which underpins and informs Narrative Play Therapy, maintains that personality development reflects both the larger society and the immediate family and other interpersonal relationships. The construction of our model of the world, the inner cognitive map, determines how a person perceives reality and how he or she will think and behave (Burr 1995; Gergen 1991, 1994). Of importance here is that when an individual's model has cognitive errors, faulty conclusions have important implications for adjustive behaviour. We all create our own world socially but, while its creators, we may also be the victims of its imprisonment because of 'its power to make up reality, rather than simply represent it' (Cattanach 1997, p.18). Language can limit or distort perceptions of the world. The rich complexity of narrative stories enables children to construct, deconstruct and reconstruct their lives. Narrative and stories can assist children in learning new ways to talk about their experiences that can ultimately change their models of the world (Gardner 1978, 1993; White and Epston 1989).

Narrative Play Therapy

Narrative Play Therapy as expounded by Cattanach 'is based on social construction theory and narrative therapy which describe the development of identity as based on the stories we tell about ourselves and the stories others in our environment tell about us' (2008, p.25). Stories allow the children to symbolically distance themselves from real life events and to explore them creatively at a distance. This includes the use of sensory and projective play material, toys and other media and dramatic role-play. Stories and play can put different events into a new perspective by re-framing the event in time or space. Children can try on a role of choice, experiencing a different reality within the role and actively constructing their own knowledge, which creates and strengthens children's identity as their world evolves (Cattanach 1997).

Narrative Play Therapy is a collaborative approach in which the partnership agreement between child and adult gives meaning to the play (Cattanach 2008, p.21). In Narrative Play Therapy the therapist 'joins' with the child in co-authoring and co-constructing the stories, entering the child's world at his or her level. The child and therapist negotiate meaning as they journey together, allowing the child to use the relationship and space to define and present him- or herself. Children tell their stories to a specific therapist who is an active listener and participant with the child and thus the co-author of the story. This approach allows the child to explore his or her narrative with the therapist's support. The 'key to the relationship is the adult's capacity to understand and reflect with the child' (Cattanach 2008, p.23).

Billy's family background

Billy was the only child of his parents' relationship. His mother was still in her teens when she became pregnant. Billy's mother had a difficult relationship with her own family and was known to the local social services department. The eldest child in the family, she was rejected by her own mother when pregnant with Billy. The relationship between Billy's parents was volatile and broke down while he was still an infant; Billy began a pattern of having contact with his father and paternal grandparents. His mother subsequently formed a relationship with another man by whom she had more children. Concerns about Billy's mother's care of him reached crisis point 18 months prior to his referral to the project. Following a social services investigation Billy was abruptly moved to live with his father and his new partner and her two daughters (one older, one younger than Billy) five days before Christmas. Billy was given 24 hours' notice but no explanation for the move. Subsequently his mother rejected all contact with him, despite having a younger son who attended another part of his school; she openly ignored him.

Billy grieved not only the loss of his mother but also his younger half-brother to whom he felt close before the move. Initially he settled well, but after six months he began testing boundaries, and relationships with the new family, particularly with his stepmother, began to deteriorate. Billy's major source of emotional support came from his paternal grandmother. He had very poor social skills, presenting in class as very demanding, and was socially rejected by his peers. He was demanding of relationships with his female teachers, seeking nurture from them indiscriminately. His teacher described him as a bright child who was seriously underachieving academically.

Billy was offered 12 one-hour sessions of Narrative Play Therapy in which to freely explore and construct stories about his world and environment. He was allowed free use of all toys and art materials in the room in the development of his stories. Within the boundaries provided by my presence and rules, the room and the time limit, Billy was able to explore in safety stories about his life. These stories, dramatically distanced from his daily life, were the basis for engaging with painful events. Within the framework of acting a story it was possible for Billy to consider alternative reasons for different events and explore a variety of endings, some happy, some sad. Working with narratives allowed Billy to explore painful past experiences, to express his emotions and at his own pace to achieve mastery over emotional events placing his experience within a context that was manageable for him, giving his life stories more cohesion.

Play therapy method, role and environment

Billy told imaginative stories in which he dramatised and fictionalised events from his daily life. My role as co-author, co-constructor and boundary keeper was to help him explore these alternative realities. It was important to acknowledge the centrality of the play as his way of making sense of the world and to allow him to explore his own narratives, which I co-authored with him.

The aim for Billy was to utilise the personal space through the relationship we constructed to develop and inform a stronger sense of personal and social identity through the stories he told (Cattanach 1997, p.8). Billy was 'object dependent' in his story telling, using mainly small toys or objects to tell his stories. He consistently returned to the same toys throughout his sessions, and it was important that the same toys were always available. His play regularly encountered disasters from which the characters did not always recover. It was important that I as co-constructor, witness and audience could bear the 'disasters' with him. The 'disasters' were a reflection via dramatic distance of his early experience in life.

Billy developed rituals around the ending of his sessions. He always finished a session wanting to leave 'his' toys out to remain there until his next session. Great care was needed to support his need to claim his own space or 'territory', reassuring him of his right to return, whilst acknowledging that the space was shared with others and therefore the toys could not stay exactly as he had left them. Evidence of the use of the room by others was met with a combination of indignation and curiosity. For Billy the certainty of the presence of the chosen toys signalled the beginnings of trust between us.

Billy's stories

In his stories Billy explored his feelings of abandonment, anger, rage and uncertainty. In his first story the baby shark was punished for disobedience and then threatened further with abandonment, a theme which had come true for Billy.

First story (from Session 3)

This story was of a mummy and baby shark. The mother shark went hunting, leaving the baby shark behind. The baby shark was told to stay inside, but he went out to play with his friends. When the mummy shark came home and found the baby shark had gone out to play, she was very angry. She smacked the baby shark and sent him to the home for naughty baby sharks. I asked how the baby shark was feeling. 'Sad because he can't go home,' was the reply. Then I asked how the mummy shark felt. 'She is cross; she does not like the baby shark.' 'Would the baby shark be allowed home?' I asked. 'No, because he was naughty,' he said.

He internalised this abandonment as being his fault because he was 'naughty'. Consumed by his loss of his mother and sibling, Billy had moved to his father and stepmother without warning or exploration. His 'narrative' had come literally true and he seemed to be stuck in a story without possibility of resolution – particularly as his mother crossed the street to avoid him. My role as play therapist was to help Billy negotiate this narrative and together to co-construct a journey towards a new ending of possibilities and hope, which seemed so lost to him. As part of this journey we navigated tricky terrain in his next few sessions. Billy was needy, he wanted more than other children; he wanted more sessions and found endings hard. As a result of his abandonment Billy's grief was palpable and was noticed by others. His classmates would not play with him unless asked to do so by the teacher and, as a female figure who offered him caring, he was often unwilling to separate from her at break-times, as this stimulated his fear of abandonment and need for attachment.

By the time of the second story Billy had had an unplanned meeting with his mother. This story revealed Billy's anxiety about his place in his world and the beginnings of stronger attachments to his new family.

Second story (from Session 9)

There was a family with a mother, a good policeman father, two girls and a boy. They went on holiday to the seaside and the boy swam in the sea while everyone else was on the sand. Then a shark started to chase the boy, he called for help, his parents tried to rescue him, and eventually after a big fight his dad killed the shark. Everyone got into a boat to escape. 'Now we are safe', they said, but they were still chased by an angry shark.

In the first part of his story, Billy's world was still subject to vulnerability. Billy's own undercurrents of emotion included concern about his safety in his new family: could they keep him safe or not? His mother remained hostile to him and Billy was aware of her anger. In turn we explored the fears of the boy as the waves overwhelmed the safety of the boat. We explored helplessness in the face of events over which Billy had no control. We explored the anger Billy felt in his abandonment whilst acknowledging the threats that the 'shark' posed to his world. Hostile mothers could not be changed but Billy began to perceive that he had a place in his new family. Through his stories Billy began tentatively to explore hope and possibility for his future.

After he had completed his 12 sessions, a review with his family and school agreed that he was making good progress and should continue in play therapy. At the beginning he lacked confidence and was an anxious, hypervigilant little boy with no friends and a vulnerable position at home. By the time he finished play therapy he was achieving academically, was popular socially (Hetherington 1989; Hetherington and Stanley-Hagan 1999) and at home he got on well with his stepsisters and had a good relationship with his stepmother, who saw him as one of her own children.

In terms of his adaptation to his parents' separation following Wallerstein's six tasks, Billy acknowledged the reality of his parents' separation and resumed customary developmentally appropriate activities. He dealt more appropriately with his feelings of loss and rejection, forging relationships with his stepmother and paternal grandmother and aunt as alternative attachment figures. His feelings of anger were acknowledged, he recognised that his parents' separation was permanent and he had more realistic hopes for loving relationships in the future.

Billy's rejection and abandonment by his mother remained real, but through Narrative Play Therapy he had a new storied self. Previously he had been angry, sad, anxious, friendless, hypervigilant, and had internalised both his parents' separation and his mother's rejection of him as his fault. He now acknowledged that these events were beyond his doing. He attached appropriately to those who were willing to care for him and in doing so flourished. Through the narrative we co-constructed Billy moved from victim to master of the story – no longer buffeted by the waves, he and his family arrived safely on the shore for a new beginning.

Shields

I used 'shields' as a pre and post assessment tool (Cattanach 1994). The first shield provides an introduction and preliminary assessment of the child's view of his or her world. The second shield illustrates whether the child has incorporated the new family structure into his or her sense of self. The shields also provide a visual representation of the child's journey through Wallerstein's (1983) adaptive tasks. The shield consists of five parts that have to be filled in:

(A) a good time with my family

(B) a hard time I had with my family

(C) why I think my parents separated or divorced

(D) something I would like to happen in my family in the next two years

(E) something special about me.

Children can find section A of the shield difficult to complete. For the play therapist it is useful to hear of a child's positive memories of his family, whether recent or in the past. In section B many children define the worst thing as being told off by a parent. Few initially would put in parental separation. Section C is particularly helpful in clarifying the child's perceptions and understanding of parental separation, including the notion of whether children are to 'blame' for their parents' separation. Section D allows for the expression of potential fantasies: have children accepted parental separation or do they continue to hold the fantasy of parental reunification? Unattached children tend to favour money or objects at this point, being unable to rely upon their parents to meet their needs. Finally section E encourages children to celebrate something about themselves.

Billy's first shield (from Session 1)

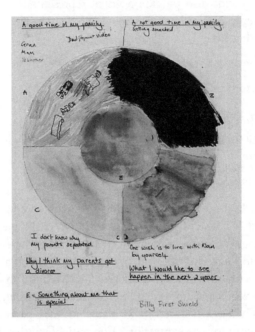

Billy had great difficulty in completing his first shield. In answer to section A, a good time with my family, he drew a picture of himself with his father and stepmother watching the television. The figures are drawn lying down at an angle, separated from each other, looking away from each other. While everyone is shown smiling there is a strong quality of disconnection in this picture contrasting sharply with Billy's desire to attach and please these significant adults. Outside the picture Billy requested that I should write the names of his grandmother, mother and half-brother. Billy was trying to include all those who were important to him. Significantly Billy did not include his stepsisters. Billy chose for the reminder of the shield to paint each section different colours and asked me to write words next to the section. For section B, a hard time with my family, Billy painted the shield black and said that he hated getting smacked. The strength of his anger was clear but he was not ready to place it directly upon the shield. Section C, why my parents got a divorce, Billy painted yellow but said he did not know why; it seemed too painful to face. In section D, the fantasy future, Billy painted green and said that he would like to live with his nan by himself. His nan appeared to be a safe person for him. Finally for section E, what is special about me, Billy painted it blue and said that he could not think of anything. I was left with the overwhelming impression of a sad, angry and insecure little boy, vulnerable in his environment and unable to find measures to cope with the pain. He wanted to attach and have security in his world whilst rejecting the available attachment offered.

Billy's second shield (from Session 12)

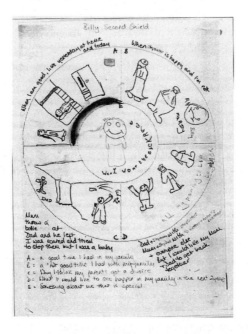

In the second shield Billy's self esteem had begun to rise. Cognitively he was able to project onto his shield details of his world, something he had previously been unable to do. He worked extremely hard and filled in every section as a complete and identifiable family picture. He also added annotations to each section of the shield. In the second shield his world shows more clarity and his pictures of family figures show clear relationships to one another. Billy's sense of safety and security had increased to the extent that he could now risk filling in his shield and staking a claim to his place in his world. In section A he was proud of his achievement of being good in the family environment. He drew himself in the bedroom he shared with his younger stepsister, a drawing that includes a good sense of perspective; he and his stepsister are shown in relationship to each other. Billy is lying on the bed and smiling and his stepsister is sulking because he has been good. In section B Billy has again drawn himself with his stepsister and shown himself as feeling unhappy, when his stepsister is happy. This was a marked contrast to the first shield where his stepsisters are not mentioned. Billy was attaching to her as a sister and a rival; they were beginning to develop a normal sibling relationship. In section C Billy was able to give a explanation of why his parents parted, due to their fighting. Billy drew himself trying to prevent his parents from fighting. In terms of scale he drew himself as the largest figure and the only one fully visible. Billy was aware that he could not have intervened in this way as he was a baby when his parents separated; it shows him trying to intervene beyond his capacity, a consistent theme for children of divorce attempting to rescue or placate their parents in order to secure their world. In section D he revealed his fantasy reunification wish; he drew himself with his parents and wrote 'all my family to live together'. Billy's mother is drawn as unsmiling. Billy was aware of how his mother would feel and showed this accurately. This picture showed Billy's wishful thinking as he began to find a place in his new world, wanting both families to unite around him. In section E Billy drew himself winning the school sack race. The process of valuing himself had begun. He was beginning to seek and accept a place in his family while continuing to hold some unrealistic expectations of himself along with his fantasy wish of parental reunification and family unity. Billy's healing process was not complete but his journey had started.

Conclusions

The play therapy intervention can be evaluated by an assessment of whether there are changes in the child's presenting problems, that is, whether the child has adapted to his new family circumstances (Wallerstein 1983). O'Connor (1991) makes the point that such adaptation will be accompanied by changes in the child's wider ecosystem.

Billy was a needy child with poor attachment, abandonment, anger, grief and loss issues. Billy had experienced developmental trauma and maternal rejection that he had been unable to process (Ainsworth 1982; Bowlby 1973, 1979, 1980). Critically he had internalised a strong sense of self-blame and badness, that is, that he must be to blame for his parents' separation and for having left his mother's care. From this perspective it was difficult for him to form alliances with other children, hence his poor peer relationships. Continuing high levels of parental discord and hostility hampered any attempts to achieve resolution of Wallerstein's six adaptive tasks and had increased his probability of referral for mental health support supporting the conclusions of Emery (1982, 1992) and Block *et al.* (1986).

A bright child, Billy used the sessions and the relationship to create a space wherein he could explore his issues of attachment versus abandonment with regard to his birth mother (Ainsworth 1982; Ainsworth *et al.* 1979; Bowlby 1980). In his first story Billy expressed anger and bewilderment at being rejected by his mother. The story with its naughty child and angry mother was a reflection of Billy's feelings of guilt and responsibility for being abandoned by his mother. Between the first and second story Billy developed much more confidence in our relationship. By the time of his second story in Session 9 Billy had begun to move on from his mother's rejection of him and had begun the process of seeking his place in his father's family. As a consequence Billy transferred his increasing confidence, albeit hesitantly, to his wider ecosystem (O'Connor 1991) improving his home life where he began to act in a more age appropriate manner with his step sibling and forging new friendships in school (Hetherington 1989; Hetherington and Stanley-Hagan 1999). Billy's desire to attach to his new family was strengthened. Subsequently he continued in play therapy to complete his journey.

Using Narrative Play Therapy Billy and I set out on a journey to explore issues that were important to him. Through the healing power of the stories we co-created, which gave meaning to the dramatic play, Billy was able to express his emotions, feelings and experience of his world. The stories enabled him to look at the painful event of his parents' separation and his struggle to cope with the process and changes involved. A crucial feature of the journey was the relationship of trust established between the therapist and the child, providing Billy with a sense of security and confidence in my role.

Some years later I met Billy's old headteacher. By this time Billy was in senior school where he was said to be popular and doing well academically. Billy was flourishing and often came by his old school. The headteacher said sadly that this was in marked contrast to Billy's half siblings on his mother's side, who now attended primary school, but who had been excluded due to their unacceptable behaviour.

References

Ainsworth, M.D.S (1982) 'Attachment Retrospect and Prospect.' In C. Parkes and J. Stevenson-Hinde (eds) *The Place of Attachment in Human Behaviour*. London: Tavistock.

Ainsworth, M.D.S., Blehar, M.C., Waters, E. and Wall, S. (1978) *Patterns of Attachment: A Psychological Study of the Strange Situation*. Hillsdale, NJ: Lawrence Erlbaum.

Block, J.A., Block, J. and Gjerde, P.F. (1986) 'The personality of the child prior to divorce.' *Child Development 57*, 827–840.

Bowlby, J. (1969) *Attachment*. London: Hogarth.

Bowlby, J. (1973) *Loss: Sadness and Depression*. London: Hogarth.

Bowlby, J. (1979) *The Making and Breaking of Affectional Bonds*. London: Tavistock.

Bowlby, J. (1980) *Separation: Anxiety and Anger*. London: Hogarth.

Bowlby, J. (1988) *A Secure Base*. London: Routledge.

Burr, V. (1995) *An Introduction to Social Construction*. London: Routledge.

Cattanach, A. (1994) *Play Therapy where the Sky Meets the Underworld*. London: Jessica Kingsley Publishers.

Cattanach, A. (1997) *Children's Stories in Play Therapy*. London: Jessica Kingsley Publishers.

Cattanach, A. (2008) *Narrative Approaches in Play with Children*. London: Jessica Kingsley Publishers.

Emery, R.E. (1982) 'Interparental conflict and the children of discord and divorce.' *Psychological Bulletin 92*, 310–330.

Emery, R.E. (1992) 'Family Conflict and Its Developmental Implications: A Conceptual Analysis of Deep Meanings and Systemic Processes.' In C.U. Shanty and W.W. Hadup (eds) *Conflict in Child and Adolescent Development*. London: Cambridge University Press.

Emery, R.E. (1999) *Marriage, Divorce and Children's Adjustment*. London: Sage.

Gardner, R.A. (1978) *Therapeutic Communication with Children: The Mutual Storytelling Technique*. Lanham, MD: Jason Aronson.

Gardner, R.A. (1993) *Storytelling in Psychotherapy with Children*. Lanham, MD: Jason Aronson.

Gergen, K. (1991) *The Saturated Self*. New York: Basic Books.

Gergen, K. (1994) *Towards Transformation in Social Knowledge*, 2nd edn. London: Sage Publishers.

Hetherington, E.M. (1989) 'Coping with family transitions, winners, losers and survivors.' *Child Development 60*, 1–14.

Hetherington, E.M. and Stanley-Hagan, M. (1999) 'The adjustment of children of divorced parents: A risk and resiliency perspective.' *Journal of Child Psychology 40*, 1, 129–140.

Jennings, S. (1993) *Playtherapy with Children*. Oxford: Blackwell.

O'Connor, K.J. (1991) *The Play Therapy Primer*. New York: Wiley Interscience.

Office for National Statistics (2010) 'Divorces: Couples and children of divorced couples, 1981, 1991, 1998 and 2001–2008.' Available at www.statistics.gov.uk/downloads/theme_population/Table4_Divorces_Couples_and_children_of_divorced_couples.xls, accessed 1 December 2010.

Rodgers. B. and Pryor. J. (1998) *Divorce and Separation: The Outcomes for Children.* York: Joseph Rowntree Foundation.

Rutter, M. (1981) *Maternal Deprivation Reassessed.* London: Penguin. (First published in 1971.) London: Psychology Press.

Sandler, I.N., Kim-Bae, L.S. and MacKinnon, D. (2000) 'Coping and negative appraisal as mediators between control beliefs and psychological symptoms in children of divorce.' *Journal of Clinical Child Psychology 29,* 3, 336–347.

Sarrazin, J. and Cyr, F. (2007) 'Parental conflicts and their damaging effects on children.' *Journal of Divorce and Remarriage 47,* 1, 77–93.

Stevenson, M.R. and Black, K.N. (1995) *How Divorce Affects Offspring.* Madison, WI: Brown and Benchmark.

Taylor, R. and Andrews, B. (2009) 'Parental depression in the context of divorce and the impact on children.' *Journal of Divorce and Remarriage 50,* 7, 472–480.

Wallerstein, J.S. (1983) 'Children of Divorce Stress and Development Tasks.' In N. Garmezy and M. Rutter (eds) *Stress, Coping and Development in Children.* New York: McGraw-Hill.

White, M. and Epston, D. (1989) *Literate Means to Therapeutic Ends.* Adelaide: Dulwich Centre.

Woodward, L., Ferguson, D.M. and Belsky, J. (2000) 'Timing of parental separation and attachment to parents in adolescence: Results of a prospective study from birth to age 16.' *Journal of Marriage and the Family 62,* 162–174.

Further reading

Bemard, J.M. (1989) 'School Interventions.' In M. Textor (ed.) *The Divorce and Divorce Therapy Handbook.* Lanham, MD: Jason Aronson.

Cattanach, A. (1992) *Play Therapy with Abused Children.* London: Jessica Kingsley Publishers.

Cattanach, A. (2003) *Introduction to Play Therapy.* London: Brunner-Routledge.

Freeman, K.A., Adams, C.D. and Drabman, R.S. (1998) 'Divorcing parents: Guidelines for promoting children's adjustment.' *Child and Family Behaviour Therapy 20,* 3, 1–27.

Grych, J.A. and Finchau, F.D. (1992) 'Interventions for children of divorce toward greater integration of research and action.' *Psychological Bulletin 3,* 3, 434–454.

Hett, G.G. and Rose, C.D. (1991) 'Counselling children of divorce: A divorce lifeline programme.' *Canadian Journal of Counselling 25,* 1, 38–49.

Hetherington, E.M. (2005) 'Divorce and the adjustment of children.' *Paediatric Review 26,* 5, 163–169.

Jennings, S. (1999) *Introduction to Developmental Playtherapy.* London: Jessica Kingsley Publishers.

Johnston, J.R., Campbell, L.E.G and Mayes, S.S. (1985) 'Latency children in postseparation and divorce disputes.' *Journal of the American Academy of Child Psychiatry 24,* 5, 563–574.

Kroll, B. (1994) *Chasing Rainbows: Children. Divorce and Loss.* Lyme Regis: Russell House Publishing.

Kurdeck, L.A. (1989) 'Children's Adjustment.' In M. Textor (ed.) *Divorce Therapy Handbook.* Lanham, MD: Jason Aronson.

Lee, M. (2001) 'Marital violence: Impact on children's emotional experiences, emotional regulation and behaviors in a post-divorce/separation situation.' *Child and Adolescent Social Work Journal 18,* 2, 137–163.

Lengua, L., Wolchick, S.A. and Sandler, I.N. (2010) 'The additive and interactive effects of parenting and temperament in predicting adjustment problems of children of divorce.' *Journal of Clinical Child and Adolescent Psychology 29,* 2, 232–244.

Main, M. and Weston, D. (1982) 'Avoidance of the Attachment Figure in Infancy.' In C.M. Parkes and J. Stevenson-Hinde (eds) *The Place of Attachment in Human Behaviour.* London: Tavistock.

Sandler, I.N., Wolchik, S.A. and Braver, S.L. (1988) 'The Stressors of Children's Postdivorce Environments.' In S.A. Wolchik and P. Karoly (eds) *Children of Divorce: Empirical Perspectives on Adjustment.* London: Psychology Press.

Sirvanli-Ozen, D. (2005) 'Impacts of divorce on the behaviour and adjustment problems, parenting styles and attachment styles of children.' *Journal of Divorce and Remarriage 42,* 3, 127–151.

Smith, H. (1999) *Children, Feelings and Divorce.* London: Free Association Books.

Textor, M. (ed.) (1989) *The Divorce and Divorce Therapy Handbook.* Lanham, MD: Jason Aronson.

Vygotsky, L.S. (1978) *Mind in Society: The Development of Higher Psychological Processes.* Cambridge, MA: Harvard University Press.

Wallerstein, J.S. and Blakelee, S. (1989) *Second Chances: Men, Women and Children a Decade after Divorce.* New York: Ticknor and Fields.

Wallerstein, J.S. and Kelly, J.B. (1980) *Surviving the Breakup.* New York: Basic Books/ Harper Collins.

Weyer, M. and Sandler, I.N. (1998) 'Stress and coping as predictors of children's divorce related ruminations.' *Journal of Clinical Child and Adolescent Psychology 27,* 1, 78–86.

Wolf, D. and Gardner, H. (1979) 'Style and Sequence in Early Symbolic Play.' In M. Franklin and N. Smith (eds) *Symbolic Functioning in Childhood.* Hillside, NJ: Erlbaum.

Chapter 8

Journey into the Interior

Narrative Play Therapy with Young People Who Sexually Harm

David Le Vay

The notion of childhood sexuality, of children as sexual beings, is challenging for many of us and can provoke strong feelings of anxiety and uncertainty. Clearly, sexuality is a natural, healthy and integral part of children's development, although within our sometimes socially neurotic and media-aroused culture the concept of childhood, and indeed parenthood for that matter, is often challenged and impinged upon by the dominant social discourse of the time. And of course social discourse is not fixed; it's an ever changing, shifting social conversation that is continually being driven and shaped by the prevalent values, attitudes, beliefs of the time. Looking back, we can see that the social construction or prevailing narratives of childhood, certainly within western society, have changed greatly over time, oscillating between children as fragile, delicate creatures that need to be cosseted from the dangers of the 'big wide world' to children as 'mini-adults' who need to be disciplined, seen but not heard and sent out to work. Employment law, compulsory education, social policy and child protection legislation have all over the years shaped the values and attitudes we hold about children within our society, and of course shaped how children perceive their own place within the community around them. But it's clear that within both past and present society there has, and continues to be, a deep social ambivalence within the expressed attitudes and beliefs regarding children and young people. As Cattanach (2008) says, there seems to have been a split in the construction of childhood, an ongoing narrative between the child as 'innocent victim' and 'little devil'.

Nothing quite captures this societal ambivalence more poignantly than the issue of children who display sexually harmful behaviour. It is an area that provokes a powerful and complex emotional response and can engender a deep sense of unease for parents, professionals and the wider public. It is simple enough for adult sexual offenders to be publicly named, shamed and vilified as dangerous, 'evil monsters', but how do we respond to children who sexually abuse other children? Through what social lens can we, and should we, view and understand this behaviour? This sense of social unease and anxiety around children's developing expressions of sexuality is further compounded within a culture where the line of what is and is not appropriate is being continually redrawn. In this sense, one has to wonder about the prevailing social narratives around children and sex, as portrayed through sections of popular culture and the corporate world. There is something just a little disturbed about a society that demonises adult sex offenders whilst at the same time seeking to eroticise our children, blurring the lines between child and adult through a process of sexual objectification. At best, children are inadvertently subjected to a bewildering array of sexual imagery through the multiple forms of media at their disposal. And at worst, there is a process little short of corporate paedophilia as children and young people are consciously and explicitly targeted as sexual objects by elements of the clothing, music and media industry. Little wonder that families are referred to our therapy service expressing confusion and uncertainty about what is 'normal' sexual behaviour.

Within this debate it is also important to acknowledge how the last decade has seen a virtual explosion in information technology that has had a hugely significant impact upon our culture as a whole, but probably most of all upon the children and young people who have known little else. The territory that young people have to negotiate as they begin to explore the world beyond their immediate family is increasingly complex. The all-pervasive presence of the internet and the plethora of social networking sites have opened up a world of opportunity that could only be imagined just a few short years ago. Exciting, tantalising and brutally direct in its immediacy, this new technology allows children and young people to engage with others in a way that often precludes the presence of any kind of meaningful relationship (as we might traditionally understand it). The landscape of the inter-personal has changed and children and young people can engage with parts of themselves, outside of any kind of coherent social context.

This access to an 'online' world challenges the traditional notion of the acquisition of sexual knowledge as a gradual, incremental process, whilst also disempowering parents and eroding their role as educators. The process of a child's psychosexual development, which once might have been thought of in linear terms, as new information is gradually integrated into a developing identity and mediated through the parental and peer relationships, is now something more fragmented and incoherent. It is as if one is reading a novel and jumping ahead to see what will happen without having a true sense of the plot; you know what happens in the end, but not how you got there. Within our team, children tell us every day that they learn about sex by viewing pornography on the internet. There is a sad irony in the notion that within our risk averse, health and safety conscious society, young children can sit in their bedroom and be just three clicks away from all the violence and hardcore pornography their parents or teachers could ever imagine. Of course, the vast majority of children have the balance and emotional sensibility to place this material in a context, but for young children and children with histories of abuse, trauma and disturbed attachments the exposure to pornographic and violent imagery can have a significantly damaging impact.

My aim within this chapter is to explore and describe the process of Narrative Play Therapy in the context of my work with children and young people with sexually harmful behaviour, to explore how this approach can help both the child and the therapist to begin to make sense of the complex and dualistic feelings that feature so strongly in young people who have been both victims and victimisers. I will do this by telling the story of my work with one particular young boy, Alex, and the journey that we made together, travelling back in time and deep into the interior of his inner world. But before that I will put this work into something of a context by talking a little about the meaning and prevalence of sexually harmful behaviour amongst the younger population and then touch briefly upon some of the theory that underpins the practice of Narrative Play Therapy.

Sexually harmful behaviour can be defined as 'a wide range of behaviours that are not part of the child's normal sexual exploration and development. This can range from sexually aggressive language to indecent exposure through to rape. It covers both the forcing or coercing of another person into the watching or taking part in inappropriate or harmful sexual behaviour' (NSPCC 2009). Studies indicate that something between 25 and 40 per cent of all alleged sexual abuse involves young perpetrators (Cawson *et al.* 2000; Horne *et al.* 1991; Kelly, Regan and Burton 1991; Morrison 1999). Of course many of the children who are referred to our service are under the age of criminal responsibility and do not feature in the majority of research or statistics that have sought to ascertain the prevalence of sexual abuse carried out by young people. Clearly, as the figures suggest, we are talking about a very significant number of young people who are displaying harmful sexual behaviour from an early age, but it is really only over recent years that the scale of this issue has been fully recognised, along with the development of appropriate assessment and treatment services. Early intervention in this area is critical and play therapy, alongside other treatment approaches, can be a valuable and effective treatment intervention in enabling children to begin to manage the very complex feelings that underpin their offending behaviour. Without early intervention, children may develop fixed entrenched behavioural patterns and dominant internalised narratives that may ultimately provide a pathway into adult sexual offending. However, it is also important to state that available evidence indicates that only a small percentage of young people who display sexually harmful behaviour go onto sexually offend as an adult (Glasser, Kolvin and Campbell 2001).

It is perhaps important also to say a few words on the subject of terminology, as this has been a subject of some debate and can have significant implications regarding the negative labelling of children. It is not uncommon for children with sexual behavioural problems to be viewed as 'embryonic paedophiles' 'or 'young abusers' and it is the responsibility of all those working with these young people to challenge some of the pervasive myths that can be generated within this area. As Pithers and Gray (1998) so succinctly stated, 'labelling these children in a manner that even remotely implies that they may have a lifelong problem with sexual assaultiveness and that denies their potential to make amazing contributions to the social good is simply wrong and should never be done'. Throughout this chapter I will use the term 'children and young people who display sexually harmful behaviour'. Rather than labelling the child this term aims to identify the specific behaviour that is harmful, both to the perpetrator and victim of such behaviour.

Traditionally, the greater extent of treatment services for young people displaying sexually harmful behaviour has trickled down from work with adult sex offenders, the nature of which has drawn heavily upon a cognitive-behavioural methodology that seeks to identify and modify the cognitive distortions that can establish and reinforce fixed, repetitive patterns and cycles of sexual offending behaviour (Finkelhor 1984; Lane 1991). Whilst this approach can be effective and clearly has its place, it carries its own prevailing narratives around the need for offenders to experience guilt, responsibility, remorse, shame and victim empathy. Of course, these qualities are significant markers in the evaluation of risk but for many children and young people, who have traumatic histories, this form of structured cognitive, behavioural and primarily verbal therapy may not always be the most appropriate. Indeed, the therapeutic needs of these children are complex and more often than not their sexualised behaviour is merely one part of a much wider picture, for example trauma, domestic abuse, multiple placements and disrupted attachments. Many of the children and young people referred to our service are overwhelmed by an intense sense of anxiety and shame to the point that they struggle to verbalise their feelings.

So when considering appropriate treatment approaches, it is important to acknowledge that the causes of sexually harmful behaviour are multifaceted and complex and include developmental, physiological, cultural, ecological and psychological factors. Within this context, intervention approaches need to address the entirety of the child's experience, taking into account their socio-cultural and family contexts, the needs of carers and parents and also be developmentally appropriate and based upon sound, age-appropriate assessment. Within this, it is also important that the child's own experiences of abuse and victimisation, sexual and otherwise, are taken into account. The notion of trying to 'fix' just one aspect of a child's sexual behaviour without addressing the underlying causes is always, in my view, going to be limited in outcome. Whilst then, sex-offence specific and cognitive/behavioural work may be the most appropriate approach for some young people, it has been our experience that a non-verbal, arts and play therapy based approach can also be a very effective form of therapeutic intervention.

Narrative Play Therapy is about the use of externalised play narratives, facilitated through the symbolic and metaphorical nature of children's play. It enables a degree of emotional, aesthetic distance through a process of externalisation so that the overwhelming or intolerable feelings are projected onto objects and into stories and dramatic enactments. In this sense, it is no longer about the internalised 'bad parts' of themselves but something 'out there' with which they can play and control, so protecting their necessary defensive strategies. Through story and metaphor children can engage with parts of themselves, within the safety of a therapeutic relationship and in a way that does not threaten to overwhelm their very fragile sense of being.

Narrative Play Therapy draws much upon the notion of a reflexive stance to therapy, a position that is influenced by the work of the narrative therapists like Anderson (1992), Hoffman (1992) and White and Epston (1990) amongst others. The term 'reflexive' in this sense alludes to the idea of something 'folding back upon itself', a circular process akin to Linesch's (1994) model of the 'hermeneutic spiral' – a concept that reflects the 'unending dialectical process of understanding'. In this sense, the relationship between therapist and client facilitates the emergence of a co-construction of meaning, providing the basis for new meaning to emerge alongside the potential for change.

An understanding of the notion of narrative and specifically a narrative model of identity is offered by Lax, who stated: 'The narrative view holds that it is the process of developing a story about one's life that becomes the basis of all identity and thus challenges any underlying concept of a unified or stable self' (1992, p.71). So, through narrative, we shape the world in which we live, creating our own subjective realities within a social community of others. Lax proposes that narrative identity, our storied sense of self, is created not only through our discourse with other but is our discourse with others – 'we reveal ourselves in every moment of interaction through the ongoing narratives that we maintain with others'.

Within a narrative model of play therapy children create stories about themselves and those around them within the context of the therapeutic relationship.

> Play Therapy in this sense is about the facilitation of a child's narrative identity so that they are enabled to explore relationships, both positive and abusive, through the symbolic and metaphorical imagery that is co-constructed during the process of their play. Play is also a healing process, and the healing narratives become embedded within the relationship between child and therapist and allow both to begin to sequence, order and make sense of the complex, dualistic feelings that are such a feature of the victim/victimiser dichotomy. (Le Vay 2005, p.254)

The reasons why children display sexually harmful behaviour are complex and more often than not the result of multiple factors. The majority of young people referred to our service have been victims of abuse, not just sexual abuse but also of physical, emotional abuse and neglect. Children's early histories and experiences of victimisation are key to understanding why they might be displaying problematic behaviour in the present. For children who have been sexually abused their behaviour might be viewed as 'sexually reactive', in the sense that it is a physical, emotional and psychological response to their own experience of abuse and is being acted out within the context of their social relationships. For children who have experienced early neglect, their sexualised behaviour might be more about the need for comfort, self-soothing and self-regulation, for example children who might compulsively masturbate.

Children who have experienced traumatic victimisation are often overwhelmed by confusing, unbearable and intolerable feelings and one way to manage these feelings is to project them onto other children, through acts of abuse. The identification with the role of aggressor and the internalisation of the abuser role may enable the child to experience some sense of power and control and achieve temporary relief from feelings of helplessness. Finkelhor and Browne's 'Traumagenic Model' (1986) and Bentovim and Kinston's 'Cyclical Dynamic/Systemic Model' (1991) are both helpful psychodynamic models for understanding why some children, who have experienced abuse and trauma, will go on to abuse others. As Bentovim states, 'the compulsion to act rather than experience and digest, is a characteristic of both abusers and the abused. Traumatic patterns of dissociation and addictive repetition of abuse is a characteristic phenomenon, which occurs in the face of unbearable levels of anxiety and helplessness' (Bentovim 1993, p.15).

There are many other factors that may contribute to a child displaying sexually harmful behaviour, for example discontinuity of care and disturbed attachment histories. Research also indicates that exposure to domestic abuse is one of the most significant contributory factors (Skuse et al. 1997) and it is easy to see how early experiences of parental violence, inter-personal and often sexualised adult aggression will impact upon a child, especially at the point of puberty and pre-adolescence, when their emerging sense of sexuality is underpinned by an aggressive and fearful internalised world. There are also some very specific issues regarding children with learning disabilities who display sexually harmful behaviour, for example in relation to developmental issues, the need for educative support and difficulties around inter-personal dynamics. Children with learning disabilities are if anything over-represented in terms of referrals regarding sexualised behaviour and it is important to consider why this might be. These young people are often isolated and marginalised, sometimes infantilised by the community around them and also, of course, very vulnerable to abuse themselves. Some of the societal issues around child sexuality discussed earlier are perhaps compounded for children with learning disabilities and they often have very limited opportunities for sexual expression.

As stated then, the contributory factors for sexually harmful behaviour are complex. But, clearly, this behaviour is never simply about sex. It is about anger, anxiety, envy, control and a host of other complex feelings and the key to engaging, assessing and treating these children and young people is to understand their behaviour within the context of their overall life experience.

Alex's story

Alex was a 12-year-old boy who had been placed in foster care at the age of seven as a consequence of the chronic abuse and trauma he had experienced as a young child. His father left when he was very young and his mother struggled with drug and alcohol addiction and associated mental health difficulties. Whilst his mother clearly loved Alex and cared for him as best she could, case files documented a relentless account of traumatic neglect and abuse, including Alex being sexually abused by one of his mother's boyfriends and witnessing the rape of his mother when he was around five years old.

Alex was referred to our service following his sexual abuse of a younger child within his foster placement, as well as concerns from school about aspects of his behaviour. His foster mother also disclosed that Alex had been taking her underwear, soiling and using it to masturbate with and hiding it in his room, sometimes along with knives that he had taken from the kitchen. Understandably, this disturbed sexualised and somewhat fetishistic behaviour left the foster mother feeling deeply anxious and she spoke of her feelings of shock and disgust, as well as the sense of herself being 'soiled' by Alex's actions, to the point that she was unsure whether she could continue to care for him. Following his referral, I worked with Alex for around a year, involving individual, weekly therapy sessions. Alongside this work, support was also provided to the foster mother as well as consultation to the wider professional network. However, for the purpose of this chapter I will essentially be focusing upon the therapeutic process inside the playroom.

Within the context of his history, Alex's experience of trauma cannot be separated from his harmful sexual behaviour; they are both parts of the same entangled narrative threads of his experience, one an expression of the other. Alex was spending long periods on his own in his room, cutting himself off from the rest of his foster family and losing himself in fantasy and dissociation; perhaps as Levine (1997) might say, 'an isolated, lifeless world of private obsessions' (cited in Lahad 2005, p.136). Lahad (2005) described trauma as a 'subjective experience of inner terror' (p.135) and was interested in the notion of daydreaming, dissociation and fantasy as aspects of how the traumatised mind seeks to protect itself. There was a sense that Alex, in a deeply troubling and problematic way, was seeking to manage some very overwhelming feelings.

Alex was unable to find words to describe these feelings, let alone talk about the behaviour that was causing so much concern. His narrative identity, his 'self-story', was underpinned by intense feelings of anxiety, mistrust, anger and, most of all, shame, which meant that he was unwilling and most likely unable to talk about his behaviour on any kind of conscious, cognitive level. Indeed, I am not sure that Alex himself understood his behaviour on any kind of rational level and why he felt the way he did. For young people like Alex, the experience of being both a victim and victimiser is inextricably linked, entwined together in narrative threads so knotted that it is hard to know where one ends and the other begins.

Erikson talked about shame as a form of internalised rage. 'He who is ashamed would like to force the world not to look at him, not to notice his exposure. He would like to destroy the eyes of the world. Instead he must wish for his own invisibility' (1977, p.227). This is the shame of both the abused and the abuser. As we sat together in the playroom for the first time, coat drawn up around him and hood pulled down over his eyes, Alex sought to hide from me in the face of his own shame, wishing himself (and probably myself) invisible. And as he perched precariously on the edge of his chair, ready to run and anxiously cracking his knuckles, the sensation of trauma in the room was palpable as the neurological tide of adrenaline and cortisol ebbed and flowed, threatening to engulf us both.

In the face of this intense anxiety I recall my own feelings of helplessness, my words feeling punitive and piercing as they threatened to breach Alex's fragile defences. Like being lost in the woods, the temptation for the therapist in these situations is to run ever faster, searching for a way out but only ever losing oneself more and more in the process. As I write this, I am reminded of the story recounted by Ann Cattanach (2008) about the hungry elephant that found a tender palm by the edge of a deep swamp. In his eagerness to eat the food the elephant dropped the palm heart into the water and the more he thrashed around with his trunk the more he was blinded by the mud that was stirred up in the thick swamp. A little frog, sitting on a lily pad, called out to the elephant – 'listen'. The elephant didn't hear and thrashed at the water even harder. The frog called out again – 'listen' – and this time the elephant heard the frog and stood perfectly still, curious, and as he stood the water gently cleared and the elephant found and ate the tender palm.

. Like the elephant, I could feel myself beginning to 'thrash around', trying to work harder in the face of Alex's frozen anxiety but only muddying the waters further. As Samuels (2006) said, sometimes as therapists we can try too hard to effect change; sometimes we just need to make contact with 'what is'. And so I reflected upon what was happening in the room, Alex cracking his knuckles, the sound they made, the physical sensation, whether it hurt and harmed his fingers and also how his actions made me feel physically. I am not sure if I was really aware of it consciously at the time, but on reflection there was perhaps something about talking about Alex's physical process that connected with his experience of trauma and how these feelings can be experienced and held at a bodily level. He was unable to receive any kind of cognitive reflection but by connecting on a physical level our process was much more about attunement and emotional regulation; a physical way of connecting that helped reduce the anxiety he was experiencing.

Alex told me that nothing ever really hurts him, that he doesn't really feel pain and proceeded to show me how he could crack his wrists, nose, ankles and even neck, enjoying the somewhat winced response he drew from me. We talked about the idea of being 'double-jointed' and about escapologists like Harry Houdini and the feats of physical endurance performed by David Blaine. This led us into a conversation about the accidents and injuries that he has had over the years, Alex showing me numerous scars caused by jumping off a high wall or cutting himself on a piece of rusty wire as a young child. I had a couple of small marks on my hand and lower arm that I showed to Alex and we joked about how we were like Richard Dreyfuss and Robert Shaw in the scene from *Jaws* where they compare their shark-inflicted battle scars. On reflection, I wondered about my decision to point out my own 'scars' to Alex. Why had I allowed myself to do this? What kind of boundary transgression was this or was it one at all? What would my supervisor say? Self-disclosure, or the 'use of self' within play therapy is perhaps another story in its own right, but essentially it needs to be understood within the context of a therapeutic intervention. In this sense, and in the moment of the session,

I think it was about connection and collaboration, of finding a way to exist together, a point where I could momentarily join Alex in his story. As Alex showed me his battle scars, going right back to when he used to live at home with his mother, a narrative developed (or more to the point, was constructed between us) about aspects of his childhood, about fear and fearlessness, injury, risk, the tolerance of pain and ultimately the notion of feeling unprotected and uncared for. The natural inclination to story personal experience is an integral part of the human condition and in our own way Alex and myself had begun to find a way to put some words around his intense feelings of shame and vulnerability and to enable him to tell something of a story about the pain of growing up.

In the following session Alex again sat perched on the edge of his chair, shielded from me by his coat and hood, the intimacy of our presence together seemingly unbearable. He sipped water from a glass and I had a fantasy of him hurling it against the wall in rage, his own repressed anger spilling out into myself, leaving us both struggling to manage something that felt barely containable. I had a feeling that if Alex left the room at this point I would be unlikely ever to see him again and so I took a risk and moved over to the sand-tray and suggested that he might like to use the sand, showing him the various trays of objects that sat beneath the tray. To my relief, Alex moved to the sand-tray, sat on a beanbag and began to look at some of the objects, toys and shells. I wondered if he might like to use the objects to create a landscape or a world and he started to select and place objects into the sand-tray, beginning with a shark that he buried under the sand (making me think a little about our scene from *Jaws* in the previous session). It was a cautious and hesitant few minutes, but out of his struggle to find words Alex had himself taken a risk and begun to play. When he had finished, I wondered whether there was a story to be told about the world he had created and so he dictated his story to me.

> The sand shark lived under the sand. Suddenly, it burst out of the sand into the open. There was a person who had been exploring the caves underground. His leg was sticking out of the sand. There was a bear cub close by and it became frightened by the shark and ran away. The bear found its brother and they stood watching the shark, afraid to move. There was a friendly dog that kept watch for them.
>
> A family of polar bears, a mother and her two cubs, came along and started drinking from the pond. They were not frightened

of the shark. Then the shark sank back beneath the sand and a monster suddenly burst out. It had eaten most of the man who had been exploring the caves and just his leg was sticking out of the monster's mouth. An elephant walked into the land. It was injured, but nobody knew how.

I was curious about this story; about the notion of exploration and the dangers of travelling too far into this subterranean world. I wondered what this might mean in terms of Alex's internal world and my own role as therapist, an explorer of sorts. The symbolism of trauma and pain were also very present within the story, the bear–child frozen with fear and the injured elephant, as well as the symbolism of the dog, a benign protector. Through sandplay and narrative Alex was able to begin to externalise and make visible some of the powerful feelings that dominated his world, feelings that he was not able to verbalise or express in any kind of cognitive way. The play therapy space is a transitional space, both real and imagined, in which unconscious feelings are projected onto the play objects, contained within narrative structures and visual imagery, and held through the relationship with the therapist and safety of the play space. Through the safety of symbolism and aesthetic distance, Alex could engage with both the abused and abusive parts of himself but in a way that didn't threaten to overwhelm him.

Alex continued to use sandplay now and again throughout our work together and I would be curious about the stories contained in his worlds. Unusually he sometimes liked to dictate the stories to me, word for word. There is a regressive quality to sandplay that taps deep into the unconscious and this is the place that Alex would go to during these sessions (Figure 8.1).

Deep underground in a monster's lair there were four sacred stones warning that anyone who pushed the stones in the correct order would wake up the beast. The ancient gods who put the stones in place built a fence surrounding the beast's pit. There was only one main entrance into the pit and two semi-entrances through gates in the fence.

A World War II bomber plane had crashed in through the roof of the cave and was half buried in the ground. One man had already been devoured by the beast and all that was left of him was an arm sticking out of the ground. An expedition of cave explorers had gone down to the cave a year and a half before. Twelve men had gone down and 11 had been devoured by the beast. One man had fought for his life against the huge demonic destroyer. The demon had bitten off his left leg.

The men escaped from part of the demon's pit but when they got close to one of the semi-entrances the beast burst out of a creature-made mound. The man crawled to the huge main gates leading out of the pit. When he was about ten inches away, the great stone door closed.

Figure 8.1 The monster's lair

Through the powerful and unconscious process of sandplay I had the strong sense that we were journeying into the interior of Alex's world, the place where he was literally battling his demons. And the warning signs were ever-present, that any explorers who venturing too far into this subterranean world might not live to tell the tale. Alex's anxiety was clear, his own fragile capacity to survive the darker places of his internal world. Alvarez (1992) talks of the need for children to be able to forget their experiences of trauma before they can safely begin to remember. Alex was not able to verbalise his fears at this stage in his therapy, but through the process of sandplay and the metaphor of story, he was beginning to be able to conjure with fragments of his experience, to begin to remember within the safety of symbolic distance and through being 'held' by the therapeutic relationship. So often in this work I am reminded of the story of Theseus and the Minotaur, and of Ariadne who spun the ball of red fleece that enabled Theseus to slay the Minotaur and find his way successfully back out of the labyrinth. So much of the therapy process is about 'holding and being held' – as I hold the thread for Alex so I am held by my own supervisor as she is by hers, much like the cave explorers in Alex's story; tied together by the safety rope as they venture into uncharted territory.

Often within Alex's play therapy, we played versions of the Squiggle Game and over time it became a regular feature at the beginning of the sessions, a collaborative, playful process that seemed to ease Alex's transition from the 'outside world' and into the therapeutic space. It felt very much a relational activity, as we found a way of being together that didn't provoke too much anxiety. He enjoyed creating ever-harder scribbles and sliding them across to me with mock disdain, challenging my capacity to create something from the tangle of lines as if it were a puzzle I had to solve. From these squiggles emerged myriad versions of riddles, codes, ciphers, mazes and secret languages, much like the secret combination of 'sacred stones' in Alex's sand-world, and I increasingly experienced my own role as something of a code-breaker, wondering whether I would ever find the right combination.

After one session of the Squiggle Game, Alex began turning the various shapes left behind on the paper into different creatures and being curious, I wondered about these creatures, what they were like, how they survived and where they lived. Alex explained that one of them was a deep-sea anglerfish that 'lured' in its prey with pretend 'bait'. Alex was interested in the kind of life that might exist at the very bottom of the sea, where he said there was no sunlight and the pressure was so great that any creature would die were it to be brought up to the surface. Alex said that it would be a very difficult 'area to research' and as he talked I wondered about this place – dark, cold and unknown. Like his sandplay, there was a powerful metaphoric narrative at play that to my mind connected strongly with the dark waters of Alex's own unconscious, the place of his fantasies, fears, compulsions and the place that linked very much with his own identity as both a victim and victimiser, his disturbed masturbatory fantasies, sexualised behaviour and aggressive maternal feelings that were being played out towards his foster mother. Again, these feelings were far too difficult for Alex to talk about at this time and to have attempted to get him to do so would have only led him to feel more anxious and emotionally defended. But the symbolism of the images and stories that emerged from our 'squiggles' together provided a way in which Alex could begin to externalise his feelings whilst keeping his sense of self intact.

As we talked about this strange underwater world Alex told me that we, humans, were 70 per cent water and I wondered about the meaning of his words, what he might have been telling me in his own, coded way. That he was part of this world perhaps? That it was a part of him? Of us? I reflected gently with Alex upon the 'unknown' creatures that seemed to be present for him and how his stories about the underwater world reminded me of his sandplay stories. Increasingly, I wondered about Alex's fantasy world, the periods of withdrawal into his bedroom, disturbed sexual thoughts and hidden knives (probably more as a source of protection than any kind of threat). Interestingly Levine (1997) talked about fantasy as a kind of failure of imagination, making a clear distinction between the two. Levine says that fantasy refers to the 'kind of daydreaming that walls the person up in his or her internal world and leads to no form of doing. Imagination, on the other hand, is the means by which we reach out and connect with otherness' (p.33). Play therapy is about active imagination, not fantasy, a place of creative transformation where Levine's 'isolated, lifeless world of private obsessions' instead becomes a place of connection, a place where the meaning and value of a relationship can be discovered through play.

More creatures emerged from the squiggles and I again wondered about them aloud with Alex, asking little questions to develop a narrative, to find out what the story was about these strange beings. One of them was called 'Spike'. It had spikes on its back and lots of teeth – pointed and blunt. I reflected that it seemed like Spike would be able to protect itself if need be, perhaps from danger, but that it also looked like it could also attack if it had to. Alex said that it might be schizophrenic. 'Oh,' I said. 'So there might be different sides to it, frightened and dangerous.' Alex was able to acknowledge these reflections as we stayed within the metaphor. I wondered about Spike's strange teeth and Alex said the blunt teeth were passive and the sharp teeth were aggressive. I was very curious about Alex's language; so clinical and adult, as if he himself were making a diagnosis of this unusual creature. We talked a little about how difficult and scary it might be if one had to approach a creature like Spike. It seemed unpredictable, so that you could never be sure what it might do, or when or how. It would be difficult to know whether it was safe or dangerous. I wondered if Alex had ever met something like Spike – he laughed anxiously and said, 'I don't know'. Breaking the metaphor and making a link with Alex's 'real' world was too difficult. But the metaphorical narrative of this creature made me think about both Alex and his experience of his mother, a woman who struggled with drug and alcohol addiction and issues around her mental health. Alex was a bright boy with a keen interest in the world around him. He knew about his mother's struggles and what they meant for him and in a sense perhaps this creature was a composite of the both of them.

Other creatures appeared on the paper, like 'Blob' which Alex explained was a 'passive' animal, looking frightened and scared. In the sessions stories appeared fleetingly about all these creatures but Alex took time to colour them in and then photograph them for his box (Figure 8.2). These creatures were important, an expression of Alex's internal world – the seabed or the subterranean cave – and the symbolism of these metaphoric narratives was poignant. The magic of the therapeutic space is that it is both real and not real; the creatures exist in a temporal void – a psychic space – and as I sat with Alex there was a shared but unspoken and half-known sense of the meaning of these creatures and of the stories that he told about them.

Figure 8.2 Spike and Blob

As Alex's sessions continued he began to bring other, more concrete stories into the playroom. We spent two sessions talking about Batman, one of many characters that held a fascination for Alex, not in a simplistic sense but more as a deep fascination with the dark mythology of the character, and in particular the 'backstory' about Batman's childhood and the trauma that he experienced as a child and which made him into the flawed, troubled hero of Gotham City. It seemed clear that the narrative of this character held a significance for Alex, albeit on an unconscious level, and I felt truly engaged as he took me back over the course of Batman's life, revealing an encylopaedic knowledge of the story. During another session, Alex recounted in detail the plot of a film he had seen, called *The Butterfly Effect*. Essentially, the film is a dark psychological/paranormal tale of a young man with suppressed memories of his very abusive childhood. As he grows up he experiences blackouts and flashbacks arising from childhood and then, as he begins to remember, he finds a way to recall these memories and travel back in time to try and alter and undo the trauma of the past. Like Batman, it was a story that gripped Alex and I was struck by the metaphorical re-working of childhood trauma that Alex was bringing to his therapy sessions. Following his elaborate account of *The Butterfly Effect* I wondered with Alex what he might do if he could travel back in time like the character in the film. He said he would go back and talk to himself – about what he knew now about his parents. The stories were less distanced now, closer to reality, but I felt that it was only through the symbolic process of the sandplay, drawing and, ultimately, the stories within his play that Alex was able to make these forays back in time to versions of his own childhood.

Over the course of time, Alex's narratives became increasingly less distanced and more concrete until, following one of our usual rounds of Squiggle and code-breaking games he began to draw maps of the area in which he used to live as a child. He told me stories of going on day trips with his mother, holding her hand as they caught the train. Later he drew pictures of the outside of his house and the layout of the driveway and immediate neighbourhood. His narrative accounts had now firmly moved from the symbolic and metaphorical to the reality of his childhood memories and there was a clear sense of a mist gently lifting, allowing him to see something that for so long had been shrouded in fear, anxiety and shame. It was if, having been allowed to forget, Alex was indeed able to slowly begin to remember.

A couple of weeks later I met with Alex for his session and he sat with a beanbag on his lap, feeling the little polystyrene balls inside. I commented upon his curiosity about the inside of the beanbag and he told me that he had once lost a little toy inside one, just like this. I remembered that he had mentioned this once before and invited Alex to tell the story again. He said that when he lived at home with his mother he was playing with a little metal lorry and it disappeared amongst all the thousands of tiny polystyrene balls and he couldn't remember ever finding it again. There was something very poignant about this theme of 'the search for something lost' and the notion of the beanbag, womb-like and maternal perhaps but also about something deeply internal in relation to Alex himself. I made a reflection about things from his childhood that had been lost and Alex responded by telling me that he could remember the exact layout of the house he used to live in with his mother. He started to describe it and then began to draw it out on paper, adding more and more details as he remembered them.

As he drew Alex recounted memories that came to him and I was taken aback by the level and detail of Alex's recall. It was as if within the intensity of his early experiences, within all the anxiety, vigilance and hyper-arousal, the images had become imprinted in his mind, seared into his memory. Alex recalled good memories of his parents but also spoke about his mother's drinking and drug use, how he used to hide the bottles in the garden so that she couldn't find them and of finding her slumped on the floor, unconscious, so he was terrified she was dead.

The stories tumbled out of Alex as if he really had found something that had been lost inside him, like the little lorry inside the beanbag, or that perhaps together, after all these weeks, we had found the right combination to unlock these hidden parts of himself. Alex was able to connect with the intense feelings of anger he held towards his mother, the anger of being left unprotected, the anger about her addictions and the anger that she could have another child whilst he languished in the care system. Of course, Alex also loved his mother and was fiercely loyal towards her and as a child his survival was dependent upon her. This is the curse of Winnicott's 'false self' (1960), Alex protecting the image of a 'good enough' mother at the expense of his own.

Toward the end of Alex's therapy, without any prompting, he chose to use the sand one final time. He created a scene that involved a dinosaur attacking a giraffe, whilst a little figure hid in the leaves of a nearby tree, watching (Figure 8.3). I wondered aloud with Alex about the scene he had created and he told me about a time when he had been walking back from the train station with his mother and a man had followed them and then sexually attacked his mother whilst he ran away and hid in a tree. My guess was that this was the incident of Alex witnessing the rape of his mother that was recorded in the case files. Perhaps now Alex had gone back as far as he could, but the fact that he had needed and wanted to show me what had happened all those years ago, that I could be a witness to this terrible crime just as he was, was a testament of the courageous journey he had made.

Figure 8.3 Alex's final sandplay

As I have hoped to convey in this account of Alex's therapy, the storying of experience is a core element of the human condition, both on an interpersonal and intrapersonal level. From the frightened young boy who first sat in the therapy room, huddled in his coat and perched tentatively on the edge of the chair, Alex had been able to make stories through his play and embark upon a long journey deep into his interior world, to a place filled with feelings of shame, anxiety, anger and hurt. But he was also able to make the journey out again and begin to link these feelings to his relationships in the outside world. Research indicates that the more coherent and organised an account an individual creates in relation to past trauma the greater the likelihood of beneficial gains (Pennebaker and Seagal 1999) and indeed that the creation of a coherent story around an experience of trauma and integrating this into one's sense of self-representation is fundamental to successful interventions regarding post traumatic stress (Brewin, Dalgleish and Joseph 1996; Herman 1992; Van der Kolk and Fisler 1995). Through a process of Narrative Play Therapy, Alex was able to engage in a process of story-telling; metaphoric narratives that were emotionally distanced enough to protect his fragile sense of self. And through this process he was able to safely remember and place these memories in a narrative context; to sequence, order and place his experiences in a way that made some kind of sense.

The disturbed sexualised behaviour that Alex was displaying within his foster placement seemed linked to very early feelings of anger, envy and the need for comfort, intimacy and indeed the presence of a mother figure. As a young adolescent, these feelings perhaps became enmeshed with Alex's developing sexuality and expressed in fixated, obsessive and problematic ways. From a Kleinian perspective, this behaviour might be understood as having its roots in disturbed object relations in early life, later becoming re-enacted in a sexually distorted manner. But from whatever language one might choose to describe it, it was clear that Alex's disturbed sexualised behaviour had its roots in his early childhood experiences. But he was able to make the connections between his unexpressed anger towards his mother and the displaced anger towards his foster mother. We were finally able to talk about his sexually harmful behaviour and, most importantly, Alex was able to make links between his thoughts, feelings and actions.

The therapeutic process was not an easy journey and there were many twists and turns along the way. At one stage Alex expressed some worrying suicidal thoughts and feelings and this was a challenge to our relationship due to my need to take these concerns outside of the room. The relationship between Alex and his foster mother got to the stage where it was not retrievable and so he moved to live with another foster carer, but this was managed in a planned way and worked out well for Alex. Our own work together ended at a point when Alex was managing well, settled in his new placement and making plans for a college placement. In many ways I was indeed Ariadne to Alex's Theseus, as he found his way into the heart of the labyrinth, fought the Minotaur and found his way back again. And it was through a process of Narrative Play Therapy that Alex was able to begin to make sense of his past and construct some form of coherent story, a narrative thread that he could hold onto. Young people like Alex so often cannot find the words to describe the overwhelming nature of their experiences, but he found another way to tell his story and whilst I am under no illusion that Alex will not have many more battles to fight I can only hope that this experience has given him some strength along the way.

References

Alvarez, A. (1992) *Live Company: Psychoanalytic Psychotherapy with Autistic, Borderline, Deprived and Abused Children*. London: Routledge.

Anderson, T. (1992) 'Reflection on Reflecting with Families.' In J.K. Gergen and S. McNamee (eds) *Therapy as Social Construction*. London: Sage.

Bentovim, A. (1993) 'Children and Young People as Abusers.' In A. Hollows and H. Armstrong (eds) *Children and Young People as Abusers: An Agenda for Action.* London: National Children's Bureau.

Bentovim, A. and Kinston, W. (1991) 'Focal Family Therapy.' In A. Gurman and D. Kniskern (eds) *Handbook of Family Therapy.* New York: Basic Books.

Brewin, C.R., Dalgleish, T. and Joseph, S. (1996) 'A dual representation theory of posttraumatic stress disorder.' *Psychological Review 103,* 670–686.

Cattanach, A. (2008) *Narrative Approaches in Play with Children.* London: Jessica Kingsley Publishers.

Cawson, P., Wattam, C., Brooker, S. and Kelly, G. (2000) *Child Maltreatment in the United Kingdom: A Study of the Prevalence of Child Abuse and Neglect.* London: NSPCC.

Erikson, E. (1977) *Childhood and Society,* 2nd edn. St Albans: Triad/Paladin.

Finkelhor, D. (1984) *Child Sexual Abuse: New Theory and Research.* New York: Free Press.

Finkelhor, D. and Browne, A. (1986) 'Initial and Long-Term Effects: A Conceptual Framework.' In D. Finkelhor (ed.) *A Sourcebook on Child Sexual Abuse.* Newbury Park, CA and London: Sage.

Glasser, M., Kolvin, I. and Campbell, D. (2001) 'Cycle of child sexual abuse: Links between being a victim and becoming a perpetrator.' *British Journal of Psychiatry 179,* 6, 482–494.

Herman, J.L. (1992) *Trauma and Recovery.* New York: Basic Books.

Hoffman, L. (1992) ' A Reflexive Stance for Family Therapy.' In J.K. Gergen and S. McNamee (eds) *Therapy as Social Construction.* London: Sage.

Horne, L., Glasgow, D., Cox, A. and Calam, R. (1991) 'Sexual abuse of children by children.' *Journal of Child Law 3,* 4, 147–151.

Kelly, L., Regan, L. and Burton, S. (1991) *An Exploratory Study of the Prevalence of Sexual Abuse in a Sample of 16–21 Year Olds.* London: Polytechnic of North London, Child Abuse Studies Unit.

Lahad, M. (2005) 'Transcending into Fantastic Reality: Story Making with Children in Crisis.' In C. Schaefer, J. McCormick and A. Ohnogi (eds) *International Handbook of Play Therapy: Advances in Assessment, Theory, Research and Practice.* Lanham, MD: Jason Aronson.

Lane, S. (1991) 'The Sexual Abuse Cycle.' In G. Ryan and S. Lane (eds) *Juvenile Sexual Offending: Causes, Consequences and Correction.* New York: Lexington.

Lax, W.D. (1992) 'Postmodern Thinking in a Clinical Practice.' In J.K. Gergen and S. McNamee (eds) *Therapy as Social Construction.* London: Sage.

Le Vay, D. (2005) 'Little Monsters: Play Therapy for Children with Sexually Problematic Behaviour.' In C. Schaefer, J. McCormick and A. Ohnogi (eds) *The International Handbook of Play Therapy.* Lanham, MD: Jason Aronson.

Levine, S.K. (1997) *Poiesis: The Language of Psychology and the Speech of the Soul.* London: Jessica Kingsley Publishers.

Linesch, D. (1994) 'Interpretation in Art Therapy Research and Practice: The Hermeneutic Circle.' *Arts in Psychotherapy 3,* 185–195.

Morrison, T. (1999) 'Is There a Strategy Out There?' In M. Erooga and H. Masson (eds) *Children and Young People Who Sexually Abuse Others: Challenges and Responses.* London: Routledge.

NSPCC (2009) *Children and Young People Who Display Sexually Harmful Behaviour.* Available at www.nspcc.org.uk/inform/research/briefings/sexuallyharmfulbehaviour_wda48213.html, accessed on 1 April 2011.

Pithers, W.D. and Gray, A. (1998) 'The other half of the story: Children with sexual behaviour problems.' *Psychology, Public Policy and Law 4,* 1–2, 200–217.

Pennebaker, J.W. and Seagal, J.D. (1999) 'Forming a story: The health benefits of narrative.' *Journal of Clinical Psychology 55,* 1243–1254.

Samuels, J. (2006) Lecture Seminar. Institute of Arts in Therapy and Education (unpublished).

Skuse, D. *et al.* (1997) cited in A. Bentovim and B. Williams (1998) 'Children and adolescents: victims who become perpetrators.' *Advances in Psychiatric Treatment 4,* 101–107.

Van der Kolk, B.A. and Fisler, R. (1995) 'Dissociation and the fragmentary nature of traumatic memories: Overview and exploratory study.' *Journal of Traumatic Stress 8,* 505–525.

Winnicott, D.W. (1960) 'Ego Distortion in Terms of True and False Self.' In *The Maturational Process and the Facilitating Environment: Studies in the Theory of Emotional Development.* New York: International UP Inc.

White, M. and Epston, D. (1990) *Narrative Means to Therapeutic Ends.* New York: Norton.

Chapter 9

Narrative Family Play Therapy

Play as a Context for Family and Child Stories to be Told, Heard and Re-authored

Ann Marie John

Introduction and theoretical framework

Lenses

This chapter is a story or construction about my work with families. The story is being created through the lens of a person who is a white middle-aged heterosexual woman who is still connected enough with her student days and Marxism not to admit to calling herself middle class but nevertheless holds many of the privileges associated with the concept. I invite you to think about how this story might be told by a young black male or an Asian lesbian pensioner. I invite you to consider your own lenses and how you would tell this story or indeed your own story of your work. I talk of lenses because they are a key concept to social constructionist and narrative thinking. Hoffman (2004) created the terms to help us understand how our view of the world impacts on how we see and talk about our lives. The context from which a story is told, impacts on what is being told, particularly in relation to the stories that families bring to therapy. It also affects the manner in which the story is heard by the therapist. By using the term 'story' I am immediately placing myself in a narrative tradition because this term developed by White and Epston (1990) assumes that there is little value in trying to establish truth in a story as a retelling of an experience is just one of many stories that can be told. This places narrative therapy in a philosophical position whereby the concept of looking for truths is not helpful and the aims of therapy are more suited to the uncovering of a multiplicity of narratives.

I have described the story of my work as 'Narrative Family Play Therapy' as this seemed to best describe the essence of working with both the family narratives and the stories of individuals within the family in order to find some coherence. However this is, if you like, a working title and is not yet (and might not ever be) at the stage of describing a new model.

The stories told are composites of families I have worked with and do not describe particular families or pieces of work.

Stories and narrative in family therapy

Stories about what should happen in families and child rearing are particularly powerful as they are often created by groups of privileged people and may exclude those who don't conform, for example single parents who have to work and take young babies to nursery.

The philosopher Michel Foucault (1975) referred to these powerful stories as 'discourses' and commented on how they impact on individuals in society. White and Epston (1990) took these ideas further, challenging the idea of how problems are defined, often in blaming and excluding ways. White and Epston (1990) suggest that families often come to therapy with 'problem saturated stories' suggesting that the role of the therapist is a 'literary role' to help families re-author their own stories that are non-blaming and which highlight tales of resilience and coping rather than blame and failure. In narrative therapy the therapist might for example help the family by finding what White refers to as 'unique outcomes': examples of stories when the family or individual have been able to cope with the problem or prevent it from happening.

Stories and narrative in play therapy

In the field of play therapy the late and terribly missed Ann Cattanach (1992) adapted the narrative approach to individual work with children, proposing a model of therapy that enabled a child to re-story their experience through play. In taking a social constructionist/narrative position in children's psychological therapy Cattanach created a fundamental shift in the field of child therapy because a narrative model offered an alternative to the deficit model (a model whereby the child was damaged by trauma and needed to have therapy to recover). Instead the narrative model of play therapy allowed for the child's story and identity to be re-worked in play in a modality that the child had control over. In Narrative Play Therapy the therapist must speak the child's language of play. This is important because the telling of the story can happen non-verbally or metaphorically and the child can then maintain their defences. This approach also avoids the risk of the child being re-traumatised by having to tell their story.

Interweaving stories

As a therapist trained in Narrative models in systemic family therapy and Narrative Play Therapy I have over the years developed a practice in which I integrate both approaches. It is not possible for the purposes of this chapter to give an overview of systemic family therapy and there are several excellent texts available (see Burnham 1986; Dallos 2006). However, the concepts of systemic family therapy that I feel are relevant to this chapter and my work are concerned with how patterns of communication and action within the family are organised and how the patterns of organisation contribute to difficulties and problems.

The story of the problem and how it developed between family members is therefore important in considering how to help. Equally important is a view that a problem with one member of the family will affect everyone in the family, so it is helpful that all members of the family need to be included to find helpful solutions.

Dallos (2006) described a similar way of working to my approach, which he calls 'pragmatic' in that it is geared to client needs. Although I initially tried to keep the disciplines separate I have found this impossible and if a session was analysed I would guess it would be difficult to say when I was doing family therapy and when I was doing play therapy, as I am in a way doing both and also something different.

Although this has created questions in terms of interdisciplinary boundaries (particularly with regard to confidentiality between the child and the family) I have worked with these dilemmas rather than remain purist, as I find that the contexts in which I have been working in the UK, particularly Child and Adolescent Mental Health Services (CAMHS), private practice and in the charity sector, require me to be flexible, and in some cases I have been employed because I am able to use different therapeutic modalities creatively.

This approach has therefore been the best fit for me with regards to creating a way of working that is useful, inclusive and accessible for clients. Dallos (2006) points out a number of difficulties with systemic family therapy, one of which is the consideration of the individual in the process in the family. My experience of play therapy and my experience of individual work with adults enable me to address this in my work.

Although Dallos is specifically referring to his work integrating narrative and attachment theory (2006) my position is slightly different in an integration of Narrative Play Therapy and narrative family therapy. I am also interested in integrating individual experiences and family experiences but I see these as an integrating or weaving of narratives.

Of course many practitioners work across disciplines. For instance Wilson (1998) bringing playfulness and creativity into systemic family therapy in order to include the child in the therapeutic process (a critique often made of systemic family therapy) in what he refers to a 'child focussed practice'. Eliana Gil has also developed her own model of Family Play Therapy (1994). However, I have not yet come across a narrative integrative model that fits with my way of working with individual narratives within a family narrative helping to communicate and re-author stories old and new.

Deconstructing family

In this chapter then I aim to show some of the development of my practice and the theoretical frameworks that guide my thinking. Most recently I have been working both in CAMHS and in private practice. I have found these contexts complementary to one another. Since we are thinking in a social constructionist frame it seems important to begin with what current stories are constructed around the meaning of family. Notions and definitions of family come and go but there is no doubt that the nuclear family is now the exception rather than the rule. The change in what constitutes family has been constantly challenged; 'blended families', same sex couples and fertility treatment and surrogacy are just a few developments that challenge us to think about our preconceived notions of family. As families are geographically dispersed friendships have in some ways become the new family as the wonderful term 'families of choice'. Weeks, Heaphy and Donovan (2001) illustrate that the close bonds that we create outside our birth families can be as or more important than those with whom we share genetics.

My most recent experience of social difference was on a visit to Sri Lanka with my family, travelling with friends. On arriving in the capital we visited my friend's nephew's mother in law. We were welcomed as family with coconut water and local delicacies. We were then taken to meet two other nephews and their families, a process which took up most of our day. Culturally there was an expectation that we were part of the family and would be treated as such and perhaps that there were obligations that needed to be fulfilled as a family member compared to where one is in the hierarchy. As I have suggested, powerful discourses or stories regarding what are acceptable ways of how we 'do family', particularly with regards to child rearing, permeate society and the legal framework and statutory services in the UK and it is within this context that CAMHS and indeed private practice are located. Dominant discourses about the meaning of childhood are particularly relevant as a context for family therapy in the UK as there is significant state intervention in family life, particularly in the socialisation process in education. Aries' (1962) classic work is still relevant as a critique of the modern concept of childhood by documenting that historically the concept did not exist in medieval times because even very young children were involved in the production process of work and survival. Narratives about childhood, what it means to be a child and appropriate childcare practices are socially constructed through the media and through social care legislation. Some of these need to be deconstructed when we are working with families or family members who feel blamed or disempowered by stories that don't fit with their experience or exclude them. Narrative Family Play Therapy acknowledges that social discourses impact on families' lives and that families may feel excluded and blamed when they come to therapy.

Approach

Narrative Family Play Therapy then offers an approach that views families as essentially resilient and able to find solutions to their difficulties. Walsh (2006) has written extensively about family resilience and how to help families to build on strengths.

In a similar way to Michael Rutter's concept of psychological resilience in childhood (Rutter 1985), Walsh (2006) asks how some families are able to cope with adversity in a way that others are not. Walsh's research highlights the importance of belief systems in families – their outlook on the world and their beliefs about their abilities to act within the world. Walsh's ideas are similar to those of positive psychology, suggesting that some families view adversity as part of the challenge of everyday life; a positive attitude and belief in coping abilities help to create resilience. Resilient families are also able to make meaning out of working together to deal with difficulties in a way that continues their story of themselves as a strong family. Walsh also comments on the importance of story-telling as a way of communicating and integrating experience within the family and as part of healing rituals and making sense of experience. Part of this process is the way that the organisational elements in the family, the 'rules' that govern behaviour are developed. This aspect of Walsh's thinking fits very well with my experience in therapeutic work of how stories of family behaviour are organised. For example I have found discussions about the rules or stories about what can be said and not said in families often are often a very important part of the therapy. I am interested in the stories that guide communication in the family and what stories can be told by whom and to whom. There is not space here to do justice to Walsh's detailed account of coping with different kinds of difficulties but I would place her work firmly within a social constructionist and narrative frame and fundamental to the principles that guide my work.

I view families coming to therapy as predominantly resilient and able to cope. My position is that sometimes things get stuck and families' narratives become, as Michael White suggests, 'problem saturated'.

At times of change in terms of the family life cycle, families may need to re-group and reconfigure new stories. Sometimes the current family stories may no longer fit the individuals within the family. The therapy process can create a space whereby different members of the family can tell and have stories heard that don't fit with the family narrative.

The stories in the family therefore may need to be recalibrated and rebalanced so that change can be integrated. Play, playfulness and humour often allow for stories to be told that a family might not usually be able to hear. Gregory Bateson (1972), an anthropologist, developed the idea of the family as a system that is self-regulatory. This accounts for why in early family therapy one member of a family's symptom would get better but another member would then develop a new symptom. Bateson (1972) commented that it was important to change the meaning or context to elicit change in a system and play provides a means of communication that can provide this contextual change that allows the unsaid and sometimes the unsayable to be said. Dallos (2006) describes the role of providing a different space for clients as an adjudicator. I prefer the term facilitator, but I have also found that my role as an adult witness that is slightly outside the family allows talking that might not usually happen. I have found that children may find the courage to tell a story that they may not have had the opportunity to have told and heard. The combination of the therapist as an adjudicator and the possibility for play and playfulness provides a context for re-editing the family and individual stories. In the following descriptions of how I go about this work, I have organised sections into referral process, assessment, the Narrative Play Therapy process, endings and evaluation as this is the way in which my thinking is organised in terms of my narrative.

Referral process

I have included the referral process because this is what I refer to as the 'first story' we are told about a family, which may be a form or a phone call. In CAMHS the first story may contain some relevant information but it often doesn't tell us what the family think about the idea of coming for therapy. We also may not know if the family know what has been written about them. We usually learn something of the story of the problem in the referral process. In CAMHS this is often written in terms of one of the children's behaviour; indeed, this is often the only reason why a parent has agreed to ask for or agreed to a service. Moreover the parent or carer may want a solution that doesn't fit with a narrative model, so the idea that the aim of therapy is to integrate or tell stories may not fit with the expectations of a parent wanting a solution to their child's challenging behaviour, for instance, a diagnosis. For example, Jan came with her 14-year-old daughter Meg, as the school had referred Meg for a possible diagnosis of Attention Deficit Disorder (ADD) on account of her impulsive behaviour. It became apparent when I met Meg and her mother that there were great issues of loss in the family and that this was a difficult time in terms of the family life cycle. However, Jan said that she did not want help from a family therapist; she had raised three children herself. In this initial session I was curious about the family's ability to cope with their difficulties and about Meg's abilities to cope, particularly in school where she had been known for impulsive behaviour (throwing chairs and destroying school property and was hence struggling with the prospect of exclusion). As we talked I found many 'unique outcomes' examples of Meg walking away from conflict in school. She explained this in terms of her strong identity as a 'coper' like her mum. I was curious about these and also about the way they seemed to contradict Jan's ideas of Meg as always being a problem. Meg also began to tell a story of how she was struggling with her grandmother's terminal illness, a story that her mother had not heard before as Meg had always presented as tough.

As the family did not want a family therapy service and the screening for ADD was negative there was not much I could offer, yet the family said that the talking had been good and that something had changed between them – they felt stronger together. The first meeting therefore is key to coming to some kind of story about the purpose of the therapy. It is important to mediate between the referrer's and the family story of the 'problem' which is often located within a child.

In private practice descriptions are often looser, as they do not necessarily have to conform to a criteria but the child's behaviour is usually part of the problem story. The child or children in the family often have no idea why they are coming to see a therapist and I usually try to talk with parents about what to tell the child; usually the carer can help with this as they know the child. I usually suggest something about a person who helps families get talking again when they get a bit stuck but I have used all sorts of metaphors, for example a referee who makes the talking fair (useful) in a sporty family, a relationship plumber (things get stuck). However, I often find, despite these conversations, that the family have not spoken to the child or children and so they have no real story of why they are coming for therapy, hence the need to explore this in the first session. Deconstructing the story of the referral and the creating a family story of what the family wants from therapy is an important element of beginning the work that impacts on the future relationship. The first session can be very therapeutic in picking up unheard stories of resilience and also in allowing untold and sometimes painful stories of individuals to be heard.

Assessment

Assessment has many different meanings in different contexts. In my experience of CAMHS assessment means making a clinical decision about which professional discipline/disciplines the most appropriate for the type of problem is/are based on the National Institute for Clinical Excellence (NICE) guidelines and evidence-based practice. While this approach is in some ways in conflict with the idea that professional narratives are stories rather than truth there are ways of making this process useful to the family in a way that clarifies what they want from therapy. In essence the formulating of the problem with the family while information gathering can often be done in a very therapeutic manner as it allows the family members to each tell their stories. I have found that the assessment process for Narrative Family Therapy needs to have certain components in order for the different stories of family members to be told and to understand how family stories are organised between family members. By components I mean different kinds of sessions. Usually the first session is a family session so that it is possible to meet each member of the family on equal terms (each member is a potential client). After this I also have one session with the parent, carer or parental/caring couple to discuss issues that may not be suitable to discuss in front of the child. Here I also make a contract regarding how I share information both with colleagues in outside agencies. If there is a child protection issue or the situation is complex I would usually see the carer/s first. If I feel that carer/s are able to support the child speaking confidentially I also spend some time alone with the identified child and/or children to obtain their view of things. They may raise issues that they wish me to help them discuss in the family. I am also very clear about sharing information practices with parents as this will determine how much the child feels free to speak. In this section I will describe the Family Shield Assessment as this is a major part of how I begin to understand the family in the assessment process and think about how I might be of help to them.

THE FAMILY SHIELD ASSESSMENT

In the family session part of assessment I have adapted Ann Cattanach's shield assessment (1992), developed as a creative tool for assessment for child identity, as an assessment tool to consider family narratives about resilience, and to consider individual narratives that might need attention. I often explain in the first session that they are the experts on their family and I would like to learn a little about how the family works and I invite the family to make a family shield.

The shield is drawn and divided into six sections by myself, adults or the children depending on abilities and preference.

Section 1 – A family emblem

I refer to coats of arms held by families in the olden days and for the first task I ask the family to choose an animal as an emblem of their family and draw/write or make a symbol about it in the first section. This question can sometimes also help to define what needs changing. For example, one family I worked with described the family animal as a dragon, always fighting and shouting. One of the children in the family wanted this to be a whale which would be peaceful and quiet. However, in looking for new stories I wondered was there anything about the dragon they liked and they felt that the dragon was strong and proud and would fight for the family as well as being a pain.

This process also engages the family in a collaborative activity in which they may need to negotiate. It helps me understand the stories or rules about who has the right to be heard in the family and how child and adult negotiations take place. This small part of the task means that the family have solved a problem together and in my experience fits with the idea of a family belief system as constructive.

Section 2 – A family motto

The element of working together is continued in the second section when I ask them for their family motto. Again I give examples from other context that might fit with the family, sometimes from literature ('all for one and one for all' is a favourite). This can be helped by asking what their friends would say they were like as a family. Sometimes we use speech bubbles or newspaper headlines to make things more fun. The Kumar family came up with the term 'lost in space' to describe how they felt that they had got lost as a family and this facilitated a conversation about how they had found their way before when lost and a whole series of maps were drawn as a development of this with signposts. Sometimes these are more resilient; 'mad but happy' is a memorable one. The process of constructing mottos is often humorous and helps families relax and be honest with one another.

Section 3 – A memorable family story

In the third section I ask families to write a good family memory or time they were together. These might be birthdays or holidays but sometimes just a day in the park. They often reveal what each member of the family really values from their relationship with one another. I asked Tim (age nine) what it was about the football game that was so special. He told me they all played until they were worn out – he explained how he didn't have to stop to do something else, it made him even be fair with his sister.

Section 4 – Stories of problem solving

I ask families how they solve problems as a family and how they work together. This often reveals stories of coping and ways of sorting things out or what Michael White refers to as 'shy stories' that have not been talked about recently, with the emphasis on problems.

Susan (10) told me about family meetings they had to discuss what was happening and how she was the secretary and wrote everything down.

Section 5 – The story of change

In the penultimate section I ask them what they would like to change about their family and finally I ask them to draw what they would be doing as a family when the problem has been sorted out. This helps to set goals for the therapeutic work and is more geared to solution focused therapy (de Shazer 2005) but it also helps with evaluation and identifying how far a family get with the changes they want to make.

Section 6 – The story of the future

In section six I ask families to describe what they will be doing with one another when they no longer need to come to therapy. Again this is a future orientated element but often families come up with activities they will be doing together instead of arguing or dealing with the stress of the problem.

The shield can help to show conflict between the family stories and individual stories but it is not fixed and can be re-written or added to as therapy proceeds. Sometimes the shield is not completed and it just becomes a springboard for conversations about the aims for the therapy. Sometimes families refer to the shield constantly and create a number of them, which is a very useful way to document the therapeutic process.

The process of Narrative Family Play Therapy

The process of Narrative Play Family Therapy in CAMHS and private practice is affected by different constraints. In my experience the number and frequency of sessions is limited unless there is complexity. In private practice things are usually more flexible but the family may have limited resources or an insurance company may only fund six sessions. Once I saw a family three times in one week, as this was the only week in the month that both parents were able to attend. (I would not be able to do this in my CAMHS practice as management of resources would not allow for such a frequency of sessions.) In CAMHS the therapist has a pool of expertise in their team and an organisation to support them with a complaint. In private practice the therapist is a lot more vulnerable. As the parent is often the commissioner of the work the therapist is directly accountable to the family. I have used my experience in CAMHS to devise a written contract (Appendix 1) to clarify the expectations of the therapy in terms of safety and risk. I also obtain permission from the families to contact their general practitioner (GP) and let them know that the therapy is happening. I show all copies of letters to families before sending them, as I would in my CAMHS practice. The following examples of practice are fictional vignettes created from my experience. They do not represent real families and although this is somewhat limiting I hope it gives a flavour of the work.

FAMILY PLAY PROCESSES

As I suggested earlier, play can provide a different context for old stories to be explored and new ones to be created. In her developmental model of play therapy, Sue Jennings (1999) created the terms 'embodiment projection' and 'role' to describe how play activity develops in infants and children. I have found this model invariably helps my thinking in relation to a child and also in relation to how families play together. Families have their own developmental process in the way that they are able to play or not play together. Some parents have difficulty playing with their children. Some children are taught that play is 'childish' from a very early age (nine or ten or even younger) and they often apologise for 'finding pleasure in the sand tray', 'I know it's a bit babyish'. This seems to be particularly the case in families where there are very strong stories about the importance of education, particularly in a family where parents may have jumped a social class or had their life choices improved by education. Giving the families the opportunity to play together can help them to remember having fun together and be reparative in relationships that have been under stress. It is important to discuss this with parents or carers first as it may be a bit too different for them. However, most parents understand that it can be helpful and will give it a go.

The playrooms I work in are quite small so it is not always possible to have the whole family meeting in the playroom but I always have paper, pens and puppets ready in sessions. A violent puppet show (a bird and a crocodile) between two brothers saw their mother at first angry at yet more fighting between them but as we froze the play and replayed the sessions we were able to understand the bird's and the crocodile's feelings and also have a conversation about what the difference was between normal rough and tumble and violence where someone got hurt. This seemed very important as the mother seemed to have a very aroused reaction to the boys' play.

In sessions three and four, when I think the family are feeling safe enough to play together, I have at least one family session in the playroom where I have embodiment play equipment, essentially slime, sand and water. The children almost immediately want to use this equipment and encourage their carers to join them. Carers are sometimes less enthusiastic although I will always let them know that we will be doing messy play beforehand. I have found that the development of being able to engage in messy play in families can often coincide with an improvement in relationships between carers and children and also between siblings.

PLAY AS A WAY OF EXPRESSING AND HAVING FEELINGS ACCEPTED IN FAMILIES

Tricia and Tony brought their six-year-old son Callum to CAMHS to ask for help with parenting. Callum was diagnosed with attention-deficit hyperactivity disorder (ADHD) and was on medication and as a result this behaviour had improved slightly in school but the parents struggled to cope with his angry outbursts. Callum began to play with the figures in the doll's house and both parents told him to stop playing and to talk to me. I explained that I would be interested in Callum's play as a way of understanding the angry feelings he expressed. As the play developed Callum began shooting all the figures while I made elaborate dying noises to his absolute delight and after a while the parents were invited to join in. Clearly this child was able to channel some of his aggressive feelings through the play and I encouraged the parents to go with this as a safe way of expressing anger.

After three sessions of playing together like this with me modelling acceptance of feelings through play Callum's mother said that he had become calmer. She realised that she had been putting a lot of pressure on him with regard to academic development and realised that he needed to play and she needed to play with him. I suggested that she told Callum this in our sessions as I thought it would be a relief to him. We also talked about other ways that Callum could communicate with his mother and father other than angry outbursts when he was feeling under too much pressure and the family developed a book to write things in. While things were not perfect there had been enough change in the way the family communicated for new stories to develop in the family about having fun and playfulness as a serious part of their life. I also noticed when the whole family came that stories about Callum's younger sister were that she was the 'good' one and that it seemed that Callum was very aware of this and this was part of his anger. The couple were receptive to this idea and created the idea that Callum was 'good at playing'; this created a new story for him that meant he didn't have to resent his sister so much. Things improved as the family stories slowly moved to more positive and creative ones and as the communication improved. Some families can pick up the potential of playing together for their child.

I saw Cleo (age 11) in my private clinic. Her mother Jane, who had been unwell, was concerned about how her illness had impacted on Cleo. Cleo started to play mother and daughter stories in the sand tray when the daughter in the play would worry for her mother. Jane was very sensitive to the meaning of the play, immediately picking up that their daughter was able to express her feelings about this in the sand tray when she played about burying mothers, and got out her old sandbox at home and refilled it. This also led to a discussion about some of the questions Cleo had about her mother's illness and Cleo's fantasies were much worse than the reality. Cleo's mother was able to see that it would be helpful to be more open with Cleo and they had regular plays in the sand at home where they would do a mixture of playing and discussion.

PLAY AND THE MEANING OF MESSINESS IN FAMILIES

The Jay family came to my private practice because of the two sons' constant fighting. Steven, his brother Clarke and their mother Rae and father Jim played in the sand with the water. I noticed that despite the fact that I had said that they could get the sand wet and messy, their mother was very concerned about the boys getting the sand wet or sand on the floor accidentally. She also found it very difficult to play in the wet sand and was very directive in telling the boys what to do to make it work. Jim was very protective of Rae, telling the boys not to get Mum messy as she didn't like it. This gave me a great deal of information about the story of the relationships in the family.

After this session I talked to the couple about it. Rae had been surprised at her reluctance to play with the children and get messy and began to think about her own family stories about messiness and play. She had been the only girl in her family of origin and never been allowed to get messy. We had some further sessions in which Rae got more involved and was able to give the children more space to develop the play. The family began to have regular play times at home and the aggressiveness between the children lessened. As the parents became more able to accept the messy play and respond to it the children began to feel safer and so did not need to express their anxiety through aggression. The carers reported feeling more in control as playing in the sand tray became a metaphor for the parents being able to contain the boys and respond to their feelings while keeping the boundaries. The couple worked long hours and so playing helped to create a story for the boys of their parents acting together and this also contributed to them feeling safer.

PLAY AND EXTERNALISATION

I saw a couple, Tunda and Marie, who were struggling with their nine-year-old son Adeola's 'naughty behaviour' which involved hiding things and chucking his parents' personal belongings in the bin. Both parents were working long hours and finding it hard to cope with understanding and responding to his behaviour.

While Adeola played with the green farty putty I suggested that there might be a green pooh monster and we discussed how the monster spoiled things by making him do naughty things. It turned out that the whole family had monsters and Mum had learned to control her silence monster and Dad had a temper monster. I commented on how crowded their house must be with all these monsters. We agreed it was hard to get rid of the monsters because even if you flushed them down the toilet they hid in the pipes. We agreed that the family would have to work together to outsmart the monsters. This approach is very similar to Michael White's (White and Epston 1990) account of using externalisation with a boy who smears faeces – the infamous 'sneaky poo'.

Working in this way involves a willingness in the parents to be playful and it's important to have this conversation with them. Sometimes parents find this approach strange as they want to deal with the child's behaviour directly and feel that therapy should not be 'fun' but be serious. I explain that although I know that the behaviour is stressful, it's more helpful if the child doesn't feel blamed for the behaviour. Often, this conversation can elicit painful material of how they were blamed in their childhood which helps them understand why they may want to engage with stories of blame about the child. I have known parents say they find it very painful that a child is having fun in the therapy as they would have been blamed for the problem.

PLAY IN COMPLEX FAMILIES

Play can often reflect the primary concerns of members of the family. While working with a family, the play of two of the siblings revealed concerns about being left at home alone. This led to a much needed family discussion about how children can be kept safe and how people who do 'bad things' get punished. Nurture play then emerged that included both sibling and parents. This seemed important to the family as a way of keeping the family identity and keeping alive the story of the family as healthy, nurturing and 'normal'.

When the children felt safe in the therapy environment they began to tell stories of the abuse they had experienced. This offered the children an opportunity to share their story with their parents and have their parents witness their relief at being able to share this story. The therapeutic space was safe enough for the children to move away from fantasy and to begin to talk about things that had been too difficult to tell. In Narrative Family Play Therapy, we can also chose to explore resilience factors. These can include the narrative of the bravery of the child in telling their story and the importance of the parent in believing the story.

Endings and evaluation

Narratives about the meaning and significance of termination of therapy are very different in play therapy and systemic therapy in general. Play therapy to some extent regards endings in the therapeutic relationship as an opportunity to heal previous endings in relationships that have been painful. Endings in play therapy are planned. Endings in Narrative Family Therapy are also planned but there is less emphasis on process. Endings and evaluation often are interlinked. Jo (age eight) had asked to come to therapy because of a complicated relationship with her stepfather in which she felt she was being left out of the family. She was able to speak about her concerns and her mother Maya became thoughtful and spoke with her partner about the difficulties. After a few sessions things were a bit better but there were still issues in the family. Maya was clear that she did not want to explore her own experience of being parented as this had been very difficult. Although I respected this I felt that this would be the next step in helping her to understand the stories about behaviour she brought from her family of origin. Maya felt that she had gone as far as she could and that she did not see how further work could be helpful. We agreed that this would be the last session. Although Jo was reluctant to say goodbye I agreed that the family could probably get along well enough without us now and congratulated Jo and Maya on working together to resolve issues. While Jo was sad to say goodbye, we acknowledged this and I commented on her bravery and ability to speak out about her concerns. I asked if I could tell other children that come to the service about her bravery as I explained some children find it very difficult. This process is similar to White's ideas of 'bringing it back' (White and Epston 1990) in that families become experts and consultants to others in re-authoring stories in their community. Although I do not bring families into sessions as consultants I ask if I can tell others about their bravery/ability to solve problems and I sometimes use these examples disguised to help other families. This raises ethical considerations regarding narrative approaches particularly regarding confidentiality and I have found this to be an issue both in narrative therapy and in creating a context in which family and child narratives may need to be separated for a while.

Ethics
Who is the client in the family?
Working with families rather than the individual child is complex as everyone in the family is a client and the therapist has to balance the needs of each client, a skill I think I learned in my family therapy training, as I found at the beginning of my training I was focusing much more on the child's process. The question of who is the client and the responsibility of the therapist to address for example the couple relationship (sometimes necessary before other issues can be addressed) or an adult mental health issue (often referring on but nevertheless a factor to be thought about in the therapy) can be extremely complex and I think training in systemic therapy is important when working with families just to be able to understand how the family works.

The voice of the child in the family
It is common practice to see children on their own as part of any assessment, medical or psychosocial. I find that children often voice views in the individual sessions that they would like voiced to their parents and then I support them in voicing their view in the session. Sunita, age ten, told me that she really didn't want to see the boy who she had had a cuddle with that had gone too far as she found it so embarrassing (he was part of their community). I asked her if she wanted us to discuss this with her parents and she agreed. When the family heard this they were surprised but immediately agreed to her request.

Similarly sometimes it is helpful for a child's play to be brought back into a family session. Raul and Maria were concerned about their child Lilly (age ten) who tended to please everyone. I saw a very feisty Lilly when we played together; in fact her characters could be quite mean and ruthless. I was curious about this with Lilly and asked if we could mention it to her family. She was quite keen to do this and her mother in particular was pleased by this new story about Lilly's ability to be mean. This impacted on her sister Jay (14) who began to think of examples of when Lilly was able to put herself first and not think of others.

The decision to share information across boundaries is important and depends on the child's age and ability to express what they wish with a therapist. I always check things out with a child and if I am ever unsure I wait as there is usually another opportunity.

Therapist's position

Although I like the idea of families of experts sometimes I have been quite directive with families where I think there is a difficulty in the way family narratives are organised. I have found in some family stories that parents are reluctant to go against a child's wishes to keep something private or secret and I often have to challenge families, particularly when keeping a secret compromises child safety. Similarly current narratives of 'child centred' parenting often leave children struggling confused with decisions that are their parents' to make. The position of the therapist when working with families requires the tenacity to challenge, as well as support, and while playfulness and humour can play a part in this sometimes, there is a place for taking a professional position and making and communicating judgements. This is not an easy task and requires a balance of respectfulness and professional distance that can sometimes be lost as we get to know families and build relationships. Although we join families in our work I often ask myself how much I have become part of a family as too much distance and too much involvement can be equally unhelpful.

Summary and critique

In this chapter I have attempted to describe how I have worked integrating Narrative Play Therapy and family play therapy and I hope given some thoughts about how family and individual narratives can be told, heard and re-authored. There have been critiques and counter critiques of narrative, summarised by Haywood (2003), which are worth considering but unfortunately there is not space here to discuss them in depth. My story has been told from the view of a white middle aged woman, who is also a parent, and I ask the reader to reflect on about how this influences the stories I have chosen to tell and what stories I might have missed. The process of writing has helped me to clarify how I work and I am curious to hear other stories of a similar nature.

Appendix 1 Child and Family Consultancy Information and Contract for Parents/Carers and Professional Philosophy of Care

I am influenced by many models of practice but my overall philosophy is humanistic. I believe that families and individuals are usually resilient and good at solving problems. My experience tells me that sometimes communication gets stuck or life events trip people up so that their usual resources need a kick-start. I see my role as a facilitator; often this has involved helping families and young people communicate and learn about themselves in their context of their lives. I am very interested in learning about social difference so please let me know if there are religious or cultural or any other aspects of difference that I may need to pay attention to and please let me know if I make assumptions or get things wrong; hopefully this won't happen very often.

Services

FAMILY THERAPY

The aim of family therapy for me is to help to re-establish helpful communication in the family so that everyone feels heard. A child may present with a behavioural symptom that is expressing something that is not being expressed in the family. Family therapy can help to untangle this. Family work may involve a certain amount of couple work to strengthen the parenting relationship which can help the child feel contained by the parents. In practice it may also involve some individual child sessions and some parent child sessions. Usually family therapy lasts six to ten sessions and is fortnightly to three weekly. This is to give space to the changes that might be happening at home.

ASSESSMENT PERIOD

Usually there is a three to six session assessment period to decide what is the best approach and if the therapy would be helpful.

CONSULTATION

Sometimes thinking about what is going on for a child in the first instance can be useful to parents and professionals. This can be to help develop strategies or thinking about possible therapeutic input.

Terms and conditions

AIMS

I aim to offer a safe, professional, transparent and respectful service which is also good value. I therefore work to a written agreement that sets out the terms of the therapeutic work and mutual responsibility. It is a condition of the contract that I let the child/families' GP know of the work by standard letter. This is a health and safety consideration so that I can let the GP know of any urgent concerns. All copies of letters to GPs are provided for parents/carers and children if age appropriate. I may also ask questions about risk at the start of the therapy so that I can assess need appropriately.

I also take my written notes to my own clinical supervision which helps me to think about the child/family and my work in depth which contributes to the quality of the service.

CORRESPONDENCE

Correspondence is by phone or letter.

RESPONSIBILITIES: THERAPIST

I will work within the Code of Practice of the British Association of Play Therapists (BAPT), United Kingdom Council for Psychotherapy (UKCP) and Health Professions Council (HPC) (copies available on request).

RESPONSIBILITIES: CARER/PARENT

To endeavour to come to sessions /bring the child to sessions on time.

In child therapy refrain from asking the child about the session but allowing a space if the child wants to talk.

Let the therapist know if there are any changed circumstances that may affect the child, for example health, bereavement, school.

Pay fees promptly or let the therapist know if there are circumstances where payment has become difficult so that special arrangements can be made.

Parent(s)/carer(s)/person(s) with parental responsibility (PWPR)

Name . . . .

Signature . . . . Date . . . .

Name . . . .

Signature . . . . Date . . . .

Type of work: Assessment period
Dates of therapy sessions planned:

Date of review . . . .

Proposed cost . . . .

Therapist . . . .

Signature . . . .

Date . . . .

Information sheet to be completed by parent/carer/PWPR

Child's name . . . .

Date of birth . . . .

Parents'/carers' names: 1.
                           2.
Address:

Address 2 (if relevant):

Contact permission sheet to be completed by PWPR/parent(s)/ carer(s)

GP name and address and phone:

School name and address and phone:

Does your child have any current health issues that it would be useful for me to know about?

Can you briefly describe your main concerns about your child/family at this time, if relevant?

Please circle:
Permission to contact all agencies (social care/GP/school, etc.):
Yes/No

You will be consulted if I feel it is necessary to contact another agency.

Permission to contact GP: conditional YES

Permission to contact school: Yes/No

Permission to contact social care: Yes/No

Permission to contact CAMHS: Yes/No

References

Aries, P. (1962) *Centuries of Childhood*. New York: Vintage Books.

Bateson, G. (1972) *Steps to an Ecology of Mind*. Chicago, IL: Chicago Press.

Burnham, J. (1986) *Family Therapy*. London: Tavistock.

Cattanach, A. (1992) *Play Therapy with Abused Children*. London: Jessica Kingsley Publishers.

Dallos, R. (2006) *Attachment Narrative Therapy: Integrating Narrative, Systemic and Attachment Therapies*. Buckingham: Open University Press.

de Shazer, S. (2005) *More than Miracles: The State of the Art of Solution-Focused Therapy*. Binghamton, NY: Haworth Press.

Foucault, M. (1975) *The Archeology of Knowledge*. London: Tavistock Press.

Freeman, J., Epston, D. and Lobovits, D. (1997) *Playful Approaches to Serious Problems*. New York and London: W.W. Norton.

Gil, E. (1994) *Play in Family Therapy*. New York: Guilford Press.

Haywood, M. (2003) 'Critique of narrative therapy: A personal response.' *Australian and New Zealand Journal of Family Therapy 24*, 183–189.

Hoffman, L. (2004) 'Constructing realities: The art of lenses.' *Family Process 29*, 1, 1–12.

Jennings, S. (1999) *Introduction to Developmental Play Therapy*. London: Jessica Kingsley Publishers.

Rutter, M. (1985) 'Resilience in the face of adversity: Protective factors and resistance to psychiatric disorder.' *British Journal of Psychiatry 147*, 598–661.

Walsh, F. (2006) *Strengthening Family Resilience*, 2nd edn. New York: Guilford Press.

Weeks, J., Heaphy, B. and Donovan, C. (2001) *Same Sex Intimacies. Families of Choice and Other Life Experiments*. New York: Routledge Taylor and Francis Group.

White, M. and Epston, D. (1990) *Narrative Means to a Therapeutic Ends*. New York and London: W.W. Norton.

Wilson, J. (1998) *Child-Focused Practice: A Collaborative Systemic Approach*. London: Tavistock.

Chapter 10

Narrative Play Therapy with Adopted Children

Carol Platteuw

Introduction

Adopted children have many narratives to make sense of. They may be told they are special and longed for – but if this is true why were they given up in the first place? They may be told their birth parents loved them but could not look after them – was this because of anything they did? Adoptive parents have stories of their own. They may have waited a long time to decide that adoption is the way to form their family – but their adopted children may be completely different personalities with completely different interests and outlooks from themselves. One of my colleagues (Kerr-Edwards, a play therapist and a member of the British Association of Play Therapists) has described adoption as two styles of music coming together – it may be classical and heavy rock – how will they find a rhythm and begin to be melodic?

This chapter will explore how therapists working with adopted children can use narratives to provide structure and meaning to help children make sense of their own early experiences. McLeod (1997) describes the purpose of storytelling as:

- to bring order, sequence and a sense of completion to a set of experiences

- to problem solve by providing a causal explanation for something that happened

- to develop a sense of perspective by placing a single event into a broader context.

Children who have been placed for adoption have usually experienced significant harm in the form of serious neglect or abuse and their early care was chaotic, inconsistent and frightening. Infants and young children need nurturing and attuned early care, in order to feel valued, loved and worthy of care in their own right. This early sense of security forms a model or pattern for relationships with people and affects how children see themselves in relation to others. This inner working model affects a child's thoughts, feelings and behaviours. So often I have worked with adopted children who do not feel worthy of care, who spoil things when they are taking part in an enjoyable family outing or control things to such an extent they never enjoy the moment or the experience.

Approaching Narrative Play Therapy with adopted children

Attachment theory, trauma theory and cognitive/developmental issues influence my work with adopted children.

Attachment behaviours serve the primary function of ensuring safety and protection. Attachment theory is based upon the premise of the infant displaying attachment seeking behaviours to maximise the closeness of the main care taker, either physically or emotionally, when the infant is under stress. Infants who indicate such needs and who receive a prompt response learn that their main carer will be a reliable, consistent source of comfort. As the infant grows older the attachment figure becomes a safe base from which the child can gradually venture to explore the world. Attachments provide connections with others and help develop a sense of self. Infants begin to develop mental representations, or inner working models regarding their own self worth, based on adults' availability and their willingness to provide care and protection. Attachment behaviour may be organised or disorganised. Three organised patterns of behaviour are secure, avoidant and ambivalent (Howe *et al.* 1999).

When the caregiver is consistent, attuned and responsive, a secure attachment pattern will develop. The infant experiences the adult as loving, attentive and nurturing when he expresses a need such as hunger, discomfort or pain. The infant begins to show a preference for his attachment figure; he feels safe and comfortable in the attachment figure's presence. A child who is securely attached has an inner working model that he feels loved, valued and cared for in his own right.

When the caregiver is consistently inattentive and unavailable, either physically or emotionally, an avoidant attachment pattern will develop.

In this pattern the parent may be consistently unavailable to the child through mental health difficulties such as depression. The infant's expressed needs are ignored and the infant begins to accept that the parent will not be responsive and starts to minimise expressing his attachment needs; he may become quiet, withdrawn and as he grows older he may appear independent and self reliant. A child who has an avoidant attachment has an inner working model that his needs are not important, he is not worthy of care, others are not to be relied on; he has to look after his own needs.

When the caregiver is inconsistently inattentive and unavailable, an ambivalent attachment pattern will develop. In this pattern the parent may be inconsistently available to the child through alcohol or substance misuse. The infant sometimes experiences responsive care but sometimes does not. The infant therefore organises himself to maximise his attachment seeking needs. He may therefore present as crying excessively, clinging or being overly demanding. All behaviours are designed to draw attention to him in order that his attachment figure notices him and meets his needs. A child who has an ambivalent attachment has an inner working model that his needs are not important, he is not worthy of care, he has to work hard to get noticed and valued.

When a caregiver is frightening or abusive the infant cannot organise a response to get his attachment needs. The attachment figure that he should be able to approach for comfort is a source of fear. These infants display a range of different behaviours including frozen responses. Later the children may present as very controlling; having experienced such a chaotic, frightening early life they need to take control of their current world. A child who has disorganised attachment has an inner working model where he views the world and adults as unpredictable and scary. He is confused about himself and how to behave in relation to others.

Adopted children with insecure or disorganised attachments benefit from narratives which contain key messages that all new born creatures are unique and worthy of care.

Experience of trauma during a child's early years may put the child at risk for developing psychological problems. Research in brain development tells us that a child who has experienced trauma has over activation of important neural systems during sensitive periods of development (Perry 1995). Two response patterns may be observed in traumatised children:

- hyperarousal leading to fight or flight behaviours; this response may be reactivated when a child is exposed to a specific reminder of the traumatic event

- dissociation leading to freeze or defeat or giving up behaviours.

The younger the child is when the trauma is experienced the more likely he is to use a dissociative response.

Children who have suffered neglect and abuse commonly struggle with object permanence and cause and effect. When their parents are no longer physically present, they become cognitively and emotionally lost to the child. If the child's early experiences were unpredictable and lacked any form of routine they often find change – of any kind – highly anxiety provoking. Children become anxious at separations from parents, changes to the school day and changes within the school day, the change from school term to school holidays and trips away with the family. Transitional objects are important, as are photographs for the child of their parents.

Cognitively children develop more of an understanding of their adoptive status as they reach middle childhood (Brodzinsky, Smith and Brodzinsky 1998). At around six years old, children learn that families are formed in different ways – by being born to and being adopted by – they may use the word 'adopted' but lack any real understanding of what 'being adopted' means. In the following years, as children begin to see situations from the perspective of others and begin to develop problem solving skills, they may question the reasons why they were placed for adoption (e.g. if my birth mother took drugs why didn't she stop and if she has stopped now will I be able to return to her care?). At seven to eight years, adopted children become more aware of biological connections; if they are not biologically connected to their adoptive parents and have birth parents elsewhere they may experience anxiety and confusion about their security and status as members of their adopted family. Logical reciprocity is identified by Brodzinsky as another important development which influences their adoption adjustment. They recognise that to have been placed for adoption one first had to have been relinquished (voluntarily or involuntarily) by birth parents. The researchers point out that adoption is therefore associated with loss (Brodzinsky 1990). In my work as a play therapist with a post adoption team, the majority of children that are referred for play therapy are eight years old and very much in this middle childhood developmental stage of making sense of what adoption means, wishing to have more information regarding why they were placed for adoption, and wanting to explore thoughts about their birth family.

Assessments

When working with adopted children, comprehensive assessments are essential. Gathering information about their early life prior to placement for adoption and discussions with their adoptive parents regarding the child's day to day functioning provide key information. Reviewing with the adopters the child's early history and exploring the trauma events he has experienced is, in my view, the beginning of the therapeutic intervention. Adoptive parents have often forgotten crucial details of their child's history, and thinking with them about their child's likely attachment pattern and the effect the early trauma would have had on their development, often raises empathy in adopters and a determination to rise to the challenges that parenting adopted children often pose.

The Narrative Story Stem Assessment Technique originally developed by Hodges (1992) at the Hospital for Sick Children at Great Ormond Street, London, is an excellent tool to use to assess children's expectations and perceptions of family roles, attachment and relationships, without asking them direct questions about their own family. The story stem assessment consists of a structured series of 13 narrative stems. These present children with a range of different family scenarios as the beginning of a story, using doll and animal figures. Children are then invited to complete the stories in whatever way they like. Children's responses are then rated (Hodges, Hillman and Steele 2002) according to the themes in their stories regarding whether they portray adults as sources of comfort and protection or as frightening or unconcerned figures. Responses are also rated for stories which may contain bizarre elements or ones that may be considered catastrophic fantasies. Such responses are felt to be highly likely indicators of disorganised/controlling children who are likely to have experienced trauma or to have been parented by caregivers who have unresolved issues in relation to past trauma or loss (Main 1995).

This is an example of one of the story stems:

The lost pig story. This is a situation which requires empathy/helping behaviour from another character. In this scenario, the child telling the story may or may not articulate the little pig being upset at being lost and/or concern from the mother pig that her baby is missing. The little pig also needs to show some resilience.

The therapist starts the story: 'Once there was a little pig and it lived here with all the other pigs, big ones and small ones. The cows lived here, the sheep lived here, the horses lived here and the crocodile lived here. One day the little pig went for a long walk. He went a long way, past the cows, past the sheep, past the crocodile and past the horses. Then he said, "Oh I'm lost. I can't see the other pigs. I don't know how to get back."' The therapist asks the child to show and tell what happens next.

George, aged five years, responded by getting the crocodile to wander over to the little pig and eat him all up and spit him out in the corner of the field. The therapist prompted George and asked whether the mummy pig had noticed that the little pig was missing. George said, 'No, cos she likes the quiet.' This was a consistent theme throughout all of George's stories – mother figures who were unconcerned and unavailable to their children.

Involvement of the child's parent

With all the adopted children I work with, I have the adopter present throughout all the sessions. My aim is that the adoptive parent can be a co-therapist, but most importantly to enhance the attachment between the child and his parent. By having the parent present in the therapy session opportunities are provided for the parent to become more 'mind minded' (Howe 2005). Parents can be exposed to children's (often incorrect) thoughts or (sometimes distorted) feelings about their past. Clarifying the child's inner working model helps parents understand the reasons underlying their children's behaviours. 'Parents who focus on their children's subjective experiences help them understand their psychological states and so promote mental well being. This lays the foundation for affect regulation' (Howe 2005, p.20).

Therapy involving the child and his parent is advocated by Hughes in his model of dyadic developmental psychotherapy (Hughes 1997). In this model the primary therapeutic approach is one of playfulness, acceptance, empathy and curiosity. The therapy session creates a safe place where the child can begin to explore a wide range of emotions and experiences that are frightening, harmful, avoided or denied. The safety is created by the therapist and parent providing reflective and non-judgemental dialogue along with empathy and reassurance. Hughes argues that co-regulating of affect and co-constructing meaning produces therapeutic progress. Parents are encouraged to respond to their child's affective states, with congruence eventually enhancing capacity in the child for reflective thought. Hughes calls such a response 'intersubjectivity'. When such moments occur within the therapy session they are both powerful and moving. I worked with eight-year-old Brenda and her mother. Brenda experienced an early life dominated by an alcoholic birth father, domestic violence between her birth parents, and she suffered serious injuries when she was caught in the cross fire between her parents. She was finally removed at the age of two years. Brenda presents as an anxious, vigilant little girl, who her adoptive mother described as emotionally shut down. In one session, Brenda was playing with baby dolls. She was the mother and the adopter and I were the grandparents. In the role of grandparents, the adopter and I began talking about how beautiful the baby dolls were, how they needed love, cuddles and to be kept safe. Suddenly the adopter burst into tears and said how sad she felt when she heard of babies who had not been taken care of properly or had been hurt. Brenda looked at her mother and asked her whether she was thinking about how she – Brenda – had been hurt as a baby. Her mother confirmed this and said how scary the world must have been for Brenda as a baby with a father who drank and parents who were always fighting. As her mother continued crying Brenda began to cry and – for the first time – really let her mother hold her and rock her like a baby. The mother reported this session as a turning point in their relationship, Brenda began to let her mother nurture her and she started to participate in shared family activities which she had previously avoided.

Process of therapy

The materials I have available in the playroom when I work with adopted children include a selection of baby dolls that can be bathed, changed, fed and put to bed. I have a baby bath, baby bubble bath, baby cream, talcum powder and nappies, bottles to feed the babies, bibs and clothes, blankets and pillows to make beds and a musical night light for bedtime. I find children love the sensory experience of caring for the baby dolls with real lotions. Playing with babies naturally creates opportunities to talk about the special care that all babies need and deserve.

I have a sand tray with a range of small figures and I find adopted children make a lot of use of the sand tray. It feels safe to create stories in a very contained space at the same time as having the sensory experience of the sand.

Puppets are also used a lot and adopted children make good use of the possibility of starting a narrative with one puppet and then using another to tell the story from another person's perspective.

I usually begin working with a child by inviting him to tell me stories, using small figures, in the sand tray. Common themes that emerge in stories created by adopted children involve small figures that are lost or have to fend for themselves. Often the narratives are very aggressive, chaotic and there are never any resolutions. An example of this was with a five-year-old child called John. He had been removed from his birth parent at the age of two. He spent a year in foster care and was placed with his adoptive parents at the age of three. His adoptive parents separated six months after his placement, his adoptive father left the home and the adoptive mother had to return to work. John's stories always involved the use of black slime; small creatures became trapped in the slime and needed rescuing. However, any potential rescuers always failed and the little figures drowned or disappeared from view. It took many sessions before John accepted the small creatures could be rescued and find ways to escape the slime forever.

I have created my own therapeutic stories for children based on Sutherland's (2000) model.

This model suggests that the therapist:

- establish the issue the child is struggling with

- create a character, place and situation that can provide a metaphorical structure for the identified difficulty. The main character should also be struggling with the same issue as the child

- describe the main character using coping strategies for the issue similar to those used by the child. Show how these lead into difficulties in relation to how the child sees himself or sees others, eventually leading to a crisis

- describe a pathway out of the crisis to a solution. Someone or something will usually enter the story to enable a different approach or different way of managing. This changes the way the character feels about himself and others. This shift makes the world a better place to be.

The following story was co-constructed with a child's adopter using Sutherland's model. The child, Clare, is six years old. She was exposed to domestic violence when in the care of her birth parents. She was removed to foster care at the age of three years but she experienced several changes of foster placement before being placed with her adoptive mother at the age of five. Clare's adoptive mother found her very independent. She would often start talking with strangers; when taken to the park she would quickly disappear out of sight and try to join a group of children but with little success as her overtures were disruptive and irritating.

The Story of the Little Mouse

There was once a little mouse who lived with his family on a farm. The mouse was an adventurous little mouse who loved going off and having adventures on his own. He often went to watch the pigs and when they were asleep he would crawl over their big fat tummies to wake them. He liked teasing the farmyard cats and would pull faces to annoy them. When the cats chased him he always reached a tiny hole he could squeeze into just in the nick of time. He liked nibbling the food that the farmer left for the chickens but the chickens began to realise he was pinching their food and when they saw him they clucked and flapped their wings to scare him away. He liked going into the farmhouse to sit in the middle of the kitchen floor. The farmer's wife did not like mice and she always screamed and chased him out with a broom.

The little mouse often spent all day out and about getting into various scrapes. When he went home he was always covered in mud and very tired. His mum got so cross with him. She was not cross that he was dirty as she liked him to enjoy himself and have fun. She was not cross that he was tired because he always slept well and did not snore when he went to bed tired. She was cross that he never told her where he was going and she was worried that one day he would get hurt. When she talked to him about her worries the little mouse said 'Don't worry, Mummy, I can look after myself, nothing will ever happen to me.'

The little mouse's mummy thought very hard. I need to make sure my little mouse is safe when I can't see him, she said to herself. She decided to go round to all the animals in the farmyard to ask them to keep an eye on little mouse for her. They said of course they would. They all liked little mouse very much, even though he could be very mischievous.

One day little mouse was watching two robins on a bird table. The farmer's wife came out and put some bread and bits of cheese out for them to eat. Little mouse felt a bit hungry. He jumped up onto the bird table and swished the robins off the table with his tail. But the bird table was very old and rickety and suddenly there was a loud creaking noise and it fell to the ground, landing on little mouse and trapping him. He was very scared, his leg was trapped, and he began to squeak 'help' as loudly as he could. The ducks, on a nearby pond noticed the bird table had fallen; they went over to help but could not move it. They waddled off to tell Mummy mouse. The farm dog heard the crash and came over; he tried to push the table off the little mouse but it was too heavy for him. He scampered off to tell Mummy mouse. The farm horse wandered over; he was so big and strong that just one kick of his hoof lifted the table off little mouse.

Little mouse was so pleased the heavy table was off him but he couldn't move. His leg was broken. Just then Mummy mouse arrived followed by the ducks, the dog and three chickens who had heard the news. All the animals helped Mummy mouse carry little mouse home. Little mouse had to have some wooden splints around his leg to help it mend and he had to stay at home to get a lot of rest. Mummy mouse was very kind and bought him lots of tasty things to cheer him up and she played games with him when he got bored. Lots of the farmyard animals came to see how he was; the chickens brought him some of their chicken food as a treat, the robins brought him some bits of cheese and bread that the farmer's wife had left out for them and the baby piglets came to tickle him with their curly tails.

It was a big surprise to little mouse that so many animals liked him and cared about him. He did not realise he had so many friends. Also little mouse liked all the spoiling from Mummy mouse and the big cuddles she gave him when his leg hurt. After a few weeks when little mouse's leg was better he went out to play but he decided to invite some of the animals to play with him and he found he could have twice as much fun when two animals played together.

Mummy mouse decided to give little mouse a necklace with a little bell on it which he could wear around his neck. She said it would tinkle when he ran around and it would remind him that she was thinking about him having fun with his friends. Mummy mouse bought a big loud bell for herself. She told little mouse that when she had not seen him for a while, or when she wanted to let him know that his dinner was ready or when she wanted to tell him that she loved him, she would ring the bell as loudly as she could and she wanted him to scamper home as quickly as she could.

All the animals on the farm got used to hearing Mummy mouse ring her loud bell. When it rang they thought:

'Oh – it must be little mouse's dinner time' or

'Oh – Mummy mouse must be checking to see how little mouse is' or

'Oh – Mummy mouse must be telling little mouse how much she loves him again.'

The End

The messages that the adopter wished to impart to the child in this story was that she respected her daughter's resilience but, as a mother, it is her job to look after her and keep her safe. She always had her daughter in mind and as their attachment grew she hoped her daughter will keep her mother in mind too. The child loved this story and it became a bedtime favourite. The mother obtained a number of key rings with photograph holders into which she placed photographs of herself and the child. She attached them to her handbag, the child's school bag, PE bag, music bag and this assisted the concept of holding each other in mind whenever they were apart.

I have found use of narratives particularly helpful for adopted children in the following situations:

When children have no information about their early life

It is now accepted good practice that all children who are placed for adoption should have a life story book which is essentially a brief chronology of their life from birth including some details about their birth parents with basic reasons why they were placed for adoption. In practice, it is my experience that there are still many children who have no life story books because their social worker left without having completed the task of compiling their book, or children may have an album of photographs but no narrative to accompany it, or children may have been adopted from abroad and very few details are known about their early life. In these situations, adoptive parents often are anxious about saying the wrong thing and put off telling children that they are adopted altogether. I have had adoptive parents of children aged ten years and above who have consulted me feeling they must tell their child about their adopted status but were at a loss to know how to start.

I had 20 sessions with ten-year-old Stacy (a quiet, anxious child) and her mother, to tell her that she was adopted and to support her as she learnt the reasons for her placement. Stacy loved dogs and her mother and I decided we would use stories about dogs as the basis for our work with Stacy. In early sessions we introduced stories where puppies lived in different kinds of families; one puppy lived with his parents, one puppy lived with his grandmother and one puppy lived with an aunt and uncle. Stacy's neighbour was pregnant and we introduced the concept of children joining families in different ways; being born into a family and joining a family in other ways – one puppy was living with his grandmother because his parents were living abroad. We introduced the role of the Royal Society for the Prevention of Cruelty to Animals (RSPCA). In the family where the puppy lived with his aunt and uncle, his mummy had not fed him and he became very thin. A RSPCA inspector heard about this and took the puppy to this new family who gave him all the milk he could drink and he soon became well and bouncy. His aunt and uncle loved him so much that he stayed with them until he was grown up. This scenario was played out a number of times with us all having an opportunity to be the aunt – who was delighted to have such a lovely puppy to live with her, the mother who was sorry she did not know how to look after little puppies and pleased that someone else was taking such good care of her puppy and the puppy who was sad and angry that the mother had not cared for her well. In session eight Stacy's mother felt able to tell Stacy that she had not grown inside her tummy, but she had come to live with her adoptive family when she was nine months old. Stacy immediately asked whether she had been very thin through not being fed properly. Her mother confirmed this was the case, her birth mother had suffered severe post natal depression, and she lived in an isolated, rural place and had not been able to take care of herself, let alone a tiny baby. A postman delivering a package had heard Stacy crying and had alerted the authorities, which resulted in Stacy being admitted to hospital and then to foster care. Stacy's birth mother was also admitted to hospital but unfortunately her mental health did not improve significantly and she has required ongoing periods of inpatient treatment throughout her life. Stacy learnt that she had been well cared for in her foster home and was fascinated to hear the story of the first time her mother went to meet her in the foster home. She requested this story be retold many times.

Within the play therapy sessions we created a life story book for Stacy using the model created by Rees (2009). This model starts with the present detailing information about the child in her current family, and then explores the past by including details about her origins. It returns to the present by explain why, and by whom, decisions were made for the child to be placed in her current family, and ends wondering what the child's future holds and what adventures might be in store for the child with her family.

When a child loses a sense of self, particularly if part of a large sibling group

As discussed, all adopted children should have a life story book and basic information about their origins. However, when a child is part of a large sibling group, there is often a sense of the child's individual story being lost. Ben Brown is eight years old and is the oldest child of four boys who are known as 'the Brown boys'. His birth mother was a substance abuser from a young age; Ben was born drug addicted and removed at birth. He spent some weeks in a special baby care unit and was discharged to foster care. He was placed for adoption at the age of ten months. His birth mother went on to have three more boys, each only a year apart in age, and the adopters took all four boys. Ben only had six months on his own with his adoptive parents before his second sibling arrived, followed shortly by the third and fourth. His adoptive mother explained that the second and third siblings had medical complications through being exposed to drugs during pregnancy and they required a lot of her time and attention. Ben became progressively more bossy and controlling within the family until his adoptive mother became exhausted and asked for therapeutic help.

In the play therapy sessions Ben loved playing with the baby dolls and quickly wanted to explore why he had been 'given away', why his birth mother could not stop taking drugs, and whether many families had turned him down before this one took him in. His adoptive mother was amazed at the torrent of questions Ben articulated. Ben was very clear he only wanted to hear about his early experiences, his placement for adoption and how he had been as a baby. A narrative was provided for Ben about him as a unique individual; his mother told him all the stories his foster carer had told about him as a small baby. She also told him that on one of his first visits to her home she had put him down on the floor in the living room, but when she returned he was not there. Where had her baby gone? Then she heard a sound from under the table; Ben had managed to crawl under the table. She described how proud she was that

Ben had decided to make his first crawl at her home. Ben's face shone with delight at this recollection. As we played with the baby dolls each week, and talked about Ben as a baby he began to ask whether he could have a bottle of milk at night when his mother read him his bedtime story and whether he could have his blanket comforter again that he used to snuggle when much younger. Ben's mother realised how much Ben had missed out, having three younger siblings placed so quickly and two with special needs. As Ben accepted the early nurture from his mother that he had missed out on, and as he began to feel valued and special in his own right, his bossy and controlling behaviours reduced significantly.

When a child's behaviour is so challenging the adopters despair of ever being able to form an attachment

For such children 'claiming narratives' can help a child accept that all children are born equal, and they all deserve unconditional love and care. Stories involving what parents would have given these children, had they cared for them as babies, can help change a child's inner working model. 'In the claiming narrative the child's original life story is not being denied, instead alternate possibilities are being presented. This begins the process of shifting those negative beliefs to a healthy model that will help the child begin to trust and feel secure in his new family' (Lacher, Nichols and May 2005, p.71).

Tyler, aged seven, was born with a number of medical problems to two teenage parents. He required a number of surgical interventions in his first year. He has a life story book which described him as a 'baby who often cried because of all the operations he had to have'. He had various braces fitted to his legs which made him heavy to carry around and he was left with a slight limp. The way the life story was written, it portrayed Tyler as a difficult baby to look after and too hard for two very young parents who decided he would be better off being adopted. The strong message that Tyler had been given was that he had been difficult to care for, unlovable and thus had been abandoned. He was an angry child in his adoptive placement and had tantrums over the slightest thing.

Tyler was another child who loved bathing the baby dolls. It emerged when exploring his early experiences with him that his birth parents had never stayed with him when he was hospitalised, and his birth mother was anorexic and could not carry him when he had his braces fitted, as she was not strong enough. His adoptive mother told Tyler stories about how she would have cared for him had she been there for him when he was born. She described how she would have wanted to stay close to him wherever he was, taking her own sleeping bag into a hospital so she could have stayed the night with him, she talked about being fit and healthy and how she would have been strong enough to carry Tyler close to her and been there 'in a flash' if he was in pain or discomfort. Slowly these repeated stories of 'how it could have been' changed Tyler's inner working model of himself, from that of a demanding baby to a baby who should have had a parent there he could have relied on to soothe him and comfort him when he was distressed. Tyler's anger began to be expressed towards his birth parents. He used puppets to tell them what he thought and said he thought they were too young to have a child, selfish to want to stay in their own beds when their baby was all on his own on the hospital, and his mother should have eaten properly once she had a baby to take care of. Tyler physically changed over the course of 30 play therapy sessions. He had arrived a tense, angry child; he left a much more relaxed, affectionate boy.

Endings

When ending a play therapy intervention with a child, I usually suggest we review our work together by thinking about the sessions as a journey. We think together what had brought the child to play therapy, what questions, dilemmas or issues he was grappling with at the beginning of the journey, whether he has found any answers or resolutions, and what or who has helped him in this process. I suggest we draw a river or a road, with obstructions to represent the difficulties and bridges, buildings and people to represent the resolutions or helpers. If the child wishes, a final story can be created using these metaphors. For the last session I print out all the stories the child has made and put them in a special folder for him to take home.

Conclusion

In conclusion, I have found co-constructing narratives with adopted children and their parents to provide rich opportunities to address issues for adopted children which centre around where they belong and who they belong to. Stories can be deconstructed, used to explore and amend distorted beliefs and then reconstructed providing new perceptions of self and others and new possibilities for the future.

References

Brodzinsky, D.M. (1990) 'A stress and Coping Model of Adoption Adjustment.' In D.M. Brodzinsky and M. Schechter (eds) *The Psychology of Adoption.* New York: Oxford University Press.

Brodzinsky, D.M., Smith, D.W. and Brodzinsky, A. (1998) *Children's Adjustment to Adoption: Developmental and Clinical Issues.* London: Sage Publications.

Hodges, J. (1992) 'Little Piggy Story Stem Battery.' Unpublished manuscript.

Hodges, J., Hillman, S. and Steele, M (2002) *Little Piggy Narrative Story Stem Coding Manual.* London: Anna Freud Centre/Great Ormond Street/Coram Family.

Howe, D. (2005) *Child Abuse and Neglect: Attachment, Development and Intervention.* Basingstoke: Palgrave Macmillan.

Howe, D., Brandon, M., Hinings, D. and Schofield, G. (1999) *Attachment Theory, Child Maltreatment and Family Support.* Basingstoke: Macmillan Press.

Hughes, D. (1997) *Facilitating Developmental Attachment.* Lanham, MD: Rowman and Littlefield Publishers.

Lacher, D.B., Nichols, T. and May, M.C. (2005) *Connecting with Kids through Stories.* London: Jessica Kingsley Publishers.

Main, M. (1995) 'Recent Studies in Attachment: Overview, with Selected Implication for Clinical Work.' In S. Goldberg, R. Muir and J. Kerr (eds) *Attachment Theory: Social Development and Clinical Perspectives.* Hillsdale, NJ: Analytic Press.

McLeod, J. (1997) *Narrative and Psychotherapy.* London: Sage Publications.

Perry, B. (1995) 'Childhood trauma, the neurobiology of adaptation and "use dependent" development of the brain; How "states" become "traits".' *Infant Mental Health Journal 16*, 4, 271–291.

Rees, J. (2009) *Life Story Books for Adopted Children: A Family Friendly Approach.* London: Jessica Kingsley Publishers.

Sutherland, M. (2000) *Using Story Telling as a Therapeutic Tool with Children.* Oxford: Speechmark Publishing.

Afterword

Aideen Taylor de Faoite

This book presents an understanding of Narrative Play Therapy as a branch of play therapy and its practice within a theoretical framework that has been influenced by narrative therapy and social construction theory. The aim is not to present some 'grand theory' but to develop a therapy practice that reflects the pluralism and reflexivity of postmodern thought (McLeod 1997). In so doing the authors and practitioners are presenting their 'developing maps of practice' (Hayward 2003). As Hayward has identified, the 'telling of stories or showing of practice is a safer and more reliable way of generating curiosity, but practice without theory makes skills and knowledge too context-specific and less transferable to others' practice situations' (2003, p.188). As proposed by Hayward this book offers some theory that it is hoped will make this model of Narrative Play Therapy more transferable to the practice situation of the reader. The stories of practice are offered as a demonstration of the practice of Narrative Play Therapy and reflect a number of the techniques utilised within its practice. Examples of the practice of Narrative Play Therapy are considered in different contexts and different working environments throughout the book. The ethical issues and practicalities of working with children in this way are also considered through the book.

In the writing of a number of the chapters, a co-constructing approach has been adopted between authors in Chapter 5 and between the author and client or parent of the client as exemplified in Chapter 10. While in these two chapters it has been very successful, this approach was not without its difficulties and had to be abandoned in other chapters. The conflicting elements of co-authoring or co-constructing and personal agency have been identified as the primary reason for any difficulties that might have arisen. While the stories presented are the stories as co-created between the child and the therapist, some details have been changed to protect the anonymity of the client and his or her family.

The process of writing has been useful in clarifying the 'lived' practice of Narrative Play Therapy and the development of each contributor's theoretical framework in which he or she practises. As noted by Ann Marie and David in Chapter 5, therapists will begin to privilege different parts of the therapy. This may be influenced by their own stories, experiences and perception of what is a 'good fit' for them as practitioners. The shaping of a theoretical framework for the practice of Narrative Play Therapy is an evolving process. As more therapists begin to practise within this model of play therapy, their contribution of their local knowledge on the helpfulness of this model for their clients will help to expand, elaborate and shape the practice of Narrative Play Therapy.

Some approaches to assessment and evaluation are presented in this volume, and over time these can begin to inform research on the effectiveness of the intervention based on the client's perspective rather than some externally imposed construction of what is effective. It is the role of practitioners, as they expand the practice of Narrative Play Therapy, to translate information of the effectiveness of this approach of therapy in a language that can be understood by policy makers and service providers. This is the challenge for the future.

References

Hayward, M. (2003) 'Critiques of narrative therapy: A personal response.' *Australian and New Zealand Journals of Family Therapy 24*, 4, 183–189.

McLeod, J. (1997) *Narrative and Psychotherapy*. London: Sage Publications.

The Contributors

Ann Marie John works as a family therapist (UKCP) in a tier four Child and Adolescent Mental Health Service (CAMHS) unit, as a couples relationship therapist and as a play therapist with looked after children. She is currently interested in the meaning and prevention of self-harm in adolescents. She has many years of experience as a supervisor and trainer and is training to become a qualified family therapy supervisor. She also attempts to write, or 'wright', plays when she has play time.

Kate Kirk is registered with the Office for Standards in Education (Ofsted) as an adoption support therapist. Her specialist fields are play therapy, assessing parent/child and sibling groups and children's attachments, and providing individual therapy to troubled children. She works in private practice as a therapist and in her secondary role works as an adviser in the Family Courts.

She holds a Bachelor of Arts degree in social studies, a Master of Arts degree in play therapy, a Master of Science degree in psychological research methods, a Certificate in child observation and assessment, and Diplomas in applied systemic theory with families and work with attachment disorder. Kate has done extensive additional training in attachment theory, as well as learning how to use and apply recognised measures to give a view of relationship patterns and styles.

Kate is a registered social worker and a former registered mental health nurse.

David Le Vay is a qualified play therapist, dramatherapist and social worker and works with children and families who have experienced significant trauma, loss and abuse. For the last nine years David has worked specifically for an organisation that provides a therapeutic service for children and young people with harmful sexual behaviour. David is also a senior lecturer on Roehampton University's MA Play Therapy programme and has his own independent therapy and supervision practice. David is registered with the Health Professions Council and is a member of the National Organisation for the Treatment of Abusers (NOTA), the British Association of Play Therapists (BAPT) and the General Social Care Council (GSCC). In his other life, David is a jazz pianist, cricket player and allotmenteer.

Sharon Pearce is a registered play therapist and supervisor for the British Association of Play Therapists. She has many years experience of working with vulnerable children and their families and with children placed in substitute care by local authorities. She runs an independent play therapy practice and has a special interest in working with children with attachment and trauma issues along with their carers and wider networks. Sharon has a developing interest in animal-assisted play therapy, in which she has undertaken training, and in understanding animal and human communication. Much of her spare time is taken up by her six rescue rabbits. She is a member of the Rabbit Welfare Association.

Carol Platteuw is Director of Play Therapy Services Ltd, an organisation that provides a range of therapeutic services for children and their families. She is a qualified social worker and play therapist and supervisor for the British Association of Play Therapists.

Aideen Taylor de Faoite is a freelance educational psychologist and play therapist, and has been working as a play therapist in private practice for over 15 years. She has devised a number of play therapy training programmes and has lectured internationally on the subject. Aideen lives in County Clare, Ireland.

Alison Webster trained as a play therapist and dramatherapist and has extensive experience of working within paediatric services. She has also worked in school counselling and CAMHS. Alison has delivered a range of training and presentations to diverse populations in voluntary and statutory services, both at home and abroad, and has also developed various family programmes. As a consultant play therapist and service manager, she is developing early intervention and preventative mental health services in schools, training staff, and supporting children and families at the earliest opportunity.

Subject Index

Page numbers in *italics* refer to figures and tables.

Author Index